The Alchemy
of Growth

The Alchemy of Growth

Practical Insights for
Building the Enduring Enterprise

Mehrdad Baghai
Stephen Coley
David White

PERSEUS BOOKS
Cambridge, Massachusetts

ISBN 0-7382-0100-6

Library of Congress Catalog Card Number: 99-60938

First published in Great Britain in 1999 by
Orion Business, an imprint of The Orion Publishing Group Ltd.,
Orion House, 5 Upper St. Martin's Lane, London WC2H 9EA

Perseus Books is a member of the Perseus Books Group

Jacket design by Bruce W. Bond

3   4   5   6   7   8   9   10—02010099

Find us on the World Wide Web at
http://www.perseusbooks.com

To our parents, wives, and children

Contents

Preface

Our aspiration in writing this book is to encourage and assist business leaders around the world to champion growth and harness its power. Growth is a noble pursuit. It creates new jobs for the community and wealth for shareholders. It can turn ordinary companies into stimulating environments where employees find a sense of purpose in their work. In growing companies, there is a surge of personal and collective energy. People live the intoxicating experience of being on a winning team. Little wonder that such companies seem to attract the best talent.

Growth's transformative power is akin to the alchemy of old. Always a mystery, alchemy's magical blend of science, philosophy, art, and spirituality held secrets that even its practitioners found difficult to penetrate. Still, they were all drawn to its alluring aim: to transform the everyday into the exalted. The pursuit of corporate growth has prompted a similar reaction in the field of management. Although excited by growth's promise, executives are uncertain about how to capture it. Feeling ill equipped to lead a growth charge, many seek a tested approach that shows them how they can actually attain and sustain growth.

This book is addressed to them. It attempts to arm business leaders for growth by laying out a proven practical framework for the holistic management of a growing enterprise. The ideas and approaches suggested here are applicable to businesses and business units of all sizes, in all locations. They are intended to provide guidance to all levels of business leadership.

Our work was born of a two-and-a-half-year research initiative by McKinsey & Company aimed at helping our corporate clients grow. The research had a global orientation, with full-time teams in Sydney,

Chicago, and Toronto and additional resources in Atlanta, Bombay, Dallas, Dusseldorf, Hong Kong, Houston, London, Munich, and New York. As a result of these international efforts, we believe our ideas apply to a broad range of geographies and cultures.

The research began with a thorough review of academic thinking on growth, leadership, and strategy. These theoretical perspectives were then combined with examples from the real-life experience of companies pursuing growth. We investigated companies from 10 industry sectors in 12 countries from four continents. A summary of the case studies appears in the Appendix.

Some of the companies are household names: Johnson & Johnson, Disney, Sara Lee. Others are less well known, but enormously successful: Bombardier, which started out making snowmobiles but has become the world's third-largest manufacturer of civilian aircraft; Village Roadshow, which has developed from a small Australian theater operator to a world-class player in the entertainment business; and Hutchison Whampoa, which has built dominant positions in fast-growing infrastructure businesses in China. On average, the growth companies we studied increased their sales by 23 percent a year and their total return to shareholders by 29 percent a year during the period we examined. Their success stories help to bring our ideas and frameworks to life.

Our research makes it clear that very few companies sustain above-average growth for their industry year after year. Indeed, some of the companies we studied have already suffered slowdowns, and we fully expect more to do so. But these setbacks do not detract from the lessons to be learned from the sustained phases of growth; indeed, they serve to reinforce the need for new approaches to help executives keep growth going. Our own approach has been specifically developed to help companies grow throughout the business cycle – not only sailing through the upswings, but also maintaining growth during the downturns.

Another cornerstone of our thinking has been McKinsey's consulting experience. Reverse-engineering attempts to kickstart growth, analyzing efforts to sustain high growth, and assessing the obstacles faced by promising growth programs have taught us invaluable lessons. This "retrospective sense-making," as organizational psychologist Karl Weick calls it, has yielded insights into the difficulties of keeping growth going.

We have been fortunate to share our ideas with many corporations around the world. The most exciting aspect of these "market tests" over the past few years has been the positive reaction of senior executives, and their readiness to put the ideas to work in different industries and geographies. Several hundred of the world's largest and most successful corporations are already using concepts such as the "three horizons" and the "growth staircase," which you will read about in the pages that follow.

These concepts work. They have proved valuable in building new managerial and diagnostic tools and providing a common vocabulary to help executives discuss corporate growth. Executives tell us they find them powerful. Indeed, it is our experience with these leaders that has prompted us to share our ideas with a broader audience.

To make the book readily accessible, we have structured it as a leader's growth journey.

Part I, Understanding growth, introduces the three horizons as the principle underpinning sustained growth. We emphasize the need for active management of three distinct stages in a pipeline of continuous business creation so that leaders' attention to managing their core business is balanced with efforts to develop new enterprises. This section also puts forward a new growth language to help change the way leaders think and talk about their businesses.

Part II, Overcoming inertia, discusses the two essential preconditions for profitable growth: earning the right and building the resolve to grow. This section helps leaders kickstart growth programs. It also describes a disciplined yet creative approach to identifying growth opportunities by exploring all degrees of freedom and thinking expansively about them.

Part III, Building momentum, presents a step-by-step method for assembling the necessary capabilities and organizing to protect and nurture new business initiatives. It shows how companies can successfully invest in business creation.

Part IV, Sustaining growth, lays out the organizational approaches, management processes, and leadership actions that are required to foster continuous idea generation and new business development.

The goal of making a difference in business and in the lives of employees makes growth worth striving for. We hope the ideas we offer will help companies achieve it.

Acknowledgments

This book is the product of a collaboration involving many people. Our clients, colleagues, and families have all made contributions to our work.

First, we want to thank the clients who have inspired us. Achieving and sustaining growth in multibillion-dollar corporations is a huge leadership and management challenge. Our ideas derive principally from our work with executives confronting this challenge. Their encouragement persuaded us to undertake the task of writing this book and sharing our ideas with a wider audience.

Second, we acknowledge the support of our partners at McKinsey, who have funded our research effort. They have made an enormous contribution to the ideas we put forward on their behalf, and to the application of these ideas in real corporate environments. Without their intellectual challenges and the opportunity they gave us to test our ideas, no book would have been possible.

Scores of our partners have contributed to the effort, but we would like to mention specifically Tim Ling, Jürgen Ringbeck, Charles Conn, and Rob McLean, who played important roles in our research. Tim was an early contributor who blended pragmatic ideas and experience with sharp thinking. He provided inspiring direction to some of our research teams and was instrumental in testing and refining our most important ideas and frameworks. Jürgen Ringbeck worked with us to bring a Continental European perspective to the research, led case study teams, and developed approaches to apply the ideas in large corporate environments. Charles Conn and Rob McLean were central to the early development of our thinking on staircases and capabilities.

We would also like to note the leadership of Dick Foster, Herb Henzler, and Rajat Gupta, who oversaw our work and provided guidance when we most needed it. Dick in particular has been a constant source of stimulation, encouragement, and support. We have also benefited from the advice and encouragement of an informal advisory board of partners that included Peter Bisson, Lar Bradshaw, Marcial Campos, Ron Farmer, Ron Hulme, and Mark McGrath. Other leaders without whose encouragement we could not have reached so far include Christian Caspar, Ian Davis, Nathaniel Foote, Ted Hall, Tsun-yan Hsieh, Wilhelm Rall, and Günter Rommel. Finally, Asif Adil, Tadaaki Chigusa, Raoul Oberman, Tony Perkins, and Hirokazu Yamanashi made notable contributions to our Asian casework.

Rajan Anandan and Andrew Grant were our first thought partners and the leaders who guided our teams through the murkiest days of the research. Jeff Chan, Alison Deans, Brad Gambill, Henrike Garkisch Mobed, and Sarah Kaplan subsequently picked up team leadership roles and performed them just as ably. Jeff Chan has played several roles, coordinating our research and helping synthesize the findings. From leading case research efforts to responding to inquiries to running client workshops, Jeff has been a bulwark. His knowledge of the research is encyclopedic, and his contributions pervade the book.

The painstaking work of our research teams not only informed the development of our ideas, but also produced extraordinarily valuable documentation of case studies for our colleagues to draw on. At one time or another, Andrew Abela, Jake Allen, Anna Aqualina, Jason Beckstead, Scott Berg, Cedric Bisson, Antony Blanc, Nikki Blundell, Wolf Bottger, Maggie Carter, Angus Dawson, Darin Gilson, Samantha Hannah, Sallie Honeychurch, Igor Kouzine, Linda Mantia, Aaron Mobarak, Verena Mohaupt, Chad Muir, Fayyaz Nurmohamed, Aileen O'Malley, Annette Quay, Deepak Ramachandran, Hugo Sarrazin, Giri Sekhar, Rafael Simon, Luc Sirois, Stefanie Teichmann, Bay Warburton, and Scott Wilkens have all made enormous contributions to our work.

We have received tremendous assistance and support from McKinsey's communications group. Partha Bose worked closely with our publishers and ourselves during the entire research and writing effort. He has been an enduring source of encouragement, support, and "hands-dirty" assistance. In addition, Pom Somkabcharti has tirelessly labored over every aspect of production, from jacket design to copyediting. We could not have met our deadlines without her help. Finally, Bill Matassoni has been generous in dedicating these resources to our book.

On the publishing side, we would not have written this book without the interest and encouragement of Martin Liu and his team at Orion. That the book is to be launched in other editions across the world is a direct result of his vision and leadership. At Perseus, Nicholas Philipson and his team have shown excitement about the project and always acted quickly and decisively to make things happen. We would also like to acknowledge Majorie Williams for immersing herself in the manuscript, offering constructive feedback, and giving us guidance on a publishing strategy.

None of this would have been possible without the professional assistance of Desiree Clancy, Leslie Cowger, Lori DeWeerd, Mandy Nachum, Heidi Smith, and Maradene Wills, who helped us through the many versions of the manuscript. Maradene in particular acted as the highest point of quality control for our evolving drafts. We are thankful for all of their patience.

Finally, we want to thank our families for their support, understanding, and patience; they have cheerfully made sacrifices greater than ours. That Roya Baghai, Jane Coley, and Lisa White have become close friends attests to the time we have not spent with our families. We owe them everything.

Special thanks

We also want to make special acknowledgments to Allan Gold and Houston Spencer. Through many almost sleepless weeks, they helped us synthesize our thinking and express our ideas more clearly and succinctly. Gifted thought partners, they have been an invaluable source of intellectual challenge and played a genuine role in the development of our ideas. Fortunately for us, their gifts are matched by their stamina and sense of humor. They have been true collaborators and friends; without them, our work would be much less than it has become.

Part I

Understanding growth

A question: what underpins sustained growth?

The answer: a company must maintain a continuous pipeline of business-building initiatives. Only if it keeps the pipeline full will it have new growth engines ready when existing ones begin to falter. But if the answer is that simple, why aren't all companies constantly growing?

The problem is, most managers are preoccupied with their existing businesses. They must learn to focus their attention as much on where they are heading as on where they are today. But companies often lack a way to talk coherently about current businesses, new enterprises coming onstream, and future options.

To fill this gap, we offer a way of thinking about growth that balances the competing demands of running existing businesses and building new ones, and that offers a language that leaders at all levels of an organization can use. We call it the "three horizons" of growth.

1 The three horizons

Our thinking about growth and decay is dominated by the image of a single lifespan, animal or vegetable. Seedling, full flower and death. "The flower that once has bloomed forever dies." But for an ever-renewing society the appropriate image is a total garden, a balanced aquarium or other ecological system. Some things are being born, other things are flourishing, still other things are dying – but the system lives on. John Gardner[1]

Only an exceptional organization manages to sustain growth when its core business matures. Just one out of ten companies that exceed the growth of their industry in any year is able to repeat that performance every year for a decade.[2] Only one company from the original 1896 Dow Jones Industrial Average, General Electric, remains part of that celebrated stock market measure today.[3]

Wherever you look, the case is easy to make: businesses mature and decline. As in John Gardner's metaphorical garden, a business, like a flower, is born, flourishes, and withers. But the fact that a company's business blossoms and then fades does not mean that the company must die. Successful companies can and must outlive their individual businesses.

As a company's businesses and revenue streams mature, it must have others ready to take their place. If continual growth is the goal, the pace of replenishment must be faster than the pace of decline. To sustain growth, there must be a continuous pipeline of new businesses that represent new sources of profit.

What distinguishes the corporations that carry on growing is their ability to create these new businesses. They can innovate in their core businesses *and* build new ones at the same time. What they have mastered is the art of managing their pipeline so that fading sources of growth are replenished at exactly the right moment.

Imagine a company that has sustained profitable growth for more than a decade. Its core businesses are already out of the pipeline, operating as fully developed profit generators. Inside the pipeline are younger businesses that are showing substantial growth in revenue (and perhaps in profits too). Further back in the pipeline are businesses in an earlier stage of formation – as yet, little more than explorations of promising ideas. The pipeline thus contains emerging and future businesses to supplement the company's existing core businesses.

A healthy pipeline is a feature of all growth-sustaining companies. Unfortunately, companies boasting such a pipeline are the exception rather than the rule. Enterprises seeking to sustain growth cannot afford to leave gaps between the decline of one business and the ascent of another. They must not delay creating new businesses until the core collapses. Yet that is precisely what many companies do. We believe that building and managing a continuous pipeline of business creation is the central challenge of sustained growth.

Three horizons of growth

What makes this task harder is that the risks and management challenges involved change as a project progresses down the pipeline. To see how, it is helpful to break down the business creation process into three stages. (Admittedly, one could just as legitimately divide it into four, ten, or twenty stages, but not without unduly increasing complexity.)[4] A three-stage pipeline is useful in that it allows us to distinguish between the embryonic, emergent, and mature phases of a business's life cycle. We refer to these stages as the three horizons of growth.

Each horizon represents a different stage in the creation and development of a business. Each calls for radically different business initiatives. And each poses a different management challenge.

What is horizon 1?

Horizon 1 encompasses the businesses that are at the heart of an organization – those that customers and stock analysts most readily identify with the corporate name. In successful companies, these businesses usually account for the lion's share of profits and cash flow. Horizon 1 businesses are critical to near-term performance, and the cash they generate and the skills they nurture provide resources for growth. They usually have some growth potential left, but will eventually flatten out and decline (Figure 1.1). Without the support of a successful horizon 1, initiatives in horizons 2 and 3 are likely to stagnate and die.

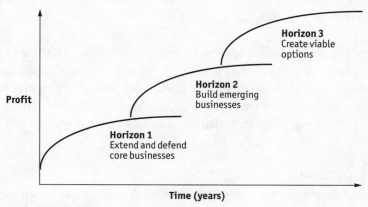

Figure 1.1 Defining the three horizons

Management's primary challenge in horizon 1 is to shore up competitive positions and capture what potential remains in the core businesses. Even when these are mature, continuing innovation can incrementally extend their growth and profitability. Traditional sales force stimula-tion programs, product extensions, and marketing changes can all contribute. Restructuring, productivity enhancement, and cost reduction measures will also help maintain healthy performance for as long as possible.

What is horizon 2?

Horizon 2 comprises businesses on the rise: fast-moving, entrepreneurial ventures in which a concept is taking root or growth is accelerating. The emerging stars of the company, these businesses are attracting investors' attention. They could transform their company, but not without considerable investment. Though substantial profits may be four or five years away, they have customers and revenue, and may already generate some profit. More important, they are expected to become as profitable as horizon 1 businesses in time.

Horizon 2 initiatives are usually characterized by a single-minded drive to increase revenue and market share. They need continuing investment to finance rollouts or otherwise accelerate the expansion of the business. In a few years, horizon 2 initiatives should complement or replace a company's current core businesses. They may represent either extensions of these businesses or moves in new directions.

Horizon 2 is about building new streams of revenue. That takes time and demands new skills. Without horizon 2 businesses, a company's growth will slow and ultimately stall. A good growth company needs to have several of these emerging businesses "on the boil," working to convert promising ideas into future earnings generators.

What is horizon 3?

Horizon 3 contains the seeds of tomorrow's businesses – options on future opportunities. Although embryonic, horizon 3 options are more than ideas; they are real activities and investments, however small. They are the research projects, test-market pilots, alliances, minority stakes, and memoranda of understanding that mark the first steps toward actual businesses, even though they may not produce profits for a decade, if ever. Should they prove successful, they will be expected to reach horizon 1 levels of profitability.

A company that thinks it has a promising horizon 3 just because it compiles a long list of whiteboard ideas at a management retreat is fooling itself. Without deliberate initiatives to develop good ideas into horizon 3 opportunities, a company's long-term growth prospects will fade. The options in horizon 3 are rarely proven opportunities, but they need to be promising and to have the support of management.

Building successful businesses means seeding numerous options. Some will fail for internal reasons; others will fall victim to shifting industry winds. Most will never grow to become successful new businesses. Given these odds, a great deal of horizon 3 activity is needed to cover the multitude of possible futures. A company's goal should be to keep the option to play without committing too much capital or other resources. The challenge is to nurture promising options while ruthlessly excising those with diminishing potential.

Managing all three horizons concurrently

Initiatives in the three horizons pay off over different time frames. When they pay off, however, has little to do with when they require management attention and investment. It is all too easy to assume that planning future horizons can be put on the back burner. If that were so, managers could attend to each horizon in turn, focusing on horizon 1 today and deferring any investment of time and energy in horizons 2 and 3.

This would be a dangerous mistake. It confuses the task of stewarding a pipeline of business creation with short-, medium-, and long-term planning. The point of traditional planning is deliberately to defer some activities to the medium and longer term. The goal of managing the three horizons, by contrast, is to develop many businesses in parallel without regard to their stage of maturity. The three horizons must be managed concurrently, not sequentially. As Ghoshal and Bartlett put it, managers are faced with the challenge of "managing sweet and sour": the "sour medicine" of operational improvements for the current business and the "sweet" agenda of revitalization for new growth activities.[5]

Managers know that businesses go through different stages of development. Yet most companies are far from having a stock of developing businesses ready to gush out of the pipeline. In many organizations, scant management attention is devoted to some sections of the pipeline, while much is lavished on others. Neglecting any horizon at any time weakens a firm's prospects of long-term growth.

If a pipeline of business creation is to succeed, management attention is required to:

- Extend and defend today's profit generators in horizon 1...

- …while simultaneously building horizon 2 businesses that will become drivers of medium-term revenue growth…

- …while also pursuing options in horizon 3 that will secure the company's longer-term future.

How concurrent management works

A straightforward example of managing the three horizons concurrently comes from Coca-Cola Amatil (CCA), a bottler of Coca-Cola beverages based in Australia. We attribute CCA's phenomenal growth to its successful concurrent management of three geographically defined horizons. In the 1960s, the company began from a modest base in one Australian state; by 1997, it had become Coca-Cola's second-largest and most geographically dispersed bottler, with a presence in the Asia Pacific region and in Europe covering half a billion consumers (Figure 1.2).

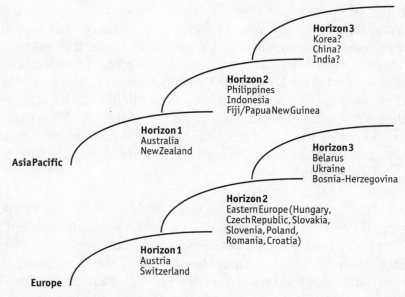

Figure 1.2 Coca-Cola Amatil's horizons, 1997

In its Asia Pacific horizon 1, CCA operates mature businesses in Australia and New Zealand, where consumers already have the soft-drink habit. According to CCA, annual per capita consumption here is greater than 150 eight-ounce servings. In these markets, incremental growth will come from cost reduction and from innovations to increase consumption and capture market share. In horizon 1, CCA is growing by introducing package sizes such as a 600-milliliter plastic bottle, products such as sports drinks, and distribution channels such as vending machines.

At the same time that CCA extends its horizon 1 businesses, it is investing heavily in its Asian horizon 2, primarily the Philippine and Indonesian markets.[6] These are markets where the proportion of daily soft-drink consumers is relatively low and growth prospects are strong, notwithstanding recent economic turmoil. Building CCA's horizon 2 businesses means investing heavily in manufacturing and distribution (for instance, by supplying cold-drink equipment to retailers in Indonesia) and finding ways to make the product more affordable (say, by using returnable glass bottles).

But CCA knows that its long-term prospects are hazy without efforts to develop horizon 3. In the Asian countries that make up horizon 3, soft-drink consumption is currently very low. But their large populations make these markets extremely tempting. Early in 1998, the Coca-Cola Company allowed CCA to buy the franchise for Korea as part of a reorganization. CCA is also positioned as well as anyone to profit from the Chinese market thanks to its relationship with Robert Kuok, the powerful Malaysia-based sugar baron and a major CCA shareholder, and thanks to its own credibility with the Coca-Cola Company. India is another potential market where CCA and its shareholders, including San Miguel, have interests.

In Europe, CCA's horizon 1 includes the established markets of Austria and Switzerland, where it emphasizes incremental growth. Horizon 2 is particularly strong, comprising growing businesses in seven Eastern European countries: Hungary, the Czech Republic, Slovakia, Slovenia, Poland, Romania, and Croatia. In the European horizon 3, CCA has made modest investments in franchises for several promising markets with low soft-drink consumption at present: Belarus, the Ukraine, and Bosnia-Herzegovina.

The rewards reaped by this geographic approach have been enormous. From 1990 to 1996, CCA's beverage business recorded 13 percent compound annual growth in sales, while annual returns to shareholders averaged 29 percent. During this period, CCA was the top performer among the 30 largest companies on the Australian Stock Exchange.

Until recently, CCA managed its operations in Asia and Europe concurrently. Early in 1998, however, it announced plans to spin off its European operations into a separately listed entity, Coca-Cola Beverages, stating that the move would enable it to focus on bottling franchises closer to home. This restructuring went smoothly and was well received by the market.

When we describe CCA's ability to manage three horizons concurrently, some say, "OK, that helps us understand how having three horizons might help us. But CCA's business isn't rocket science; they sell a simple product with the backing of the world's most powerful brand. What about us?"

It is true that selling Coca-Cola is not difficult to understand, but that is precisely what makes the CCA case a good place to start in exploring the three horizons. In essence, CCA has filled its pipeline by geography, managing three horizons of country-based businesses simultaneously. The result has been sustained growth.

As we hope to show, the three horizons approach also sheds light on the success of more complex growth strategies. Consider the financial services concern Charles Schwab. Schwab defines its three horizons by the development and introduction of new financial products and services (Figure 1.3).

Charles Schwab started his company as a full-service stock brokerage in 1971, a time when brokers' commissions were strictly regulated. In 1975, the US Securities and Exchange Commission freed brokers to set their own fees, opening up the possibility of price-based competition. While traditional full-service brokers maintained high rates, Schwab dropped its fees and introduced the concept of the discount broker. This step marked the beginning of an astonishing growth run. Schwab has since remade itself into a much broader financial services concern, with 5 million active customers and $400 billion in assets in

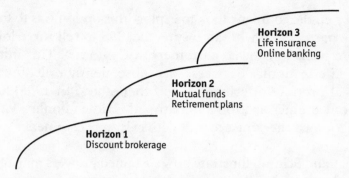

Horizon 3
Life insurance
Online banking

Horizon 2
Mutual funds
Retirement plans

Horizon 1
Discount brokerage

Figure 1.3 Charles Schwab's horizons, 1998

March 1998. Between 1987 and 1996, it achieved compound annual growth of 35 percent in shareholder returns.

Schwab's horizon 1 discount brokerage business is extremely profitable, and still growing rapidly. The company has been a pioneer in telephone, online, and Internet trading. It continued to expand in international markets with its 1995 acquisition of ShareLink Investment Services, the largest discount broker in the United Kingdom. More recently, it has opened a Latin America center and rolled out an Asia Pacific service.

To complement its activity in horizon 1, Schwab is building an impressive collection of horizon 2 businesses. In the 1980s, it launched a third-party money market fund that it has since developed into the third-largest mutual fund provider in the United States, with customer assets of $161 billion at the end of 1997 and still growing strongly. A second horizon 2 business has developed in employee defined-contribution retirement plans, an attractive growth area.

Schwab's record shows that it does not neglect the incubation of future businesses. In horizon 3, Schwab is securing options in the cash-rich life insurance business. It seeks to profit from customers' apparent fatigue with traditional life insurance agents by leveraging its own well-developed back-office technology and customer base. "If we can successfully market this, then we ought to be able to identify a profitable position for the company," said Jeff Benton, vice-president for annuities and life insurance. "And that could mean everything from starting an underwriting company to joint-venturing with an existing one."[7]

The first step the company took to explore this option was to form an exclusive partnership with an insurer in 1996 to sell three low-cost insurance plans to Schwab customers in California. This initiative, Schwab Life Insurance Services, was subsequently rolled out, with additional product offerings, to 14 other states. In 1998, Schwab announced another horizon 3 initiative, this time in online banking, and is piloting a checking account with existing customers.

Both CCA and Schwab illustrate how sustained growers manage their three horizons. In CCA's case, the three horizons are geographically defined; with Schwab, they are focused on adjacent product markets. For both companies, any failure to manage all three horizons concurrently would curtail their ascent. How much longer will CCA and Charles Schwab be able to sustain their growth trajectories? The answer depends on how well they feed their business pipelines.

Cascading the three horizons through the organization

To create robust pipelines, the most successful growers identify three horizons for each of their businesses. The corporation as a whole has three horizons of business creation, and so does each of its divisions or business units. So does each functional department within a division, as well as each manufacturing site, product group, research lab, and sales territory. The value of the three horizons approach increases exponentially when it is pushed beyond the top executive team and into the hands of managers at lower levels.

In short, every leader should have three horizons to manage. The greater the number of managers who use the three horizons, the more the growth mindset can be woven into the fabric of the business, and the greater the value of the three horizons perspective.

Among the growth companies we researched, Bombardier stands out for its ability to develop horizons across the enterprise (Figure 1.4). One of Canada's most admired companies, Bombardier has sales of C$8 billion (US $5.8 billion) that are spread across a wide range of products and services. The third-largest civilian aerospace company in the world, it is also the second-largest maker of snowmobiles and

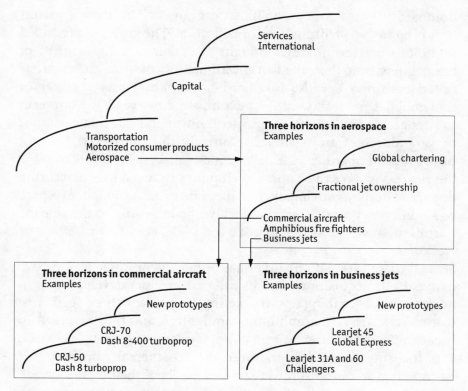

Figure 1.4 Bombardier's cascading horizons, 1998

personal watercraft, and one of the leading manufacturers of trains and trams.

Joseph-Armand Bombardier founded the company in 1942 to make and market snow-going vehicles. By 1998, Bombardier had evolved into six business groups that can be broadly classified in terms of the three horizons. Horizon 1 has three businesses: transportation, motorized consumer products, and aerospace. In horizon 2, Bombardier is building a financing and leasing business in niche markets where it has relevant product knowledge and distribution networks. In horizon 3, it is converting insights about airlines and the other industries with which it deals into a service business that includes the repair, maintenance, and overhaul of regional aircraft. In April 1998, it announced the formation of a new group designed to pursue growth in emerging markets in all lines of business.

Bombardier's aerospace group illustrates how well the three horizons have been cascaded through the organization. The group was founded in 1986, when Bombardier bought Canadair, a manufacturer of business jets, from the Canadian government. At the time, the purchase raised eyebrows because Bombardier was known as a maker of snowmobiles and trains. Inside the company, however, it did not seem so strange. "As I studied the [aerospace] business, I saw that it was not so very different from what we already did," observed Laurent Beaudoin, Bombardier's CEO. "From a management point of view, the processes were the same: developing products, manufacturing them, and dealing with highly specialized markets. Although aerospace was a different type of market, we felt we had the skills to manage the operation, so we decided to give it a try."[8]

Since the late 1980s, Bombardier has been a major force in aerospace thanks to its acquisitions and its internal product development. In horizon 1, it is making and marketing aircraft for three segments: commercial aircraft, amphibious firefighters, and business jets. To broaden the market for corporate jets, the aerospace group's horizon 2 is focusing on building a time-share ownership business for customers who cannot afford to purchase a jet of their own. Horizon 3 includes initiatives aimed at building a global charter business with Lufthansa and other carriers as partners.

But the cascade does not stop there. Bombardier is pursuing three horizons in the commercial aircraft division too. In horizon 1, there are the CRJ-50 regional jet and the Dash 8 turboprop; in horizon 2, the recently introduced stretched CRJ-70 regional jet and the Dash 8-400 turboprop; and in horizon 3, alliances for developing larger aircraft.

These horizons have not appeared by accident; Bombardier made a conscious effort to develop regional jets. "We have always been a growth company, so when we realized that Canadair had plans to develop a 50-seat passenger jet, we asked a task force to look at it," Beaudoin recalled. "Once we were satisfied with its findings, we pulled out some of the best engineers from Canadair, set them up in a separate building, and asked them to develop a regional jet. We invested some $250 million on development – about half of the company's market capitalization at that time. Today, the Canadair regional jet is a great success."

Similarly, in the business aircraft division, horizon 1 consists of the light Learjet 31A and the medium-sized Learjet 60, as well as the Challenger business jets – all models with great order books. Horizon 2 comprises the super-light Learjet 45 and the innovative long-range Global Express. Horizon 3 is composed of confidential prototypes in development.

Bombardier has made its three horizons work to maximum advantage. At most levels of the company, from the corporate office down, managers are keeping their business pipelines filled. This rich cascade of growth activity is not limited to the core businesses. Even the services group, sitting in horizon 3 at the corporate level, is pursuing its own three horizons of growth.

All in all, Bombardier's relentless focus on growth across the three horizons has yielded extraordinary results: compound annual growth of 22 percent in sales and 42 percent in shareholder returns between 1986 and 1996.

At first sight, the three horizons metaphor may seem simplistic as a way to explain the evolution of a business. But this very simplicity is its strength. It has proved a powerful learning tool for dozens of companies seeking to develop growth strategies and communicate them to managers.

The three horizons can be used to promote growth in three ways. First, as a diagnostic tool, the three horizons can help managers assess the prospects for growth at any level in an organization and reveal possible gaps in the volume and consistency of new profit sources.

Second, as a language, the three horizons approach offers a coherent way to communicate with employees and investors. Its simple terminology makes it easier for both groups to understand and discuss corporate priorities.

Third, as a management philosophy, the framework forces managers and organizations to consider the future, as well as this quarter's results.

Our experience with hundreds of companies suggests that the three horizons are intuitively easy to grasp and apply. Introducing them into an organization offers a powerful way to look into the mirror and begin the journey of growth.

NOTES

1   J. W. Gardner, *Self-Renewal: The individual and the innovative society* (W. W. Norton, New York, 1981), p. 5. Gardner is a former US cabinet secretary, a social activist, and the author of several books on values.

2   Richard N. Foster, a McKinsey director, established this success rate in comprehensive unpublished research into the impermanence of excellence. The conclusion is based on evidence from 404 single-business companies in 15 industries over 30 years.

3   The Dow Jones Web site recalls, "When Charles Dow created the Dow Jones Industrial Average, first published on May 29, 1896, it consisted of a dozen stocks. Only one of the original 12, General Electric, is in the average today. And even GE dropped out for a while – deleted in 1898 but back nine years later as a replacement for Tennessee Coal and Iron."

4   See, for example, I. Adizes, *Corporate Lifecycles: How and why corporations grow and die and what to do about it* (Prentice Hall, Englewood Cliffs, New Jersey, 1989). Adizes proposes a 10-step lifecycle curve: courtship, infant, go-go, adolescence, prime, stable, aristocracy, early bureaucracy, bureaucracy, and death.

5   S. Ghoshal and C. A. Bartlett, *The Individualized Corporation: A fundamentally new approach to management* (HarperBusiness, New York, 1997), p. 134.

6   Coca-Cola Amatil classifies its businesses as "established," "developing," or "emerging," depending on the level of soft-drink consumption per capita. Since we identify horizons by level of business development, we describe Indonesia as horizon 2 because it has strong business momentum and investment, while CCA classifies it as emerging because of its extremely low per capita consumption.

7   S. Hensley, "Charles Schwab to start selling life insurance in May," *American Banker*, April 23, 1996.

8   M. A. Baghai, S. C. Coley, R. H. Farmer, and H. Sarrazin, "The growth philosophy of Bombardier," *The McKinsey Quarterly*, 1997, Number 2, pp. 4–29.

2 Looking in the mirror

To pursue growth, leaders at all levels of an organization should first look in the mirror and ask, "How healthy are my horizons?" It is not unusual to find one, two, or even all three horizons barren. Inside the company, executives may not be devoting due attention to one or more horizons. Externally, industry shocks can overturn the fortunes of existing or developing businesses overnight. No matter why, if all three horizons are ailing, a company's growth will inevitably falter, and attempts at renewal will be an uphill struggle.

Our research shows that the vast majority of companies have a less than healthy set of horizons. That's the bad news. The good news is that an accurate diagnosis provides the starting point for a cure. Knowing the strong and weak spots in the pipeline gives managers a good indication of how to prioritize growth initiatives. In some cases, a particularly poor snapshot may even suggest that a company is not yet ready to pursue growth.

To look in the mirror, a business leader should begin with the current engines of profitability in horizon 1, and ask these questions:

- Are our core businesses generating sufficient earnings to allow us to invest in growth?

- Do we have a strong performance orientation to push profits higher in the next few years?

- Is our cost structure competitive with that of the rest of our industry?

- Has operating performance been stable?

- Has market share grown or been stable?

- Are we reasonably well protected from new competitors, technologies, or regulations that could change the rules of the game?

Next, move on to emerging businesses in horizon 2:

- Do we have any new businesses capable of creating as much economic value as the current core businesses?
- Are these new businesses gaining momentum in the marketplace?
- Are we prepared to make substantial investments to accelerate their growth?
- Is there mounting investor confidence in these businesses?
- Are the new businesses attracting entrepreneurial talent to our organization?

Finally, reflect on the options for future businesses in horizon 3:

- Does our leadership team set aside time to think about growth opportunities and industry evolution?
- Have we developed a rich portfolio of options for reinventing existing businesses and creating new ones?
- Are these ideas very different from those on the list last year? Three years ago? Five years ago?
- Are we developing effective ways to turn these ideas into new businesses?
- Have the ideas been made tangible in concrete, measurable first steps?

If a leader cannot answer "yes" to most of these questions, then the company's horizons are probably not all healthy. Exceptional companies that have managed to create three healthy horizons of growth do exist, as we saw with Coca-Cola Amatil, Charles Schwab, and Bombardier. For the most part, though, leaders find themselves in one of six other patterns (Figure 2.1).

✓ Healthy
✗ Unhealthy

Horizons	1	2	3
Under siege	✗	✗	✗
Losing the right to grow	✗	✓	✓
Running out of steam	✓	✗	✗
Inventing a new future	{ ✗ ✗	✓ ✗	✗ ✓
Generating ideas but not new businesses	✓	✗	✓
Failing to seed for the future	✓	✓	✗

Figure 2.1 Six common patterns

Unhealthy patterns

Under siege

The first and worst pattern is that of a company under siege. Here, the core businesses of horizon 1 are underperforming, threatened by competitors, or facing imminent decline. Little is happening in the pipeline, so no new businesses are available to pick up the slack. None of the horizons is healthy.

Companies undergoing a turnaround are usually under siege, as are companies blindsided by rapid industry change or deregulation. Companies under siege suffer a double blow: not only will financial markets punish them as their earnings decline, but investors will also look unfavourably at the capital investments they need to develop new businesses.

The Walt Disney Company is often cited as a shining example of sustained growth, but it was not ever thus. After Walt Disney's death in 1966, the company floundered. Despite the creative blueprint he had left behind, few new projects were undertaken, and the core businesses atrophied. Executives lived off the fat of the brand, and by the end of the 1970s, Disney had become a prime takeover candidate.

The essence of the presentation Michael Eisner made to the board of directors before he was named CEO was that Disney was a company ready to be exploited.[1] Its core horizon 1 cash generator, the theme park business, was lying fallow. Few new attractions were being added, and attendance was falling. Admission prices had risen by only 1 percent in real terms in a decade, even though $30 million could be added to the bottom line for every $1 increase in the entry ticket. No new hotels had been built since 1973. And by the time management opened the EPCOT Center at Walt Disney World in Orlando, Florida, in 1982 and Tokyo Disneyland in 1983, the cyclical theme park business was in mid-recession.

Disney's other horizon 1 engine, the film business, had also slipped during the 1970s. Once a Hollywood powerhouse, Disney had the lowest market share of the seven major film studios by 1979, having failed to release a successful animated feature in years. Its handful of annual releases fell woefully short of the industry average of 15 to 20.

To make matters worse, few new businesses were being built in horizons 2 and 3. To be sure, talks were under way to develop a theme park in Europe and the Touchstone film production company had been launched to woo young adult audiences, but Disney was falling behind in the video market, and the Disney Channel was losing money.

The stock price nosedived. Total return to shareholders showed a cumulative average growth rate of only 8.3 percent from 1974 to 1984 – half that of the Standard & Poor 500. Not surprisingly, several takeover attempts were mooted. In the early 1980s, the likes of Saul Steinberg and Irwin Jacobs threatened the company with breakup. "It's like watching your mother getting ravaged by New York thugs," is how one broker described Steinberg's takeover attempt.[2]

This was the state of the company when Michael Eisner took the reins in 1984 as the first outsider to run Disney in its 61-year history. It was undoubtedly under siege.

Losing the right to grow

An excessive focus on growth can be just as much a problem as ignoring it. While companies under siege suffer mainly because they have failed to fill their business creation pipeline, others lose the right to grow when they become obsessed with new businesses. The novelty of these opportunities can be so exciting that managers take their eyes off horizon 1, forgetting that it must be maintained in order to provide the financial capacity to drive growth.

Companies can find themselves in this predicament for several reasons. Some forge ahead intelligently with business creation, but then get stung by external events. The loss of cash generation that follows can stall growth. Others fall down by trying to do too much at once and spreading the organization's management and financial capacity too thin. If managers forget about performance in the current core, the paradoxical result may be the death of the new businesses about which they are so passionate. They should remember that since horizon 2 and 3 initiatives are seldom self-sustaining, threats to the profitability of horizon 1 may prompt drastic cuts in investment and management attention. If a company panics, growth may not return to its chief executive's agenda for years.

Nokia, the global telecommunications equipment maker, lost the right to grow simply by trying to do too much. Founded in 1865 on the banks of the Nokia river in Finland, the company was originally a pulp and paper manufacturer. In 1966, it merged with a rubber company and a cable manufacturer. In the 1980s, its then-CEO Kari Kairamo went on a buying spree, spurred by the vision of building a global corporation as European trade barriers fell: "We are all the time selling bits, buying bits, making joint ventures. Nothing is holy inside Nokia."[3] The company made 21 acquisitions between 1986 and 1989. At the peak of its diversification, it attempted to manage businesses ranging from footwear to chemicals.

There were simply too many enterprises for managers to handle, and the horizon 1 businesses, including pulp and paper, began to collapse. Nokia was left drowning in red ink. Though sales grew at 24 percent annually, net income plunged. On December 12, 1988, the European business community woke to the news of Kairamo's death, later found to be suicide. The new president, Simo Vuorilehto, inherited a company that was losing the right to grow.

Running out of steam

In stark contrast, some companies never take their eyes off their core businesses. Yet even world-class companies can run out of steam when these businesses mature and there are no new enterprises in the pipeline to take their place. Crisis may not be at hand, but it could be just around the corner.

Companies that have raised their performance by boosting efficiency and cutting costs will eventually face diminishing returns. This often happens after the completion of rigorous turnaround programs. There are also companies that have expanded their original business by gradually building market share. Once its business concept reaches its natural peak, such a company may run out of steam if it does not have the next big idea, as Wells Fargo feared.

Wells Fargo is in many ways the quintessential American success story. In 1995, it produced the highest return on assets and on equity of any of the 50 largest US banks. This result was entirely consistent with its financial performance since the early 1980s. Over the 10 years to 1995, Wells Fargo achieved annual compound growth of almost 19 percent in its net income, which translated into annual growth in market capitalization and shareholder returns of more than 20 percent. This record of profitable growth rested on ruthless cost reduction, rigorous budgeting and planning, and a strong performance ethic.

Paradoxically, these very strengths inhibited new business creation. The company's planning and budgeting process and demand for short-term profitability worked against the flow of new ideas. This did not become a problem until the first half of the 1990s, when assets and revenue declined by 2 percent a year and earnings growth slowed to 8 percent a year. Although Wells Fargo's 1995 results were far superior to its peers', diminishing returns from cost reductions were becoming painfully evident. While the bank had clearly earned the right to grow, it lacked sufficient horizon 2 and 3 initiatives to create new sources of substantial revenue growth.

Inventing a new future

Some organizations boast promising horizon 2 or 3 businesses, but no viable horizon 1. This is most common in startup companies whose business is still a few years from posting substantial profits and building market value. It can also occur in large corporations.

From time to time, industries are shaken by discontinuities: wrenching shifts in competitive structure that redefine the rules of the game and reshape players' fortunes.[4] Minimill technology transformed the steel industry, for instance, by permitting production with less capital investment, opening the door for Nucor to become an industry leader. Electronic commerce is changing the game in many industries by driving down transaction costs.[5] But discontinuities are not confined to technological change; deregulation can also reverse incumbents' fortunes. In the US telecommunications industry, deregulation meant more than the breakup of AT&T: the introduction of competition meant many players had to scramble to defend themselves against hungry attackers.

Whatever their origins, these discontinuities generally present what the strategy consultant Ian Morrison has called a "two-curve challenge."[6] Leaders confronting them must make the transition from an unattractive legacy business in horizon 1 to a new business that drives earnings and growth in horizon 2. In such cases, horizon 1 must finance the new initiatives in horizons 2 and 3, yet it is probably not generating sufficient earnings to do so. Consequently, it must be harvested and perhaps even divested to create the financial capacity to invest in the organization's future. The goal in such situations, as Morrison notes, is to manage the timing and pace of the transition.

Generating ideas but not new businesses

Another troublesome pattern occurs when companies have strong horizon 1 businesses and lots of ideas in horizon 3, but few people working to turn these ideas into real businesses. No matter how exciting the ideas may be, horizon 2 will remain empty until businesses are built. A company can find itself in an insidious situation as promising horizon 3 options lull it into a false sense of security. To complicate matters, these options can also inflate market expectations for growth far beyond the company's capacity to meet them. As the gap between market expectations and the company's actual growth widens, a steep fall in stock price becomes more likely.

This pattern tends to appear among high-technology companies and those that have traditionally lacked new ideas but have worked hard to address the gap. Such a company may have imagined that a few good ideas at the far end of the pipeline constituted a growth strategy. It may even have deluded itself that a few out-of-the-box ideas are all it takes. As market expectations mount, executives start to wonder whether the new ideas will come to anything. Under pressure, they may seek salvation in hasty acquisitions. Prompted by anxiety, these acquisitions may fill holes, but all too often they end up destroying shareholder value and stalling growth programs.

Companies that pride themselves on cutting-edge research, but do not have a good record of commercializing their ideas, are also prone to exhibit this pattern. Xerox provides a notorious example of the failure to commercialize horizon 3 research. In 1970, the company decided that its future depended on coming up with radically new ideas. Though it had a strong horizon 1 business as the world's largest maker of photocopiers, it worried about the possibility of a paperless future that would make its products obsolete. It set up the Palo Alto Research Center (PARC) in California, staffed it with some of the best scientists and engineers in the world, and gave them a broad brief: to invent the future of computing.

The specialists at PARC did just that. The array of innovations that emerged is legendary: the first graphical computer interface featuring windows and icons, and driven by a mouse; the laser printer; and the local area network. But Xerox's management failed to commercialize these ideas, leaving Hewlett-Packard, Apple, Microsoft, and others to extract the value. Many companies today are making the same mistake.

Failing to seed for the future

Organizations that launch a successful growth effort may find themselves with strong earnings in horizon 1 and promising businesses in horizon 2. This will fuel profitable growth for several years, but if they are to sustain success, they must be able to institutionalize the creation of new ideas. Without a continuous stream of new options in horizon 3, the next generation of horizon 2 businesses will not come onstream quickly enough, and growth will stall.

The demands of the stock market intensify the challenge. The success associated with healthy horizons 1 and 2 inevitably raises market expectations of growth. To meet these expectations, organizations must generate new businesses faster than before. Yet identifying and managing an expanding number of growth opportunities soon becomes daunting, and few organizations are up to the task.

One of the few is Johnson & Johnson, which scours the world to find and acquire underleveraged patents and emerging technologies. It has dozens of vice-presidents of licensing and acquisition, most with doctorates in both law and science or medicine, whose job it is to identify and nurture opportunities. They establish relationships with the venture capital and investment banking communities, scientific research establishments, medical research centers, and small entrepreneurial startups to gain access to attractive medical and health care technologies. These technologies eventually translate into the products that spur Johnson & Johnson's growth.

To complement its vice-presidents, the company has a formed a CEO-level committee on science and technology. It forges relationships with academia, leading think tanks, professional and scientific associations, and other research institutes to identify breakthrough technologies.

Defining balance

The leader who conducts our diagnosis and finds three healthy horizons is very much the exception. For most, health all around is an aspiration, not a reality. Making it happen is a matter of knowing how many initiatives to pursue under each horizon, and what kind. What does a balanced three horizons portfolio look like? What initiatives are appropriate?

Financial markets implicitly recognize the value of a balance of activity across the three horizons. While horizons 2 and 3 may account for little or no current earnings, they are crucial to how much investors are willing to pay for a company's stock. If strong, they create expectations of growth and contribute to large stock price premiums. Even though horizon 1 businesses provide the bulk of cash flow, they may account for a surprisingly small fraction of the stock price, most of which can be attributed to expectations of future growth.[7] This is especially relevant in the high-technology sector, where startups routinely command price-to-earnings ratios of 50 to 100, despite the fact that they have no horizon 1 business – just the potential for strong growth.

Achieving balance does not mean having the same number of initiatives in each horizon. The low hit-rate associated with horizon 3 options means that a large number are usually needed to yield even one successful horizon 2 business. Similarly, not all horizon 2 businesses will make it into horizon 1. Given this attrition, a balanced portfolio across the three horizons produces a development pipeline that looks more like a funnel than a cylinder.

More telling than the mere number of initiatives per horizon is the way that skilled growth companies allocate investment spending across the horizons. They tend to devote substantial sums to initiatives that are still years from paying off. Most of the growth-sustaining companies we studied commit at least one-third to two-thirds of their new investment spending to horizon 2 and 3 initiatives. But a company that pours all its energy and money into numerous initiatives in these horizons while neglecting the core businesses has missed the point. How many initiatives a company has under way is less important than whether the balance of initiatives addresses its needs across all three horizons.

If there are no hard and fast numbers to determine ideal balance across the three horizons, how should you define it? The standard is simple: balance means having the next engine of growth ready when it is needed. Applying the standard, however, is far from simple. The definition of balance varies from company to company.

Consider the following factors:

Pace of industry evolution. In hyper-evolutionary industries, horizon 3 may be only a couple of years away. The importance of what is in the pipeline relative to current performance becomes much greater. Valuations of software companies tend more than most to be driven by expectations of future growth, putting greater emphasis on initiatives in horizons 2 and 3. By contrast, the more slowly evolving basic materials industries may not see horizon 2 for a decade. Balance for them may mean a much smaller number of promising initiatives in horizons 2 and 3.

Degree of uncertainty. Related to the pace of evolution is the level of uncertainty in an industry. Unexpected changes in the environment may threaten core businesses, but they also open the door to opportunities. The uncertainty produced by deregulation, consolidation, or new technologies increases complexity, making it all the more important to have a portfolio of business-creation opportunities. The more options you have, the greater your strategic flexibility.

Managerial and financial capacity. If a company is unrealistic about the money and management time it has available for business creation, its growth program may become an exercise in frustration. The greater the financial means and management talent a company can lavish on growth, the more horizon 2 and 3 initiatives it can support. Companies seeking to grow fast should stretch themselves but not let growth initiatives debilitate horizon 1 businesses.

Shareholder expectations. If a company's investors are willing to accept volatility, its definition of balance can tilt toward the later horizons, supporting investment in horizons 2 and 3. As we saw, having many promising horizon 2 and 3 initiatives will raise market expectations, possibly rewarding a company with a higher market capitalization. Horizon 2 and 3 initiatives generate little profit and cash flow, and their returns are much more uncertain than those of horizon 1 businesses. Consequently, a heavier emphasis on horizon 2 and 3 initiatives tends to introduce more volatility into the stock. This increased risk profile may be exactly what some investors want.

A pessimist might interpret some of the patterns we have described as a diagnosis of poor health with a prognosis of dim growth prospects. A growth leader, however, will see the patterns as starting points from which sustained growth can be achieved. Growth can be the alchemy by which companies transform themselves into strong, vital organizations. Every company whose difficulties we discussed in this chapter has since pulled itself out of trouble, established healthy horizons, and grown profitably.

Under siege in 1984, Disney managed to renew itself, generating 29 percent compound annual returns to shareholders for the next 10 years while increasing net income by 27 percent a year. Nokia shed many businesses to focus primarily on telecommunications. From 1991 to 1995, its net income increased by 70 percent a year, with annual growth in shareholder returns of over 80 percent. Wells Fargo's stock increased by 54 percent in the two years following December 1995, when it made growth a goal on a par with operational performance. Its 1996 hostile takeover of First Interstate Bancorp, a large regional US bank, doubled its assets from $56 billion to $114 billion and laid the foundations for its subsequent merger with Norwest in 1998.

An objective assessment of the health of the three horizons can point to recovery and growth. Achieving them may take several years, but the journey is one full of reward and excitement. Companies must begin by filling the holes in their horizons. This is the thrust of Part II.

NOTES

1 R. Grover, *The Disney Touch: How a daring management team revived an entertainment empire* (Irwin, New York, 1991), p. 40.
2 R. Grieves, "Greenmailing Mickey Mouse: Disney buys out a threatening investor for $325 million," *Time*, June 25, 1984.
3 J. Heard and J. Keller, "Nokia skates into high tech's big league," *Business Week*, April 4, 1988.
4 For a brilliant discussion of the impact on incumbents of market-changing technology, see C. M. Christensen, *The Innovators' Dilemma: When new technologies cause great firms to fail* (Harvard Business School Press, Boston, Mass., 1997).
5 The radical reduction of transaction costs and its implications is discussed in P. Butler *et al.*, "A revolution in interaction," *The McKinsey Quarterly*, 1997, Number 1, pp. 4–23; and P. B. Evans and T. S. Wurster, "Strategy and the new economics of information," *Harvard Business Review*, September–October 1997, pp. 71–82.
6 I. Morrison, *The Second Curve: Managing the velocity of change* (Ballantine Books, New York, 1996).
7 The portion of a company's market capitalization that is due to growth is what is left after the present value of current cash flows has been deducted. Cash flow refers to normalized cash flow to shareholders; we use profit after tax as a proxy. We assume that reinvestment should equal depreciation to maintain present cash flows. The most recent consensus forecast from the Institutional Brokers Estimate System is used as the estimate for profit after tax. The cost of equity is based on the Capital Asset Pricing Model, using the company's global beta and the 10-year US bond yield as the risk-free rate. Data for this calculation are readily available from popular databases. Market capitalization and profit forecasts are available from Datastream and Global Vantage (Compustat in the United States). Global betas are used instead of country-specific betas; they are calculated directly from monthly returns.

The calculated growth premium gives a good first-order indication of how much investors expect a company to grow, but should be used with caution. The conclusion may be misleading, for three reasons. First, the capital expenditure-to-depreciation ratio required to maintain current cash flows varies substantially across companies and industries. Second, many companies are in cyclical industries, and profits after tax need to be normalized across a cycle. Third, major differences in interest rates and accounting for profit make comparisons across countries less than robust.

Part II

Overcoming inertia

We live in an era rich in opportunities. Our experience suggests that growth prospects are limited more often by management failings than by economic realities. The question for underperforming companies is thus not whether growth is possible, but whether they are prepared to take on the growth challenge.

In the next two chapters, we describe how successful growth companies lay the foundation for growth. They earn the right to grow by ensuring strong operating performance; at the same time, they build the resolve to grow both internally and among investors. As managers get their house in order, they also begin to think more expansively about new business opportunities. To do so, they must break the constraints of ingrained beliefs.

Laying the foundation for growth is likely to take between one and four years of extremely hard work. Some managers have already completed that work. For others who are ready to stop envying growers and start pursuing growth, this part discusses how to do it.

3   Laying the foundation

Profitable growth energizes people, makes for an exciting environment, and creates shareholder value. It should not, however, be the top priority for all corporations. Some are simply not ready for a growth-oriented culture. For them, growth must take a back seat to building a solid foundation of operational excellence, competitive strength, and sustainable cash flow.

Much of the corporate restructuring movement in the United States and Europe has been aimed at achieving this foundation for growth. Unfortunately, many companies, particularly in Europe and Asia, are not yet there. But restructuring and improving performance – starting to earn the right to grow, in our terminology – make up only half the picture. The other half is extraordinary leadership will.

So difficult is the task that the whole senior leadership team must share the resolve to grow. Creating this resolve is another critical part of the foundation for growth.

Many of the ideas in this chapter have emerged from our research into what we call "inflection" companies: enterprises that deliberately set out to increase their rate of growth and succeeded in doing so. These companies are distinct from our sample of 30 great growers. While the latter offer insights into how to sustain growth for a decade or more, the companies we cite in this chapter are notable for their success in overcoming inertia to kickstart growth. Not all have managed to sustain that growth.

Earning the right to grow

No growth program can begin without a strategically and operationally sound base. A successful growth program will demand management's full attention, so any major problems in the core business must be resolved before work can begin. Growth also calls for investment. A company must show that it can remain profitable and generate enough cash to sustain the investment required to pursue growth. Otherwise, funding for growth initiatives may be axed during economic downturns. Few decisions are as demoralizing as cutting back investment after a company has courageously set off down the growth path.

To earn the right to grow, a company must achieve superior operating performance, sell any distracting or underperforming businesses, and build the confidence of the investment community – three critical steps that are illustrated in the recent history of the Warnaco Group.

Superior operating performance

The growth-sustaining companies in our research base are all outstanding operators, usually enjoying market-share leadership and low-cost producer status. They recognize that the issue is not growth *or* operational excellence, but growth *and* operational excellence. Superior operating performance is the product of a strong strategic position combined with executional expertise. These conditions enable management to lead and finance growth initiatives. How companies achieve superior operating performance has been the subject of hundreds of articles and books.[1]

For more than a century, Warnaco earned a good living making bras and intimate apparel. As time passed, it branched out into men's clothing and active wear. By 1986, it had become a broadly diversified apparel maker worth $600 million, with a portfolio of popular brands including Olga, Geoffrey Beene, Hathaway, and Chaps by Ralph Lauren. Despite these business-building moves, solid growth had proved elusive for a decade, with sales increasing at just 5 percent a year. Worse, operating performance was unacceptable. Profits in 1986 were little different from those in 1978, and the company was not earning its cost of capital.

Years of cost cutting had left the business stable but only marginally profitable, and its growth pipeline empty. But this was soon to change.

Andrew Galef and Linda Wachner led a leveraged buyout of the company in 1986, and Wachner became CEO.

Faced with a mountain of debt and underperforming businesses, Wachner knew she had to act quickly. She chose to focus first on improving operations, replacing most of top management and supplying her new team with cheap spiral-bound notebooks bearing the message "Do it now." She dragged her managers along to visit stores during the holiday selling season. Every Friday night, she responded to single-page memos of problems faced by division heads. Such actions signaled the sense of urgency that Wachner wanted to create in the new Warnaco. Her strong personal leadership and the new managers she brought in enabled the company to take the necessary tough actions to improve its operating performance.

Internal restructuring improved profitability early on. The Chaps by Ralph Lauren, Christian Dior, and Hathaway divisions were combined; all intimate apparel was brought together in one division; 15 underperforming stores were closed; and Olga international operations were consolidated. Slow-selling lines were dropped, working capital was managed more tightly, and manufacturing effectiveness programs were introduced. Warnaco also acquired low-cost factories in Asia.

These measures increased profits by 250 percent in 1987. Though not yet secure enough to grow sharply, Warnaco could at least consider investing in growth initiatives. Operating performance was stable and poised to improve from a sound base.

Strategic divestment

Companies with strategically distracting or badly performing businesses must use their judgment. Should they try to turn them around, or sell them off? Chief executives of growth-sustaining companies tend to opt for divestment rather than invest time, money, and energy in improving the performance of businesses that are not central to their companies' future. Most of the 30 successful growth companies in our sample shed such businesses, as did all nine of the "inflection" companies that made a deliberate choice to grow.

Chief executives contemplating growth usually follow a logic something like this: "I can create far more shareholder value by investing senior management energy in improving our A businesses than by turning around our C businesses." Needless to say, such an approach applies only to units that are not strategically important, and entails finding buyers at acceptable prices for the C businesses.

Pruning the portfolio of businesses through divestment creates capacity for growth. Although a business unit may still be earning adequate profits, these must be weighed against the opportunity costs of management distraction and competition for resources.[2] Management attention and other resources are often more productively focused on growth opportunities than on businesses with limited potential. "We divest any part of the business we are not happy with…we are very disciplined," said Alfred Zeien, Gillette's chairman and chief executive. "We are convinced that the benefits of worldwide leadership are so great that we can't afford to waste time, money, and management talent where that leadership is not achievable."[3]

Shedding unsatisfactory businesses has the added benefit of signaling strategic intent to both stock markets and employees. Conversely, *not* pruning increasingly irrelevant businesses can send mixed messages about a company's direction and resolve to grow.

At Warnaco, Wachner quickly launched a program of strategic divestment. When she took charge of the company, it was competing in four apparel groups and operating specialist retail stores. Seeking to improve cash flow and pay down debt, Wachner chose to divest and consolidate until only two lines of apparel were left. She kept cash generators that had strong distribution, but sold cash losers that did not (women's wear and 15 stores). Active wear, a Wachner favorite, was reluctantly sold in 1990 to raise cash for debt payments. By 1992, Warnaco focused exclusively on intimate apparel and menswear, profitable businesses that have laid the foundation for the company's subsequent impressive growth.

Building investor confidence

Earning the right to grow also means convincing investors that a company's businesses are sufficiently strong and well run that diverting cash and management attention to growth initiatives is a sound investment policy. Investors look for proof that cash retained in a company will obtain better returns than if it were paid out in higher dividends or stock repurchases. Underperforming companies obviously have trouble making this case.

To gain shareholder acceptance, companies that have created a growth inflection think carefully about how they communicate with the investment community. They ensure that communications are clear, consistent, and regular. They go to great lengths to avoid contradicting public statements about corporate goals and raising expectations beyond their ability to deliver.

Superior operating performance is a key factor. Companies with a record of consistent profitability over the ups and downs of the economic cycle earn the confidence of investors. This "halo effect" enables them to endure periodic poor performance without being punished too harshly by the stock market, giving them invaluable strategic flexibility.

Money managers who understand a company's strategy and have faith in its ability to execute it bestow on management the flexibility to invest when it wants to react quickly to opportunities. That might mean investing countercyclically or moving faster than competitors when deals are on the table. To reap such advantages, the company must get its investors on board in advance. They are likely to hang on to their holdings for as long as they believe the growth story.

At Warnaco, communications with investors were frequent and relatively straightforward. Wachner and chairman Andrew Galef owned most of the equity, and debtholders were regularly apprised of progress as part of the financing and repayment terms. When describing the program of divestment and consolidation, Wachner explained to them that the businesses to be retained were strong cash generators with the potential to be low-cost manufacturers. To boost their confidence, she stressed the company's new focus on cash, profitability, and growth. This emphasis on drivers of economic value was exactly what debt providers wanted to hear. To sum up her aspirations for Warnaco, Wachner told audiences, "We want to be the Coca-Cola of the bra business."

Profitable once again, Warnaco went public in 1991. The news for investors quickly turned positive: between 1992 and 1996, Warnaco achieved average compound annual growth of 14 percent in sales and 16 percent in operating income.

Resolving to grow

Warnaco's program to kickstart growth took five years. It was an arduous undertaking. Efforts to start growing cannot simply be switched on and off; in most organizations, they demand nothing less than a transformation of the entire culture. Companies need more than the right to grow; they need a passion for growth. The resolve to grow must be built and shared. Many of the companies in our research base took years to transform themselves; all required the unflinching dedication of the management team.

What is the catalyst for creating this shared resolve? Most often, the spur comes in the form of a change in leadership – or even the threat of one. But a few enterprises have been able to create their own catalysts.[4] In resolving to grow, they typically rely on three methods: capturing the commitment of the senior team, raising the bar by setting ambitious targets, and removing organizational barriers to growth.

In 1994, the Emerson Electric Company completed its thirty-eighth consecutive year of earnings per share gains. But this manufacturer of electrical and industrial parts and systems realized that its long-standing focus on productivity improvements would not be enough to generate the rate of earnings growth that it was seeking. Emerson had become renowned as the best-run cyclical company thanks to its ability to increase earnings even during economic downturns. Its strategy of being the lowest-cost producer drove continuing cost reductions, quality improvements, and small market share gains. Its

record of sustained profitability was matched by no industrial manufacturer, and by few public companies of any sort. It had clearly
earned the right to grow.

But in late 1992, its chairman and chief executive, Chuck Knight, had
become convinced that earnings gains and stock price appreciation
would slow if new growth initiatives did not receive more attention.
Corporate planning forecasts indicated that future advances in
productivity and sales would not generate sufficient profit growth to
produce attractive shareholder returns. More top-line growth would be
required to meet Emerson's aspirations. In resolving to grow, Chuck
Knight pulled all three levers: he captured the senior team's commitment,
raised the bar, and removed organizational barriers to growth.

Gaining senior team commitment

Rallying the leadership team to growth is not easy.[5] In most corporations, it takes six months to two years of reflection, debate, and
personal development. Changes in personnel may be needed too. There
was no "big bang" that galvanized Emerson's management team.
Rather, an intense analytical process forged agreement on the need for
growth and the risks involved.

Once the commitment was made, action soon followed. Knight made
several changes in management systems, practices, and policies. The
1994 corporate planning conference put the urgent need for growth
in all Emerson's businesses firmly on the corporate agenda. The
structure of Emerson's planning process was changed accordingly. The
annual divisional planning conference was split into two parts. In one,
a senior corporate executive would lead a profitability review not
attended by the CEO; in the other, Knight himself would lead a growth
review. Such overt changes sent a clear signal to Emerson's senior team.

Though it is still in the process of transforming itself into a growth
company, Emerson's early returns are encouraging. Between 1994 and
1996, the annual revenue growth rate jumped to 14 percent, roughly
three times the average rate of the previous five years. Just as important,
profit growth rates kept pace.

Raising the bar

The resolve to grow is usually expressed in the form of new targets. Often, these targets seem to be beyond reasonable expectations. As such, they get noticed. Bold expectations serve as a rallying cry for corporate efforts.[6]

Knight announced a program aimed at double-digit sales growth. He also called on each business unit to put forward growth opportunities in two categories: "sustain and protect leadership" (driving horizon 1 growth) and "change the game" (building horizon 2 and 3 businesses). At the same time, individual divisions and the corporate office developed plans for strategic acquisitions and partnerships.

Knight noted, "Our planning sessions exceeded our expectations by identifying more growth opportunities than we expected."[7] Like Emerson, most organizations have substantial latent growth potential. Merely to ask for growth ideas – and indicate a willingness to share the risk of pursuing them – sometimes produces surprisingly good results.

Removing organizational barriers

Unseen barriers to growth hold most large companies back. Unless confronted and removed, they undermine efforts to kickstart growth. A common example is the conviction that to advance in a company, one must avoid mistakes. Who ever got fired for making budget?

Other barriers can include corporate cultures with fixed beliefs, such as "We compete in mature markets"; incentive systems that reward performance in relation to budget rather than according to the magnitude of the improvement achieved; and planning systems that propose investments and initiatives tailored to survive the annual strategy review. These things are the unintended consequences of a decade's worth of reengineering, restructuring, and downsizing. Getting started on a growth program means identifying and tearing down such barriers.

Shifts in human resources policies are a case in point. At Emerson, top-line growth became the measurement tool for more than half the annual bonuses. Employment practices changed as Emerson hired experienced marketers from such companies as Procter & Gamble, Johnson & Johnson, and Black & Decker to put more muscle into its industrial brands. It permitted divisions to budget for as many as 2,000 new growth-related positions by 1997, while making redundancies in areas that were failing to develop substantial growth possibilities. To highlight the growing importance of the Asia Pacific region, it transferred a vice-chairman to lead corporate growth initiatives there.

Building the resolve to grow throughout an organization calls for actions like those taken by Emerson: clear signals of the leadership team's commitment to a growth agenda. More important and enduring are the changes in practices and policies that affect how people work and how they are motivated. Changes to planning processes, targets and goals, incentive systems, and even organizational structure are what really convince the troops that management is serious about change.

It all takes time. Successful growth efforts must identify the organizational barriers to growth, and confront them. Leaders who fail to do so may be able to generate momentary growth, but they will not be able to sustain it.

Creating a point of inflection

The right and the resolve to grow are both preconditions for success in the pursuit of growth. However, a company's approach to these two essentials will be partly determined by its starting position. Some managers have successfully started a growth program and may be beginning to see results; for them, it is important to continue progress toward three healthy horizons.

In our experience, however, many leaders have failed to earn the right to grow, have not resolved to grow, or both. They fall into one of the three most unhealthy categories described in chapter 2: under siege, losing the right to grow, or running out of steam. In preparing for growth, they must address the missing preconditions.

If you are under siege...

 ... you need both to earn the right and to build the resolve to grow.

It is difficult to grow your way out of trouble. Companies whose core businesses are under attack should be thinking above all about earning the right to grow. Before managers get carried away with new ideas, they must achieve solid performance in their core businesses. Cost cutting, quality improvement, strategic divestment, and other performance enhancement measures will be needed to make such companies competitive.

This is not to say that growth should come off the agenda altogether. A desire to grow may well focus an organization's attention on performance improvement. Indeed, employees will find it easier to accept a performance improvement exercise if it is undertaken to realize an inspiring growth aspiration. In any event, the priority must be to achieve profitability in horizon 1. Without it, the cash and stability needed to sustain investments in growth will be lacking.

Compaq provides a dramatic illustration of how a company can kickstart growth while under siege. An early player in the IBM-compatible PC business, Compaq was stunned when cheap clones started to flood the market and attack its more expensive models. At prices some 40 percent below Compaq's, products from companies like Dell and Packard Bell changed the competitive game, turning PCs into commodities. After rising by 25 percent the previous year, Compaq's sales fell by 9 percent in 1991, and operating income halved. Compaq's high cost structure, underdeveloped sales forecasting and production planning processes, reliance on trade promotion, and inflexible culture left it ill equipped to deal with rapidly changing buyer behavior and fierce price competition.

To tackle the slump, the company laid off 12 percent of its workforce. But unsatisfied with the turnaround effort, Compaq's board of directors replaced co-founder and chief executive Rod Canion with Eckhard Pfeiffer. He led a drastic restructuring of the company in three areas: reducing operating costs, speeding up product development, and extending the product line to compete with the clones. By doing so, he was earning the right and building his team's resolve to grow.

Pfeiffer immediately set new targets for product profitability. He also took steps to develop a performance culture. Managers were held strictly accountable, and high performers were handsomely rewarded. These efforts produced an impressive turnaround in operating performance by the end of 1992. Total staff reductions amounted to 14 percent of the 1991 workforce, overhead per computer produced was down by 63 percent, and product development times were slashed.

Compaq was now poised to pursue growth, and resolved to achieve Pfeiffer's aspirations. Soon after becoming chief executive, he had announced that Compaq aimed to be the world's top designer and manufacturer of PCs, notebook computers, and servers by 1996. Having introduced no new products between 1990 and late 1991, the company launched 40 in 1992. By resegmenting its markets, Compaq was able to sharpen product planning and positioning. Prices were cut by between 10 and 30 percent – still preserving a small brand premium – and geographic expansion was vigorously pursued in Asia, Latin America, and Eastern Europe.

Thanks to these heroic efforts, Compaq became number one in PCs in 1994, two years ahead of Pfeiffer's target. Just as important, sales grew at 45 percent and net income at 58 percent a year between 1992 and 1996, while shareholder returns averaged 46 percent.

If you are losing the right to grow...

 ... you must refocus on the basics of performance improvement in your core business.

Companies that are emphasizing horizons 2 and 3 at the expense of their core business obviously have no problem with resolve to grow; indeed, if anything, their desire to grow may be the root of the problem. If they are unable to maintain performance in horizon 1, the growth businesses in horizons 2 and 3 are likely to suffer as funding dries up. While executives in such companies need not relinquish their resolve to grow, they must redouble their efforts to keep the core healthy. They must balance growth performance measures with operational ones, and ensure that sufficient resources remain dedicated to defending and extending the core businesses.

Consider the Reynolds & Reynolds Company. In 1988, it completed a decade of 16 percent average annual growth, but was on the brink of trouble. Founded in 1866 as a manufacturer and distributor of forms, Reynolds grew into an $800 million business through internal growth and acquisitions. By the mid-1980s, it was building horizon 2 businesses in information management products ranging from high-margin industry-specific computer systems to low-margin continuous paper rolls for computer printers.

In the late 1980s, Reynolds suffered several setbacks in its horizon 1 businesses: customer consolidation, a market shift to low-margin products, and heightened competition. It also had trouble digesting the Arnold Company, a large general printer it had bought in 1986 just as competition in the printing industry intensified. The acquisition had added 50 percent to Reynolds's revenue and was too large to dismiss as an obvious candidate for divestment, but it was largely responsible for a one-third decline in Reynolds's operating income. With the core in trouble, sales flattened from 1989 to 1991, and market value dipped ominously. David Holmes, who had run the division that sold business forms to automotive dealers, became chief executive and confronted the crisis.

Holmes's first challenge was to stabilize operating income in horizon 1 and regain the right to grow. He developed a strategy to focus on a limited set of customer markets – automotive, health care, and general business – and build leadership positions in them. After analyzing industry prospects and Reynolds's competitive position, Holmes decided to divest six other operating units between late 1988 and 1991. Reynolds returned to profitability, and the general business forms unit became a growth engine from 1992 to 1996 as multiple acquisitions were integrated into the now successful business.

If you are running out of steam...

 ... building resolve to start on the journey toward growth is your priority.

Companies that are running out of steam have the opposite problem of those losing the right to grow. Performance is not usually a problem; these companies are often internationally respected, high-performing organizations. If anyone has earned the right to grow, they have. It is simply unclear where future growth will come from because horizon 1 is experiencing diminishing returns and there are no new drivers of growth in horizon 2 or 3. What is needed is a dedication to growth to equal the dedication to operating performance. There is no better time to build the resolve to grow than when the core is strong.

The magnitude of the task should not be underestimated: altering ingrained behavior, changing the culture, and rallying the organization to a new cause will almost certainly require major changes in aspiration and a suite of business-building initiatives that may alienate some of the old guard. The story of Emerson Electric, which was running out of steam in the early 1990s, proves the point.

Although many senior management teams are new to spurring growth, the experience of such companies as Warnaco, Emerson Electric, Compaq, and Reynolds & Reynolds demonstrates that they can do it if the proper foundation is in place. But the tasks of earning the right and building the resolve to grow are never complete. Both are preconditions for growth, but neither is a milestone that can be passed and then forgotten. Both call for vigilance. Continuous performance improvement must go hand in hand with the development of growth initiatives. Any growth program will hit rough patches, so management's resolve to grow must be reinforced continually. Failing that, growth will simply rise and fall on the swells of the economic cycle.

While the foundation is being laid, managers must also turn their attention to identifying growth opportunities. In chapter 4, we describe productive ways to search for these opportunities.

NOTES

1   One influential book in this area is M. Hammer and H. Champy, *Reengineering the Corporation: A manifesto for a business revolution* (HarperBusiness, New York, 1993). An excellent summary of the value and impact of reengineering appears in J. Mickelthwait and A. Wooldridge, *The Witch Doctors* (Heinemann, London, 1996), chapter 1, "The fad in progress: Re-engineering," pp. 27–48.

2   See, for example, the compelling analysis of the value of focus and simplicity in the German electronics industry in J. Kluge *et al.*, *Shrink to Grow: Lessons from innovation and productivity in the electronics industry* (Macmillan, London, 1996).

3   W. H. Miller, "Gillette's secret to sharpness," *Industry Week*, January 3, 1994.

4   C. Baden-Fuller and J. Stopford agree: "Our successful transformations share a common feature: rejuvenation was generated from within, using limited outside resources." *Rejuvenating the Mature Business: The competitive challenge* (Routledge, London, second edition, 1996), p. 2.

5   Many commentators discuss the challenge of developing senior teams' commitment. See, for example, N. M. Tichy with E. Cohen, *The Leadership Engine: How winning companies build leaders at every level* (HarperBusiness, New York, 1997); C. Baden-Fuller and J. Stopford, *Rejuvenating the Mature Business: The competitive challenge* (Routledge, London, second edition, 1996), pp. 154–6; S. Ghoshal and C. A. Bartlett, *The Individualized Corporation: A fundamentally new approach to management* (HarperBusiness, New York, 1997), chapter 8; and J. Katzenbach *et al.*, *Real Change Leaders: How you can create growth and high performance at your company* (Times Business, New York, 1995).

6   The importance of stretch targets is acknowledged by managers and commentators alike. In *Built to Last: Successful habits of visionary companies* (Century, London, 1994), J. C. Collins and J. I. Porras devote chapter 5 to "Big, hairy, audacious goals," which they define as those that reach out and grab people in the gut.

In General Electric's 1995 annual report, CEO Jack Welch notes that GE set goals for profit margins and inventory turns in 1991 that were respectively 50 and 100 percent higher than the company had achieved in the past three decades. He explains the rationale: "In stretching for these 'impossible' targets, we learnt to do things faster than we would have going after 'doable' goals."

Kazuo Inamori of the Kyocera Corporation says: "Suppose that you are capable of reaching 100 percent, but you set your goal to be 90 percent, just to make sure you would attain it. Your conservatism will compound each time you set a new goal. On the other hand, if you were to set your goal above 100 percent and work hard to attain this, your next goal could be even more ambitious. This will lead to exponential growth.... In 10, 20, or 30 years, there will be a big difference between people who have set incremental goals and attained them one at a time, those who have set unattainable goals and never reached them and those who have never set any ambitious target." *A Passion for Success: Practical, inspirational, and spiritual insights from Japan's leading entrepreneur* (McGraw-Hill, New York, 1995), pp. 81–2.

7 Emerson Electric 1995 annual report, letter to stockholders, p. 3.

4　Searching for opportunities

Many leaders doubt they can make their companies grow. Advisers tell them their markets are mature, their core business is threatened, or their competitors have already commandeered the attractive territories. If they look elsewhere for inspiration, they may find the prescriptions emerging from the current debate on growth too narrow. Their advice is usually to follow a single strategic path.[1] One approach latches onto product innovation, another talks of fundamental business redesign, yet another focuses on globalization.[2] But such strictures oversimplify the manager's challenge and, if followed, are likely to yield disappointing results in the long term.

The reality is that managers impose implicit and explicit constraints on their thinking about corporate growth.[3] But it need not be that way. In our work, we have looked for ways to open managers' eyes to hidden opportunities. To this end, we have developed a tool that we call the "seven degrees of freedom." By systematically addressing each degree of freedom in turn, managers can learn to think more broadly about growth opportunities in their businesses.

The seven degrees of freedom are based on variables that describe the directions in which growth can be pursued. These are the customers served; the products and services provided; the system for delivering them to customers; the geography in which business takes place; and the current industry structure (Figure 4.1). These directions are

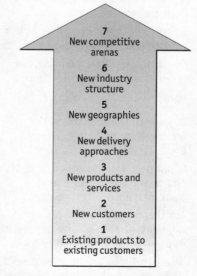

Figure 4.1 Seven degrees of freedom for growth

distinct from vehicles such as acquisition, which could be used to pursue several of them.

The first degree of freedom concerns the existing business: managers consider how the company can grow by selling more of what it already makes to current customers. The second degree looks beyond current customers to find opportunities to sell existing products or services to new customers or segments. As constraints are relaxed one by one in this way, new degrees of freedom open up. The process ends with the opportunity to step outside the industry and begin business in a new arena.

Seven degrees of freedom

1. How could we increase sales to the same customers with the same product mix?

Could new approaches to advertising or promotion persuade customers to increase the size or frequency of their purchases?

How could we increase customer loyalty and our share of each customer's purchases?

Could prices be adjusted to boost volume and net revenue?

Could other existing products or services be cross-sold to current customers of core products?

2. How could we extend the business by selling existing products to new customers?

Could new approaches to advertising and promotion capture new customers in existing segments?

Are there entirely new customer segments that might be interested in existing products and services?

How can these products or services be repositioned for new segments?

Are there partnerships or alliances we could form to increase the reach of existing products and services?

Could we bundle these products and services in ways that appeal to new customers?

3. How could we grow by introducing new products and services?

What extensions or modifications to existing products and services would fill gaps in our market coverage?

What customer need is our current product or service satisfying, and what is the ideal product or service for that need?

What fundamentally new products or services could be developed to cater for emerging or latent demand?

Are there any products or product lines that can be purchased or licensed to complement our current range?

One might ask, "Don't executives already do all that?" Frankly, no. In the heat of the commercial battle, many managers fail to con-sider all the possibilities open to them. Our experience indicates that the seven degrees of freedom framework is an effective way to identify growth opportunities. Its value as a diagnostic tool lies mainly in the fact that it forces users to consider each degree of freedom in turn. Though straightforward, it has helped companies ensure that they investigate the full range of options. Moreover, comparing opportunities across the degrees of freedom often prompts a productive debate among the management team about corporate priorities.

4. How could we expand sales by developing better delivery systems for customers?

What new sales channels have we yet to explore (direct sales, electronic channels, new distributors)?

Are there substitute channels for existing products? Is a direct channel now feasible?

Can the business delivery system be reengineered to improve time, cost, and quality?

5. How and where could we expand into new geographies?

Are there opportunities to deepen points of distribution in existing territories?

Are there opportunities to enter underserved regions within the boundaries of an existing national business?

Could production cost or quality advantages be exploited via exports?

Could global coverage drive economies of scale?

In which new markets could our business model be exploited?

6. How much could we grow by changing the industry structure through acquisitions or alliances?

Which troubled industry participants could be acquired at the right price and turned around?

Which parts of the industry could be consolidated via acquisitions? Are there scale economies or other competitive advantages in doing so?

Short of outright acquisition, what assets or sub-businesses could be bought?

7. What opportunities are there outside existing industry boundaries?

Are there opportunities to integrate vertically and create competitive advantages?

Could our business skills be used in other industries?

Do we have unique assets that could be used to create new businesses?

Could any of our relationships be used to gain access to new businesses?

Are other industries converging on our own?

Freedom in practice

Let's bring the seven degrees of freedom to life by considering how a few real companies explore their strategic options.

1. How could we increase sales to the same customers with the same product mix?

Companies that sustain growth are adept at finding new ways to expand sales of their existing products and services to their existing customers. They may design marketing and sales initiatives that increase the frequency of purchase or the quantity purchased, or cross-sell products to customers who currently purchase from a narrower range of offerings. As well as pursuing traditional approaches like these, more and more companies are growing by deploying direct marketing programs based on sophisticated databases of purchasing behavior, and by rewarding customer loyalty.[4]

Many companies with a dominant position in a slow-growing market would start to look elsewhere for growth. Not Frito-Lay, the snack food division of PepsiCo. Unwilling to concede that the snack chip category might be mature, Frito-Lay constantly breathes new life into its existing product range. Fritos, Lay's, Doritos, Cheetos, Ruffles, Rold Gold, and other products are in the cabinets of 94 percent of all US households. In the five years from 1990 to 1995, Frito recorded almost double-digit annual growth, while the cumulative share of competitors declined.

Frito-Lay is a master at boosting sales of existing products to existing customers. It employs fun mass media marketing campaigns to support its brand equity and uses effective point-of-sale promotions to tempt consumers to make impulse purchases. In addition, it leverages its 13,000-strong sales force to capture more and better shelf space in retail outlets by, for example, seeking to get its corn chips placed not only next to other salty snacks in the snack foods aisle, but also next to Mexican salsa dips in the condiments aisle.

2. How could we extend the business by selling existing products to new customers?

To focus on meeting the needs of a carefully defined target market can be the essence of effective strategy. But electing to serve only a certain group of customers can blind companies to other possibilities. Identifying and pursuing new customers can offer incremental growth or unlock attractive opportunities to serve entirely new segments. Demographic patterns and socioeconomic trends may point to pockets of latent demand. The aging of the baby-boom generation has opened up opportunities in health care and insurance for many companies. Marketers have recognized the potential in demographically defined segments such as women and ethnic minorities, or behaviorally defined segments such as "environmentally aware," "aspirational status conscious," and "price oriented/discount driven."

By adopting a consumer goods marketing strategy rather than a technology focus, Nokia has reached new segments. One of the leading producers of cellular phones, Nokia used to aim its models at high-volume business users. But it has since turned cellular phones into a fashion accessory by offering easy-to-use devices in vivid colors such as purple, opal, green, blue, and pewter. A few relatively simple modifications to the hardware met the needs of a distinct market segment, making the product a must-have among young people. "We are always looking for new ways to blend technology with today's lifestyles. What Nokia has inspired marks the transition of the phone – used not only for its function as a personal communication tool, but also as a fashion accessory," said Matt Wisk, Nokia's director of marketing.[5]

3. How could we grow by introducing new products and services? Companies seeking growth most often choose to exercise the freedom of introducing new products and services. But the results are frequently disappointing, especially in mature industries. Innovations must be carefully designed to ensure that they meet a genuine market demand; there is no point in a new product that no one wants, or that is a me-too clone. Innovation is difficult to predict or plan; it can only be made more likely to happen.

It is surprising how often chance events lead to exciting new product ideas. Recovering at home from a heart attack, Mike Harper, the former president of ConAgra, invited his vice-president of marketing over for lunch. After trying the Harper family's turkey chili, they had a sudden insight: prepared foods that are good for you can taste good too. That might not sound terribly original today, but it did in 1985. Harper's turkey chili lunch evolved into a successful range of products marketed under the banner of Healthy Choice. After four years in the R&D pipeline, these low-salt, low-fat, low-cholesterol meals were launched in supermarkets across the United States.

Determined to capture a first-mover advantage, ConAgra flooded the market. By 1992, the brand had more than 150 products. Healthy Choice moved from ninth to third among frozen entrées, enjoying sales of more than $500 million in its first three years. By 1997, the product count was over 300, and sales topped $1.5 billion.

4. How could we expand sales by developing better delivery systems for customers?

Again and again, companies with strong market positions lose out to competitors that develop a better way of delivering a similar product or service to the same customers. The revolution in communications and Internet-based commerce has intensified such competition by effectively redesigning the delivery system and allowing innovators to bypass existing sales channels. In financial services, automatic teller machines, combined with innovations such as mobile sales forces, are prompting big changes in banks' branch infrastructures. In retailing, category killers provide consumers with a vast array of specialist products at much lower cost than traditional retailers. In industry after industry, the redesign of delivery systems is providing growth opportunities for attackers and problems for defenders.[6]

Who would trade a sari for heavyweight jeans in steaming India? That was the marketing challenge faced by Arvind Mills, the world's third-largest denim manufacturer. Arvind had both to increase the appeal of jeans and to find a low-cost way to distribute an affordable product in a country with an average income equivalent to US $200 a year. It came up with Ruf and Tuf, a ready-to-sew kit of jeans components (denim, zipper, rivets, and leather brand patch) that could be distributed via thousands of tailors across India.

By early 1996, the company had organized 52 training programs showing how to stitch a pair of jeans for 4,500 tailors across 10 states.

At $6 a pair, the new jeans for the masses were far more affordable than such upmarket brands as Flying Machine and Lee, which cost $20 to $40 (and were also marketed by Arvind in India). Ruf and Tuf became India's best-selling jeans. Even after production was increased threefold, demand continued to outstrip supply – so much so that Arvind stopped advertising. Within two months of launch, sales of the new fashion sensation topped a million units. Having established its market position, Arvind is now moving toward more traditional channels for pre-sewn jeans and considering product extensions such as Ruf and Tuf ready-to-stitch shirts.

5. How and where could we expand into new geographies?
Geographic expansion is one of the most powerful options for growth, but it is also one of the most difficult. Many companies are in a position to harness growth by increasing product coverage within existing territories or entering new territories in countries where they already operate. International growth opportunities may offer even more scope, allowing companies to replicate a successful business formula in multiple markets and leverage the cost advantages of global coverage in scale-intensive businesses.

Among the many companies in our research sample to use geographic expansion as a principal driver of growth is SAP. "If you had asked 10 or 15 years ago, can a German company be renowned internationally in the software area, most people would have said no," wrote the *Financial Times;* "that is the domain of the American companies, of the Japanese."[7] Today, SAP is the largest European software company and the fifth-largest independent software vendor in the world. It has an enviable growth record: compound annual growth of 40 percent in sales and 38 percent in net income between 1990 and 1996, with sales of DM 3.722 billion (about US $2.4 billion) in 1996.

The company's early aspirations to go international have pushed sales outside Germany to as much as 67 percent of revenue, from just 30 percent in 1988. SAP moved first into familiar German-speaking territories, then systematically expanded across the world, particularly in North America. Its flagship product R/3 dominates the fast-growing sector of enterprise resource planning software and has revolutionized the way data flows between different parts of a company. The software is available in 14 different languages and can be customized to suit different local requirements. We will return to SAP in chapter 6 to see how it used its distinctive capabilities to carry out this international expansion.

6. How much could we grow by changing the industry structure?
Managers are naturally cautious about growth opportunities that involve changing the industry structure. But many of the most successful growth companies do pursue opportunities of this kind, usually by means of mergers, acquisitions, or alliances. More than half our sample of 30 companies have used acquisitions to drive growth. Pat Anslinger and Tom Copeland have shown how distinctive approaches to acquisition and integration enabled a sample of leading diversified corporations and leveraged buyout funds to grow profitably through M&A.[8]

CRH, a producer of building materials and products such as cement and concrete blocks, has used acquisitions extensively to expand its business and create a global building materials group. The company was created in 1970 by the merger of Irish Cement, the country's first cement producer, and the Roadstone Group, the local leader in aggregates and concrete products. Following the merger, CRH found itself with high market share in a small island economy, and started to look to international growth.

Much of its long record of 20 percent annual sales and profit growth was driven by the acquisition of small and medium-sized players in Europe and the United States. It adds value to these companies through operational improvements, product transfers, and synergies with existing CRH operations. Between 1986 and 1996, CRH digested about 150 acquisitions to become the fourth-largest company in the world in its sector in terms of market capitalization.

Thanks to its decentralized organization, CRH is able to provide development and entrepreneurial thrust at a local level. Many big corporations with a centralized acquisition focus might consider CRH's acquisitions too small to bother with. CRH avoids bidding wars through the patient courtship of mostly family-run enterprises, ensuring that it has a realistic valuation of its targets before purchase. For their part, owners feel comfortable with the CRH culture, and usually stay and enjoy growing their businesses within the group. This acts as an excellent reference for other prospective sellers. The company has fine-tuned this program of small acquisitions into a growth machine, gradually building strong regional market positions and giving its shareholders 21 percent compound annual growth in returns between 1970 and 1996.

7. What opportunities are there outside existing industry boundaries?

Expanding outside industry boundaries is one of the most challenging directions in which to pursue growth, and calls for especially careful consideration. Though many companies have diversified and prospered, there are still more for which diversification was a disaster.

None the less, most of the successful growth companies in our sample have stepped outside their industry boundaries. Some have created value through vertical integration either because the industry they were entering was attractive in its own right, or because integration enabled them to overcome a market failure between two stages of the industry chain. Others have been forced to compete in new arenas when previously separate industries converged, as in cable television and telephony or gasoline selling and grocery retailing. Still others have defined where they wanted to play according to the capabilities required for success rather than the product market, and have found ways to leverage their existing skills in a new setting.

GE Capital Services stands out in our sample as a successful exponent of cross-industry movement. Originating as a credit company that helped finance the purchase of General Electric products, it has grown by adding businesses at a frenetic pace. "With its multitude of businesses, GE Capital ought to have a personality as fragmented as Woody Allen's," *Fortune* remarked. "Instead, it is more like Clint Eastwood, scanning the horizon squint-eyed for a fistful of dollars."[9]

GE Capital still defines itself as a financial services company, but some of its 28 units have the look and feel of nonfinancial businesses. Over time, the company has moved from consumer and retail credit to railcar, aircraft, truck, and trailer leasing, corporate finance, credit cards, insurance, technology management, and outsourcing. Boasting more than $30 billion in annual revenue, GE Capital is the world's largest equipment lessor, with over 900 airplanes, 120,000 trucks, nearly 200,000 railcars, 750,000 cars, and 11 satellites.

Perhaps the biggest diversification has been GE Capital's successful foray into the information technology world. Its IT solutions business began with a small company in Canada. After proving the formula locally, it made a number of IT acquisitions in the United States, the United Kingdom, and Australia, building annual revenue to more than $6 billion. Its aim has been to provide "soup to nuts" computer services, ranging from financing company computers to managing entire networks and systems.[10]

Breaking the shackles

Relying on the seven degrees of freedom to identify growth opportunities will not necessarily solve the strategic problems of moribund companies. The search can easily fail if strategists have their eyes fixed on an image of the business as it is today, or if they produce a feeble list of opportunities that no one cares about. Creating a real growth strategy is impossible until managers allow themselves to see businesses in new ways and evaluate opportunities with their hearts as well as their minds.

Expansive mindsets

Corporate creativity can be a casualty of success. A company can so dominate its market that it will need a broader market definition before it can find growth opportunities.

Gillette could easily have been satisfied with its commanding 60 percent share of the global market for men's razors and blades. But an expansive mindset allowed it to see opportunities in the more broadly defined market for men's grooming products, in which its share was only 20 percent. It moved into shaving cream, deodorants, and aftershave with the Gillette Series for Men.

An even broader definition put the company in the market for personal care products, of which its share is only 5 percent. Still more unexplored opportunities emerged. Gillette moved into dental care with Oral-B, women's grooming with Sensor for Women, small appliances with Braun, and even stationery with Waterman and Parker. Its expansive mindset has allowed it to pursue all seven degrees of freedom:

Existing products to existing customers. In its blades business, Gillette has a host of products from basic disposables to Sensor blades. Its attention to distribution, advertising, and promotion generates continuing growth from core customers and products.

Existing products to new customers. Following the success of the Sensor razor, Gillette extended its brand and technology into products designed for women, introducing a specially tailored variation of the Sensor. Its success established a new growth arm in women's toiletries.

New products and services. In any five-year period, Gillette aims to have 40 percent of its sales coming from new products. In razors, the company has attempted to upgrade customers through successive generations of breakthrough products: from coated stainless steel blades, twin blades, pivoting heads, and lubricating strips to Sensor, Sensor Excel, and now MACH3, a three-blade razor. The Gillette brand has been extended into new product areas such as shaving cream and deodorants. Braun Oral-B invented a revolutionary oscillating toothbrush to clean teeth better. Satin Care for women represented the first shaving preparation not based on soap. Gillette invented the first "invisible" clear gel antiperspirant and the indicator toothbrush.

New delivery channels. After acquiring Parker, Gillette used its position in the corporate gift market to push its more exclusive Waterman pens. In dental care, Gillette leveraged two sales channels to sell its newly developed electric system: Oral-B representatives sold to dentists and Braun sold to the appliance trade.

New geographies. With operations in over 200 countries, Gillette generates more than 70 percent of its sales and operating profit outside the United States. It often enters a new country with the blade business since a shaving market usually exists, captures market share by offering superior products, and then introduces a broad range of ancillary products. The risks of entering emerging markets are minimized through joint ventures and the use of established technologies.

Improved industry structure. Gillette consolidated PaperMate's position in the stationery industry by acquiring Liquid Paper in 1979, Waterman in 1987, and Parker in 1993. It also acquired the operating assets and intellectual property rights for Wilkinson Sword's blade business throughout much of Asia and Latin America.

New competitive arenas. From its core business of blades and toiletries, Gillette stepped out into stationery with PaperMate in 1955, small electric appliances with Braun in 1967, dental care with Oral-B in 1984, and batteries with Duracell in 1996.

Not many companies are as enterprising as Gillette. It has been said that once people are convinced they know something, they stop learning about it. Corporations behave in the same way. An organizational orthodoxy often dictates what is and is not possible, without necessarily reflecting the opportunities available. There may be a widespread conviction that few new possibilities exist, or managers may simply be in the habit of looking at the company with blinkers on.

As early as 1960, Theodore Levitt condemned the limitations of companies' mindsets in his classic *Harvard Business Review* article, "Marketing myopia." He referred to the tendency of companies to imprison themselves "in the narrow grip of tight product orientation." He used the railroads as an example of inappropriate self-definition: "They let others take customers away from them because they assumed themselves to be in the railroad business rather than in the transportation business."[11]

Challenging the orthodoxy is an effective way to break out of ingrained beliefs and restrictive self-definition. Some of the most enduring growth companies defy conventional wisdom by redefining their industry boundaries and target markets. Their destinies would have been quite different had they chosen not to look beyond their core businesses.

If Disney had remained focused, it would probably still be a small animation company. If GE Capital had confined itself to financing General Electric's consumer products, it would never have become a leader in leasing, fleet management, property and casualty reinsurance, and private-label credit cards. If Bombardier had stayed with snow-mobiles, it would not be the third-largest commercial aircraft manufacturer in the world. If Hong Kong entrepreneur Li Ka-shing had heeded advice to stick to his knitting, he might still be in the plastic flower business, not heading a multibillion-dollar empire of shipping terminals, telecommunications, power, and finance.

Thinking too broadly also has its dangers, however. Harvard Business School professor and consultant Michael Porter argues that in the attempt to grow, companies too often "blur uniqueness, create compromises, reduce fit, and ultimately undermine competitive advantage. In fact, the growth imperative is hazardous to strategy." Porter contends that a company's priority should be to deepen its strategic position, not widen it, as this carries the risk of dissipating its value.[12]

Companies are right to be cautious about pursuing growth initiatives. But to let due caution prevent them considering unusual ideas is foolish. Collins and Porras strike the right balance: "We're not saying that evolutionary progress equals wanton diversification.... Nor are we saying that the concept of 'stick to the knitting' makes no sense. The real question is: What is the 'knitting' in a visionary company?"[13]

The legitimacy of passion

All companies make completely rational decisions about the opportunities they are going to pursue – at least, that is the standard expectation in the business world. As a result, planners and analysts often have undue influence on the strategy process. The methods they use are engineered to eliminate or control for bias. They should not be.

Sterile strategy documents gather dust for a reason. They have the arrogance to suggest that the will of the organization should bend to the rational elegance of a cunning strategy. But seldom is that strategy imbued with the interests, hopes, and dreams of the managers charged with making the new ideas fly. Without their passion, a strategy may be smart. It may be ingenious. It may even be right. But it may also be impotent, lacking the power to transform anything.

The assumption that a company can search for opportunities without bias is false. When tradeoffs must be made between several economically attractive ideas, executive teams are deeply influenced by what they most want to do. For this reason, passion should be explicitly recognized in the search for opportunities. Putting a value on passion acknowledges that business creation is not a mechanistic process for planners, but a human affair to which leaders bring their own emotions. It may mean assigning lower priority to some opportunities that show genuine promise, but in return, it gives the remaining ideas a better chance of success. Managers are more likely to devote their energy to ideas they believe in and care about.

Approaching the seven degrees of freedom with an expansive mindset answers the question, "What is possible?" Just as important is the question, "What are we passionate about?" Ventures about which no one cares are unlikely to flourish. Instead of wasting limited management and financial resources on opportunities that arouse little enthusiasm, leaders should shelve them or work to generate excitement around them.

The Kyocera Corporation's founder, Kazuo Inamori, believes passion to be perhaps the single most important ingredient in the success of a strategy. He started Kyocera in 1959 to make ceramics. Today, his company is the leading supplier of integrated circuit housings in the world; it is also successfully involved in telecommunications with DDI, multimedia with Kyocera Multimedia, and finance with Kyocera Leasing. Inamori's belief in passion is so deep that he recommends not seeking profit directly, but letting profit follow from the pursuit of passion. With this approach, Kyocera's net income has grown from less than ¥5 billion in 1980 to more than ¥80 billion (US $713 million) in 1996.

In his book about entrepreneurialism, Inamori asserts that "deep passion" was the reason behind the creation and eventual success of the telecommunications business DDI, in which Kyocera owns a 22 percent share. "I would never have been able to start DDI had I not been intoxicated with the dream of challenging the national monopoly of NTT. The project required a huge investment and nobody could guarantee our success. Any traditional mind would have judged the venture too risky."[14] Passion led Kyocera executives to devote private time to a speculative discovery process. Every weekend for six months, a team of six engineers would travel to Kyocera's guest house in Kyoto to "plan, dream, reflect, and argue." Following their passion paid off. On its first day of trading in 1994, DDI's market capitalization exceeded US $11.75 billion. By 1996, the company had sales of $6 billion and a market value of $18.8 billion (greater than that of Kyocera itself: $14 billion).

Putting passion on the table does not mean letting bias run riot. Biases against new ideas can be as destructive as passion can be constructive. If passion is fuel in the search for opportunities, prejudice is a brick wall. For managers, overcoming prejudice is as great a responsibility as tapping into passion.

Prejudices can be both organizational and personal. A company may simply resist ideas that are too new. It will almost certainly be biased against any that threaten to cannibalize the core. Personal prejudices can have just as much impact. A growth strategy based on expanding into China and India cannot succeed if no senior executive is prepared to spend a few years in these countries and if members of the leadership team are reluctant to pay regular visits.

The best way to combat prejudice is often the simplest. Senior leaders can create momentum around an unpopular set of opportunities simply by showing their commitment to it. Another way to fight prejudice is with fact. Taking a few small steps can give managers the information they need to make a more informed judgment about the attractiveness of an opportunity. If the steps serve only to confirm their prejudices, then that in itself is valuable. If their prejudices prove unfounded and the opportunity is promising, those first steps lend momentum.

Neither passion nor prejudice affects an opportunity's potential. But they do affect how that opportunity is perceived, and hence its chances of success. Passion magnifies; prejudice obscures. If a company takes both into account during its search for a growth strategy, it will be better able to recognize an opportunity's true potential.

There are many different ways of searching for opportunities. Some companies run workshops; others set up a strategy skunk-works at head office. Some assign five crackerjack executives to the task; others round up thousands. Whether the process is top-down or bottom-up is beside the point. It is not just the breadth of involvement that matters, but the breadth of the search. In the end, whatever the process used and resources deployed, finding attractive opportunities is always as much art as science.

Earning the right to grow, resolving to grow, and identifying new opportunities are all necessary to overcome inertia. But a compelling growth strategy calls for more than the identification of opportunities. Not all opportunities are structurally attractive.[15] And, as the proponents of the resource-based view of the firm demonstrate, new businesses can only be built and protected from competitors where attractive market opportunities intersect with relevant company capabilities.[16] Bringing together opportunity and capability to create new businesses is the subject to which we turn in Part III.

NOTES

1   See, for example, R. Whitely and D. Hessan, *Customer Centered Growth: Five proven strategies for building competitive advantage* (Addison-Wesley, Reading, 1996); M. Treacy and F. Wiersma, *The Discipline of Market Leaders: Choose your customers, narrow your focus, and dominate your market* (Addison-Wesley, Reading, 1995); and R. M. Tomasko, *Go for Growth: Five paths to profit and success – Choose the right one for you and your company* (John Wiley, New York, 1996).

2   See, respectively, J. M. Utterback, *Mastering the Dynamics of Innovations: How companies can seize opportunities in the face of technological change* (Harvard Business School Press, Boston, Mass., 1994); A. J. Slywotsky, *Value Migration: How to think several moves ahead of the competition* (Harvard Business School Press, Boston, Mass., 1996); W. C. Taylor and A.M. Webber, *Going Global: Four entrepreneurs map the new world marketplace* (Viking Penguin, New York, 1996); and J. Bleeke and D. Ernst (eds.), *Collaborating to Compete: Using strategic alliances and acquisitions in the global marketplace* (John Wiley, New York, 1993).

3   For an engaging discussion of the limitations of "managerial frames," see G. Hamel and C. K. Prahalad, *Competing for the Future: Breakthrough strategies for seizing control of your industry and creating the markets of tomorrow* (Harvard Business School Press, Boston, Mass., 1994), chapter 3, pp. 49–71.

4   The use of loyalty-based marketing to boost sales from existing customers is described in F. Reichheld, *The Loyalty Effect* (Harvard Business School Press, Boston, Mass., 1996). See also M. Treacy and F. Wiersma, *The Discipline of Market Leaders: Choose your customers, narrow your focus, and dominate your market* (Addison-Wesley, Reading, 1995), chapter 8, "The discipline of customer intimacy."

5   Reported on Nokia Web site.

6   See, for example, A. J. Slywotsky, *Value Migration: How to think several moves ahead of the competition* (Harvard Business School Press, Boston, Mass., 1996), which demonstrates how value migrates from outmoded business designs to new ones that are better able to satisfy customers' priorities. Slywotsky identifies seven interesting patterns and draws on a number of case studies. See also I. Morrison, *The Second Curve: Managing the velocity of change* (Ballantine Books, New York, 1996).

7   G. Bowley, "Silicon Valley's transplanted sapling," *Financial Times*, March 27, 1998, p. 20.

8   P. L. Anslinger and T. E. Copeland, "Growth through acquisitions: A fresh look," *Harvard Business Review*, January–February 1996, pp. 126–7. The authors studied 21 diversified corporate acquirers and 37 financial buyers. The corporate acquirers made a total of 829 acquisitions, 80 percent of which they reported as earning more than their cost of capital, and averaged more than 18 percent a year in total

return to shareholders over a 10-year period. The financial acquirers averaged 35 percent a year by their own estimates.

9 T. Pare, "GE monkeys with its money machine," *Fortune*, February 21, 1994, p. 81.

10 J. Curran, "GE Capital: Jack Welch's secret weapon," *Fortune*, November 10, 1997, p. 130.

11 T. Levitt, "Marketing myopia," *Harvard Business Review*, July–August 1960; reprinted September–October 1975, p. 44.

12 In "What is strategy?" *Harvard Business Review*, November–December 1996, pp. 61–78, Porter uses the example of Maytag, a manufacturer whose success rested on dependable washers, driers, and dishwashers. After expanding its range into refrigeration and cooking and adding five new brands with different positioning, it grew substantially but saw its average return on sales drop from between 8 and 12 percent to less than 1 percent. Though the expansion had seemed a logical way to develop Maytag's offering, the costs involved in losing brand identity and production efficiencies compromised the company's success.

13 J. C. Collins and J. I. Porras, *Built to Last: Successful habits of visionary companies* (Century, London, 1994), p. 187.

14 K. Inamori, *A Passion for Success: Practical, inspirational, and spiritual insights from Japan's leading entrepreneur* (McGraw-Hill, New York, 1995), p. 146.

15 There is a difference between an opportunity and an attractive opportunity. One influence on likely profitability is industry structure. Michael Porter popularized the "five forces" model for assessing structural attractiveness in his landmark book, *Competitive Strategy: Techniques for analyzing industries and competitors* (Free Press, New York, 1980). This work built on the structure/conduct/performance paradigm of industrial organizational economics put forward by Joe Bain in his 1956 work, *Barriers to New Competition* (Harvard University Press, Cambridge, Mass.). It asserts that an industry's profitability is determined by the nature of firms' competitive conduct (for example, pricing decisions), which in turn is driven by the structural forces at work (such as producers' market power). In turn, the average profitability of the industry affects the profitability of individual corporate strategies.

16 For an excellent summary of the theory and implications of the resource-based view, see D. J. Collis and C.A. Montgomery, "Competing on resources: Strategy in the 1990s," *Harvard Business Review*, July–August 1995, pp. 118–28. The antecedents of this view can be found in E. Penrose's 1959 book, *The Theory of the Growth of the Firm* (Oxford University Press, Oxford, third edition, 1995), and in K. Andrews's 1971 classic, *The Concept of Corporate Strategy* (Richard D. Irwin, Burr Ridge, Ill.). Other notable contributions to the development of the theory include B. Wernerfelt, "A resource-based view of the firm," *Strategic Management Journal*, September–October 1984, p. 171–80; M. A. Peteraf, "The cornerstones of competitive advantage: A resource-based view," *Strategic Management Journal*, March 1993, pp. 179–91; and R. M. Grant, "The resource-based theory of competitive advantage: Implications for strategy formulations," *California Management Review*, Spring 1991, Volume 33, Number 3, pp. 114–34.

Part III

Building momentum

The foundations are laid. You are prepared to pursue growth. But how do you get started? And if you are already growing, how can you accelerate your growth?

The art of kickstarting or accelerating growth lies in turning ideas into profitable businesses. A company cannot profit from an opportunity, no matter how attractive, if it cannot marshal the capabilities to capture and defend it. This can present a problem for low-growth companies. Most have limited skill sets, and pursuing a new business without the necessary capabilities can be a leap into the unknown that is doomed to failure.

The next three chapters describe how to identify capabilities and use them to build businesses. They illustrate a pragmatic step-by-step approach that we call "staircases to growth."

We also show how to create strong, hard-to-imitate competitive positions in an emerging business. As well as protecting young businesses from competitors, it is also necessary to protect them from your own company. We close by describing the steps growth companies take to ensure that their own organizational behavior does not stifle new business initiatives.

5   Staircases to growth

The three horizons provide a compelling snapshot of a company's current position. As such, they show only what is happening at a particular moment. The contents of a business development pipeline appear as a frozen image: the stock of a company's initiatives, each captured at a specific stage of development.

To sustain profitable growth, a business development pipeline must have not only a strong stock, but also a healthy flow. A motion picture assembled from a sequence of snapshots would show horizon 3 options flowing into horizon 2 growth engines and ultimately into horizon 1 core businesses.

Accumulating a stock of ideas is not enough: the next challenge is to take a promising idea and create from it a viable business. Too often, promising horizon 3 options fail to become horizon 2 businesses, and emerging horizon 2 growth engines fall prey to excessive spending or are preempted by competition. For models of successful business building, we can look to the companies in our growth sample. Below, we explore how, in less than a decade, American natural gas players Williams and Enron built respectively a multibillion-dollar telecommunications business and a worldwide private power generation business, and how property company Lend Lease became Australia's fastest-growing and second-biggest fund manager.

One step at a time

Executives who want to develop horizon 3 options into core profit engines face two big problems: market uncertainty and gaps in their skills, assets, and relationships. We have found that successful growers typically address these problems by taking not bold leaps, but a series of measured steps. Each step takes them a little closer to their ultimate goal, makes money in its own right, and adds capabilities that prepare them for further opportunities. When these growers look back on what they have achieved, they see not a chaotic zigzag but a distinctive staircase pattern.

While few single steps are dramatic, when linked as a staircase of sequential growth they create dramatic results. None of our sample of successful growers would claim to have known from the outset where their steps would lead, but they did have a clear view of the business they were building. Every few steps they climbed, they learned skills, secured options, and carved out a competitive position that had been beyond their reach when they stood at the bottom of the staircase. Our research base contains more than a hundred examples of successful growth stories that can be told using the staircase analogy.[1]

This "one step at a time" approach holds good for even the most dramatic business creation moves, as the experience of Williams (formerly the Williams Companies) demonstrates. In 1986 and 1987, Williams, a multibillion-dollar conglomerate based in Tulsa, Oklahoma, got out of real estate, coal, banking, agricultural chemicals, and oil production. Its aim was to focus instead on its core business: building and operating gas pipelines. But after the divestments were over, it still lacked strong growth prospects.

For some time, CEO Joe Williams and senior executive Roy Wilkens had been studying the big changes under way in the US telecommunications market. The deregulation of long-distance services and the breakup of AT&T brought new telecommunications wholesalers and retailers into the market. Voice and data traffic were booming, and high-capacity, digital-quality fiber-optic cable was becoming affordable as the United States entered the information age. Joe Williams decided to start a tele-communications subsidiary, WilTel. With Wilkens at the helm, the new company set its sights on wholesale long-distance services (Figure 5.1).

Williams had no experience in telecommunications, and the WilTel initiative represented a major departure from its core pipeline business. But Joe Williams believed that WilTel gave Williams a growth vehicle that it could marry with the pipeline business. He had realized that the company's decommissioned gas pipelines in the American Midwest

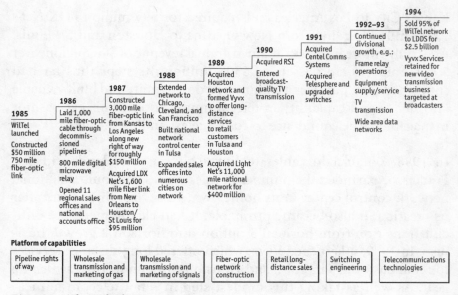

Platform of capabilities

Pipeline rights of way	Wholesale transmission and marketing of gas	Wholesale transmission and marketing of signals	Fiber-optic network construction	Retail long-distance sales	Switching engineering	Telecommunications technologies

Figure 5.1 The WilTel staircase

gave it a potential advantage in the telecommunications industry. The pipelines provided rights of way and protective sheathing through which it could thread fiber-optic cable.

Williams also had specific skills that it could apply to its telecommunications venture: experience in negotiating rights of way for long-distance pipelines, network capacity management of wholesale gas transmission operations, and wholesale commodity marketing. So it was that Williams moved from delivering gas to delivering signals.

In May 1985, WilTel took its first step on the staircase: a $50 million, 750-mile fiber-optic link in Oklahoma for internal company use and resale. In 1986, it laid another thousand miles of cable through decommissioned pipelines running from Kansas City to Des Moines and Omaha to Chicago. Stock analysts and industry experts were skeptical. What could a pipeline company possibly know about telecommunications?

Undaunted, WilTel began a second series of measured but more substantial steps. It constructed a 3,000-mile fiber-optic link from

Kansas City to Los Angeles and acquired for $95 million LDX Net's 1,600-mile fiber link from New Orleans to Houston and St. Louis. After only two years, it had attained annual revenue of $40 million, over 500 employees, and assets of $300 million. Its steps thus far had confirmed that there was a commercial opportunity and built valuable knowledge and capability in telecommunications. This gave senior management the confidence to continue expanding the network.

In 1988, WilTel laid cables to link Chicago, Cleveland, and San Francisco, expanded the number of sales offices, and built a national network control center in its hometown, Tulsa. Just three years after its creation, it also became profitable. It had clearly made the difficult transition from horizon 3 option into horizon 2 growth business. In 1989, it launched Vyvx, which offered long-distance services to retail customers in Tulsa and Houston through its own switching gear. As well as taking this modest step in retail telecommunications, WilTel made its biggest step yet in the wholesale business by acquiring Light Net's 11,000-mile network for $400 million. Expansion continued in 1990 and 1991 with the purchase of RSI, Centel, and Telesphere.

In 1991, six years after startup, WilTel had revenue topping $600 million, profit of more than $80 million, and 1,200 employees. By 1993, its step-by-step growth had created the fourth-largest digital network in the United States, with revenue of more than $1 billion and 2,000 employees. In 1994, Williams sold 95 percent of the WilTel network to LDDS (now MCI Worldcom) for $2.5 billion.

Staircase architecture

Several questions arise when a company tries to build a staircase to growth. Are there rules of proportion to guide the construction of successful staircases? Should each step be a certain size? How do you decide when to persevere with a staircase and when to give up?

No formula can substitute for managerial judgment. Even so, analysis of more than 100 growth staircases reveals a consistent pattern. Virtually all successful staircases proceed in four phases: seeding the initial growth options; testing the business model; replicating and extending the business; and managing for profitability.

This staircase architecture is closely linked to the three horizons (Figure 5.2). The first stage of the staircase, seeding growth options, is essentially horizon 3. The second stage, testing commercial viability, represents the challenging transition from horizon 3 to horizon 2. We believe that this transition deserves to be considered separately because it raises specific issues that sometimes trouble organizations. The third stage, in which there is rapid replication and extension of the business concept, is synonymous with horizon 2. The final stage of the staircase, managing for profitability, is consistent with guiding core businesses in horizon 1.

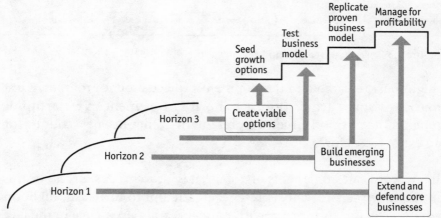

Figure 5.2 Staircases and horizons

The Enron Corporation grew from a Texas-based natural gas transporter into a leader in the physical and financial trading of gas and electricity in the United States, and in independent private power generation worldwide. Tracing the development of the staircase for this latter business will shed light on each of the four steps (Figure 5.3).

1. Seeding growth options

To start staircases, companies must secure growth options. Just having an idea for a business is not enough. An idea does not become an option until a step has been taken to establish a nascent business position. It

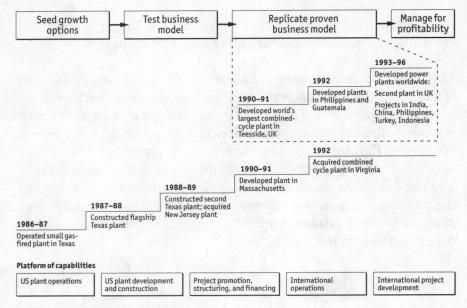

Figure 5.3 Enron's staircase in power generation

might be a research and development project, a pilot program, a test market, a small acquisition, a minority investment in a startup or potential acquisition target, a representative office in a new country, or an export sales force.

If any word can sum up this first stage, it is "search."[2] A staircase begins in unknown territory. It represents an attempt to turn a spotlight on a dark area. It calls for creativity, patience, and persistence in the face of repeated false starts.

This is a fitting description of Enron's evolution. In 1986, it created a horizon 3 option from its base in natural gas extraction and transportation. Its first step was modest enough: it acquired the right to operate an existing Texas gas-fired power generation plant. With this early step, it built knowledge and capability in private power generation, a promising opportunity that had emerged from the deregulation of gas and electricity markets in the United States. Enron knew that market uncertainty could yield a first-mover advantage for smart operators. Its first step not only confirmed the size of the opportunity but also produced insights into a business model that might succeed.

2. Testing the business model

Companies push their staircases into the next stage by testing their business models. Their aim is to develop a market-based grasp of what might work, to discover which capabilities are critical, to understand how options can be developed, and to assess the extent of the likely commercial potential.

The word that best sums up this second stage is "direction." While the first stage culminates in a clearer idea of where a staircase is likely to lead, the second stage clarifies how it will get there. Understanding the nature of the commercial opportunity makes it possible to see how it can best be captured. The second stage entails deciding how to take the business to market and validate its potential.

It usually takes at least two to four years to move a business from stage 1 to stage 3, where it may begin to take off commercially. Enron tested the commercial viability of its independent power production staircase in its next few steps. It constructed a bigger plant in Texas in 1987, following that with three more power ventures in Texas, New Jersey, and Massachusetts. Having done all that, it had validated and refined its business model and was ready to accelerate expansion.

3. Replicating the business model

If the business model proves commercially viable, the staircase can be replicated and extended in a phase equivalent to horizon 2. In this third stage of staircase development, growth accelerates. Heavy investment is needed, and bigger revenues begin to flow. This is usually the point at which the stock market recognizes that the business has more than just option value.

If there is a word that sums up this stage, it is "position." Stage 3 is essentially about securing positional advantage in the market. The accumulation and control of critical capabilities are key; so is timing. As previously proprietary insights become more visible to others, advantage flows to those who can establish a strong market position ahead of the pack.[3] For this reason, stage 3 typically consists of bold steps: large investments and major acquisitions.

Five years after entering the independent power production business, Enron found itself at the forefront of the deregulating electricity industry. In 1991, it took its first major step to replicate and expand its business concept by developing the world's largest combined-cycle gas turbine plant in Teesside in the United Kingdom. This project secured Enron's international reputation as a developer of independent power projects. With its staff of seasoned specialists, Enron replicated the concept globally, developing projects in Indonesia, Germany, China, Guatemala, the Philippines, Turkey, and India.

4. *Managing the business for profitability*

In nature, no tree grows to heaven. In business, even the most rapidly evolving enterprises reach maturity. At stage 4, the emphasis shifts from rolling out and extending the business model to managing for profitability, the equivalent of managing core businesses in horizon 1. Companies with businesses in this phase focus on extracting value from incremental extension, cost reduction, and renewal.

If one word could sum up this fourth stage, it is "execution."[4] The key to success in the last part of the staircase lies in operational excellence: a single-minded concentration on executing better than anyone else.

By 1998, Enron's independent power business had entered the fourth part of its staircase. To achieve its vision of becoming the leading energy company in the world, the company will need to be adept at managing profitability and continuing to anticipate industry trends. This will be no easy feat at a time when governments are growing savvy at playing suppliers off against each other, competitors are getting smarter, and margins are falling. To manage profitability, industry players are working to restructure fuel supply, electricity sales, and construction contracts, pushing for engineering breakthroughs in the design of plants, and making operating improvements in generation and transmission.

The value of staircases

Even when there is strong capability building at each step, migrating an idea from a horizon 3 option to an emerging horizon 2 enterprise and on to a horizon 1 core business is tricky. The advantage of taking many small steps rather than a few big leaps is that it helps companies manage the risks that arise on two fronts. First, market uncertainty makes it impossible to predict the success of a business: for every great idea, there are many that will fail. Second, new businesses call for capabilities that a company does not yet have; without them, the promise these businesses hold out will not be realized.

Market uncertainty

External forces are forever changing the strategic landscape on which a staircase is built, and attractive growth prospects can disappear as quickly as they come into view. Companies often ask, "Why can't we describe our ideal complete staircase today?" The reason is that strategies drawn up with detailed five-year budgets are rarely accurate, even for experienced players. This makes it impossible to plan a staircase more than a few steps in advance, or to know exactly where it will lead.

Failing to recognize the inevitability of market uncertainty, large corporations sometimes overcommit to a new business by sinking major investment early. The staircase approach helps them preserve flexibility. Successful staircases focus on immediate steps. There is an overall direction or aspiration, but the size of each step is small. With each one, the company builds skills and sees new opportunities open up; its field of view expands, and the range of possible next steps becomes clearer. "Bet the company" moves that lock an organization into a new business become a thing of the past. (Admittedly, in some capital-intensive industries with large minimum efficient scale plants, or in network businesses, or where competitive dynamics call for a preemptive strike, it may be necessary to make large investments with bold early steps.)[5]

The staircase approach minimizes the damage suffered when things go wrong. Not all new businesses thrive. Small steps retain flexibility, avoid excessive early commitment, and allow poorly performing staircases to be cut off. Consider the Lend Lease Corporation, an Australian growth company that started out in construction and property development. Lend Lease's interpretation of property has grown progressively over the years (Figure 5.4).

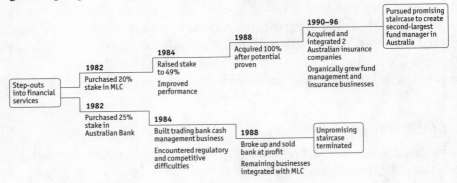

Figure 5.4 Lend Lease's successful and unsuccessful staircases

By the early 1980s, Lend Lease had developed fund management expertise through its wholly owned property trust, which financed and owned a number of developments constructed by the company. In 1982, it spotted an opportunity in the deregulating Australian financial services industry. It created two horizon 3 options in financial services by buying modest stakes in the startup Australian Bank, the country's first new retail bank in 50 years, and in MLC, an established insurance company.

The retail banking staircase did not go as planned. Lend Lease joined Australian Bank as one of several partners, taking a prudent 25 percent of the equity. The success of the new venture hinged on changes that were expected to take place in Australia's restrictive banking legislation. These did not materialize, and the business environment remained hostile to the upstart. Though the bank introduced innovative products, its performance was disappointing. In 1988, Lend Lease cut short the staircase at a small loss, broke up the bank, and took its cash management and mortgage loan portfolio and consolidated it into MLC.

Lend Lease's first steps in insurance and fund management were also modest. It had worked with MLC in property development before it bought a 20 percent interest in the company. Two years later, convinced of MLC's potential, it increased its stake to 49 percent. Over the next four years, Lend Lease cut staff numbers at MLC by 30 percent and doubled profits. In 1988, it bought MLC outright.

Under its new ownership, MLC introduced a stream of investment products, developed its sales channels, and made two insurance acquisitions, Capita and Australian Eagle. By the end of 1997, MLC had become the second-largest retail fund manager in Australia, and contributed more than half of Lend Lease's profits. Early in 1998, Lend Lease attempted to continue the staircase by merging MLC with National Mutual, the Australian subsidiary of French insurer Axa, but the deal did not come to fruition.

Lend Lease preserved its flexibility by taking as many small steps as it could before making big commitments. At some point, however, commitment becomes unavoidable. Even in industries where strong competitive positions can be built via gradual investment, there comes a time when flexibility must be sacrificed and investment ramped up.[6] The strength of the staircase approach is that the early small steps increase a company's knowledge and skills. When it decides that bigger steps are required to give the business momentum, it can make a much more informed commitment. Lend Lease's first steps gave managers the wherewithal to make sound decisions about whether to build their staircases or cut them short.

Many great growers have built new businesses in this way, capitalizing on the fact that each time they took another step, additional opportunities opened up. Managers were able to move fast enough to exploit these opportunities before competitors moved in or business conditions changed. Staircases can thus encourage managers to behave as entrepreneurs rather than bureaucrats, avoiding excessive deliberation and paralysis by analysis.[7]

Gaps in capability

The WilTel and Enron stories are salutary. Conventional thinking would have condemned the moves from gas pipelines into telecommunications and power generation as unduly risky. They were not. Both staircases involved many steps, not one dangerous leap. More important, Williams and Enron acquired new capabilities with each step they took – capabilities that acted as a base from which they could take subsequent steps.

Capabilities are at the heart of the staircase approach. Broadly defined to encompass all of the resources at a company's disposal, they are more than just core competencies. They also include privileged assets and special relationships, which we discuss in chapter 6. In starting its staircase, WilTel had the advantage of a dormant asset, its decommissioned gas pipelines. Its first step brought it new experience and knowledge of the economics and operations of wholesale telecommunications networks. With each additional step, the organization gained additional capabilities, enabling it to take further steps.

Companies rarely possess all the capabilities they need to succeed in new businesses. The newer the business, the greater the gap between current capabilities and those required in the new venture.[8] The staircase approach addresses this problem by breaking large leaps into manageable steps that allow time to build the necessary skills. For an example, consider Johnson & Johnson's approach to developing a global leadership position in disposable contact lenses.

Back in 1980, before Johnson & Johnson entered the consumer optical products business, executives engaged in a strategic review selected contact lenses as a promising new proposition, given its growth prospects, the lack of entrenched players, and the potential fit with the company's distribution strength and consumer reputation. To turn the idea into a horizon 3 option, Johnson & Johnson took an exploratory first step. In 1981, it acquired Frontier Contact Lenses, a relatively small ($50 million) company with a market share of less than 5 percent in the hard contact lens business. Frontier produced lenses using a traditional two-step molding and grinding process. This small acquisition gave Johnson & Johnson a starting point from which to learn the contact lens business (Figure 5.5).

Soon after the purchase, a manager from another Johnson & Johnson business encountered a Danish scientist who had developed a process for molding soft contact lenses. He realized that it might revolutionize the industry and called the president of Vistakon, Johnson & Johnson's contact lens business, who flew to Denmark the next day. The company snapped up the rights to a new polymer that could in theory be molded to the specification of a contact lens and cured via ultraviolet light. Produced in a new one-step process, it had the potential to slash production costs. Vistakon realized that affordable disposable lenses could be marketed to consumers frustrated with caring for hard lenses.

Johnson & Johnson still had to work out how to overcome the limitations of injection-molding technology to produce disposable contact lenses. Vistakon sought the assistance of NYPRO, one of the few companies capable of producing injection-molded lenses to the specifications required for human use.

Three years after its initial move, Johnson & Johnson had learned enough about the industry to understand the potential of its staircase. It had also acquired a distinctive technology and manufacturing skills that made the venture less vulnerable to competitive attack. Its steps had been relatively small up to that point, but in the next few years, it committed some $250 million to bring the Surevue contact lens to market and an additional $200 million to develop and launch the Acuvue daily disposable lens. By the mid-1990s, it had built a highly profitable business.

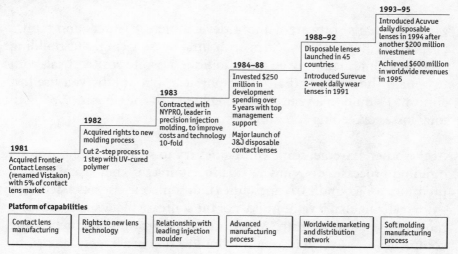

Figure 5.5 Johnson & Johnson's contact lens staircase

Each step on a staircase, be it an alliance, an acquisition, or a new marketing program, can be thought of as a business-building initiative – an investment to add a capability. Implicit in each step is a decision to build, borrow, or buy that capability. Companies can build capabilities internally by training people. They can borrow them from other organizations by embarking on alliances, partnerships, or licensing agreements. And they can buy them by hiring new people, procuring technologies, or acquiring entire companies.

Some companies try to avoid the hard graft of creating a staircase. Others make the mistake of trying to build every capability for themselves. It can be tempting to do everything in-house, but building capabilities from scratch is far more time-consuming than buying or borrowing existing capabilities. It may be more expensive, too.

Consider the problems experienced by AT&T's Medis venture, launched in 1984. Its objective was to automate patient records so that doctors and hospital staff could share information in real time at the patient's bedside or in the doctor's room. AT&T tried to create Medis by assembling all the required capabilities from inside the corporation. It brought in technical experts from Bell Labs and marketing and strategy people from the corporate center. It even forbade the Medis team to hire outside.

Medis wrote its software without development partners and built a proprietary hardware platform with little outsourcing. But building everything internally proved too ambitious. Despite positive trials with two major hospitals and an office physician group, the venture lost almost $11 million a year. AT&T finally pulled the plug in 1988 with total losses exceeding $60 million.

At the other extreme, some companies try to speed up the business-building process by buying an existing staircase. They usually pay a premium for a bundle of capabilities that someone else has assembled – not realizing that it is the builder of the staircase that usually captures most of the value it creates. When sustained growers acquire mature companies, however, it is usually to build a step in a larger staircase by assembling a missing capability. They do not try to escape the work of building a staircase, nor do they make the job harder than it need be. They use every available method of assembling capabilities, but in a balanced mix, building some themselves, borrowing what they can, and buying others.

The staircase approach reflects how entrepreneurs succeed in the real world, often despite fierce competition. Industry landscapes are changing so rapidly that it is unwise to build businesses around hazy or static views of the future. Building a staircase recognizes that growth strategy cannot be a deterministic exercise. The best a company can do under changing circumstances is to build strong capabilities and secure strategic options while retaining as much flexibility as it can.

Consider Williams and Enron. As players in the natural gas industry, they faced the same set of growth opportunities in 1984. But because growth strategy has as much to do with capabilities as it does opportunities, they proceeded to build very different staircases.

For Williams, the opportunity presented by the regulatory and technological changes in the wholesale long-distance telecommunications business was huge. Its capability consisted of its decommissioned pipelines, existing rights of way, and experience in wholesale transmission. Enron, however, built a substantial business in independent private power generation after seeing the opportunity that electricity market reform afforded. But by leveraging its capability in long-term gas supply contracts for power plants, it quickly developed more sophisticated deal-structuring skills and learned to assemble complex private power ventures.

In the next chapter, we consider how a company begins to assemble capabilities and how they may determine the success or failure of a staircase. Then in chapter 7, we describe the mechanics of taking steps up a staircase in the marketplace.

NOTES

1 Developed in 1992 and subsequently used with dozens of clients, the staircase framework was first publicly discussed in M. A. Baghai, S. C. Coley, and D. White, "Staircases to growth," *The McKinsey Quarterly,* 1996 Number 4, pp. 38–61. The analogy of a staircase is also used independently by C. Baden-Fuller and J. Stopford in *Rejuvenating the Mature Business: The competitive challenge* (Routledge, London, second edition, 1996), p. 71. They state that "the visual image of a staircase reinforces the importance of creating multiple advantages." In "Strategic staircases," *Long Range Planning,* 1991, Volume 24, Number 4, pp. 36–43, P. Williamson and M. Hay describe the value of breaking the strategic capability-building agenda into "bite-sized pieces" that bridge the "gap between strategy and action" and between senior management vision and middle-level operators. Our early thinking was influenced by D. Teece and G. Pisaro, "The dynamic capabilities of firms: An introduction," *Industrial and Corporate Change,* 1994, Volume 3, Number 3, pp. 537–56, and their earlier work with A. Shuler, "Dynamic capabilities and strategic management," CCC Working Paper No. 94–9, University of California, Berkeley, August 1994.

2 Many books and articles deal with the development of strategic options under conditions of uncertainty; see, for example, K. M. Eisenhardt and S. L. Brown, *Competing on the Edge: Strategy as structured chaos* (Harvard Business School Press, Boston, Mass., 1998), and G. Hamel and C. K. Prahalad, *Competing for the Future: Breakthrough strategies for seizing control of your industry and creating the markets of tomorrow* (Harvard Business School Press, Boston, Mass., 1994), chapter 4, "Competing for industry foresight."

3 First movers that establish early advantage can sometimes create a virtuous cycle that allows them to accrue disproportionate returns. This is especially true in industry settings characterized by increasing returns. See W. B. Arthur, "Competing technologies, increasing returns, and lock in by historical events," *The Economic Journal,* March 1989, Number 99, pp. 116–31, and Z. Achi, A. Doman, O. Sibony, J. Sinha, and S. Witt, "The paradox of fast-growth tigers," *The McKinsey Quarterly,* 1995, Number 3, pp. 4–17.

4 For a practical discussion of the features of companies with strong execution and performance discipline, see G. G. Marmol and R. M. Murray, Jr., "Leading from the front," *The McKinsey Quarterly,* 1995, Number 3, pp. 18–31.

5 In "How entrepreneurs craft strategies that work," *Harvard Business Review,* March–April 1994, pp. 150–61, A. Bhide notes that the founder of Federal Express, Fred Smith, faced the need to take big bets early in the company's staircase: "His creativity lay in recognizing that customers would pay a significant premium for reliable overnight delivery and in figuring out a way to provide the service for

them. Smith ruled out using existing commercial flights, whose schedules were designed to serve passenger traffic. Instead, he had the audacious idea of acquiring a dedicated fleet of jets and shipping all packages through a central hub that was located in Memphis.... The jets, the hub, operations in 25 states, and several hundred trained employees had to be in place before the company could open for business."

6 For a thorough exposition of the nature of strategic choices and the relative value of flexibility and commitment, see P. Ghemawat, *Commitment: The dynamics of strategy* (Free Press, New York, 1991), especially chapter 3, "Choice: Making commitments," pp. 33–51.

7 In interviews with the founders of 100 companies on the 1989 "Inc. 500" list of the fastest-growing companies in the United States, A. Bhide found that "successful entrepreneurs spend little effort on their initial business plan – 41 percent had no business plan at all and 26 percent had just a rudimentary, back-of-the-envelope-type plan." In "How entrepreneurs craft strategies that work," *Harvard Business Review,* March–April 1994, pp. 150–61.

8 G. Hamel and C.K. Prahalad have written extensively on the need to build capabilities to bridge the gap between current resources and those required to achieve a corporation's strategic intent. See "Strategy as stretch and leverage," *Harvard Business Review,* March–April 1993, pp. 75–84, and *Competing for the future: Breakthrough strategies for seizing control of your industry and creating the markets of tomorrow* (Harvard Business School Press, Boston, Mass., 1994), chapter 7, "Strategy as leverage."

6 Securing advantage

How did Gillette, a razor-blade company, justify spending $7 billion to buy battery maker Duracell? How has consumer products giant Sara Lee managed to sustain such high growth rates? And how has entrepreneur Li Ka-shing been able to pull off the kinds of deal in China about which others only dream?

The answer is capabilities: the skills, assets, and relationships that companies assemble to build competitive businesses. Our research confirms that sustained growers think broadly about capabilities. Naturally, some rely on operational skill, the traditional definition of capability. But a surprising number from our growth sample thrived by employing less obvious capabilities. We will see how Gillette employed a privileged asset to create huge value from its Duracell purchase, how Sara Lee built superb M&A skills to keep growing at a ferocious pace, and how Li Ka-shing used special relationships to build a sprawling Asian business empire.

The staircase approach suggests that it is possible to build a new business on the strength of a few distinctive capabilities. But if missing capabilities can be assembled as a staircase takes shape, then every company with a relevant capability could pursue a given opportunity. The question then becomes: who will end up capturing the value in the opportunity? Who will own the staircase?

What counts in the end is the set of capabilities each competitor brings to bear in pursuing the opportunity. The competitor with the strongest bundle of distinctive capabilities has the best chance of emerging as the winner. Long-term success is secured only by assembling a difficult-to-imitate bundle of critical capabilities through the staircase approach.

Capabilities, not competencies

When businesspeople refer to organizational capabilities, they usually mean the skills embedded in a company's people, processes, and institutional knowledge. These are so basic to survival that they are often referred to as core competencies.[1] In any competitive environment, a company must be good at what it does and possess skills that make it stand out. Distinctive competencies allow growth companies not only to make more money from existing businesses, but also to extract greater value from new opportunities.

Consider the case of the State Street Corporation. A quiet regional retail bank in the northeastern United States, it seemed in the early 1970s to have a bleak future. Not only was it sitting on a pile of bad loans, but it also had little to mark it out from a cluttered field of competitors. In 1975, new president William Edgerly pushed it to look beyond moneylending to consider a different area of banking: financial custodial services. Edgerly recognized that some of the bank's operational skills could be applied to exploit the intersection of three trends: a growing pool of retirement assets, customer demand for faster access to better investment information, and fund managers' need for efficient back-office accounting and processing systems.

In addition to money handling and safekeeping, the traditional jobs of the custodian, information processing would, Edgerly believed, be a critical operational skill. State Street's back office was a ready-made information processing operation, providing the initial capability the bank needed to enter custodial services. Over time, it transformed itself into a custodian of mutual and pension funds. By 1982, it had left retail banking and boasted $151 billion in assets under custody. Fifteen years later, that figure had risen to $3.9 trillion, and total shareholder returns had grown by more than 32 percent a year.

Today, State Street's IT skills are so advanced that Wall Street analysts see the company as more a data processor than a bank. "Information technology continues to be central to our success," said Marshall Carter, who succeeded Edgerly in 1991. "The way we develop, array, and deliver information related to our customers' securities, cash transactions, and investment portfolios is the value we add."[2]

Important as operational skills are to a company's success, too great a focus on them can stunt growth. The resource-based view of the firm observes that corporations have more than just operational competency at their disposal.[3] A broader definition of capability is required that includes all resources useful in gaining competitive advantage.[4] In addition to operational skill, our definition of capability includes three other classes of resources: privileged assets, growth-enabling skills, and special relationships (Figure 6.1).

Capability platform	Examples
Operational skills	IT management
	Research and development
	Product design
	Low-cost manufacturing
Privileged assets	Distribution networks
	Brands
	Reputation
	Customer information
	Infrastructure
	Intellectual property
Growth-enabling skills	Acquisition and post-merger management
	Financing and risk management
	Capital management
Special relationships	Customers
	Suppliers
	Partners
	Government

Figure 6.1 Elements of a capability platform

Privileged assets

Privileged assets are physical or intangible assets that are hard to replicate and confer competitive advantage on their owner. They include distribution networks, brands and reputation, customer information, infrastructure, and intellectual property.

Distribution networks. A business can use the scale of its distribution network to increase sales of its existing products and services or to reduce the cost of a new product launch. For Gillette, the principal motive for its $7 billion acquisition of battery maker Duracell in late 1996 was synergy in distribution. The distribution network that gets Gillette's razor blades into supermarkets and convenience stores – the same outlets where batteries are sold – was second to none. So big was this opportunity that investors added $4.1 billion to the companies' combined capitalization in the two days following the announcement of the deal. Gillette was able to help Duracell grow by taking it global. This strong domestic player had 50 percent of the American market but little exposure in such emerging economies as China and India, where Gillette's network was especially strong.

Brands and reputation. Strong brands can be extended to launch products without threatening the credibility of the current business. Gillette has used its brand to enter the market for men's grooming products. The Gillette Series for Men includes products such as after-shave, shaving cream, and deodorant, as well as razors and blades. Launched in 1990, the men's Sensor razor achieved $2.9 billion in sales in 1997 alone, with over 60 million users worldwide. Gillette is seeking to beat this record with its revolutionary new product, the MACH3, a three-blade multi-angled razor.

Customer information. Detailed information of all kinds can be critical to maximizing sales. Some of the most valuable is about customers' buying habits and needs. Seven-Eleven Japan's point-of-sale information system helps to ensure that it has the right product mix for every customer who walks into its stores. The company tries to extract a range of data from each sale, including the time of purchase and the gender and estimated age of the customer. The information is downloaded daily from store computer terminals to headquarters, where sales trends are analyzed. Every day, managers can gain access to current and historical data to adjust and customize the product mix for their stores. About 70 percent of an average store's 3,000 products is replaced annually in the never-ending quest for the optimal product mix.

Growth-enabling skills

Organizations that master certain generic growth-enabling skills such as acquisition, deal structuring, financing, risk management, and capital management have a big advantage in creating and sustaining growth. While operational skills tend to be specific to each of a company's businesses, these growth-enabling skills are transferable from one market or business unit to another. As we show in chapter 9, because of their broad applicability, they usually reside in the corporate center, from where they are made available to business units. Most staircases require a measure of these skills, and some would be unattainable without them.

Acquisition and postmerger management skills. Poorly executed, acquisitions can be expensive and risky. Done well, they can make climbing a staircase faster, easier, and cheaper. The ability to make and integrate acquisitions quickly and on attractive terms confers an obvious advantage.[5] It has certainly been critical for the companies in our research base.

The Sara Lee Corporation has relied on acquisitions to extend its staircases and build new ones. Under John Bryan's leadership, the company made more than 80 purchases between 1981 and 1995, while simultaneously divesting underperforming and distracting businesses. Its planning and budgetary system often sets targets that cannot be reached through organic growth alone. To meet them, managers go to great lengths to keep the acquisition pipeline full. The company sometimes courts potential targets for as long as ten years so that it can be the first to know when one of them is ready to sell.

Financing and risk management skills. Since almost every step on a staircase costs money and involves risk, these skills can improve just about any staircase. Highly developed financial and risk management skills enable some organizations to take steps that others cannot. By crafting elegant solutions to funding constraints, such companies can advance along promising growth paths that are too costly or risky for their competitors.

Although the Barrick Gold Corporation's core competency lies in the operation of gold mines, former CFO Robert Wickham noted in 1992 that "Larger [gold companies] will need to know as much about financing as they do about metallurgy."[6] Barrick has used gold bonds that index interest to the gold price as a means of financing new mines. It has also conducted an extremely successful hedging program. Through clever financial engineering, it narrows the risk of developing new mines to operational and geological uncertainties.

Capital management skills. Exceptional capital productivity skills enable managers to make a commercial success of projects that other companies might reject as yielding poor returns. Stretching capital further increases the projected return from individual projects and frees up some of a company's financial capacity for investments in other projects.

Hindustan Lever's success in Indian consumer goods rests partly on its capital efficiency skills. The company generates tremendous sales per dollar of capital through its skill in designing manufacturing plants without any gold-plating and the clever outsourcing of selected manufacturing and distribution activities.

Special relationships

Relationships are one of the most important yet least discussed capabilities. Relationships with existing customers and suppliers can provide growth opportunities and should be nurtured. Those with powerful individuals, businesses, and governments can unlock opportunities that would otherwise be shut off. In particular, relationships can facilitate entry into new industries and geographies, and bring deals to the table.

In Asia, special relationships have played a major role in the extraordinary success of groups founded by overseas Chinese families.[7] The business empire of Li Ka-shing, one of the world's richest men, is founded on special relationships. Li's powerful web of contacts has granted him early access to restricted opportunities in fast-growing infrastructure businesses. His flagship company Hutchison Whampoa has moved rapidly from container terminals into electricity generation, retailing, and telecommunications, expanding from its Hong Kong base into China, the United Kingdom, and Canada. Through joint ventures, it now operates three of China's largest container ports.

Li's access to deals comes through a network of relationships he has been cultivating in Hong Kong and China since the late 1970s. It includes close ties with governments, state-owned enterprises, financial institutions, overseas Chinese entrepreneurs, and Western multinationals. Li has nurtured these relationships in dozens of ways. He sits on the board of the Hong Kong Shanghai Bank, well situated within the Asian deal flow. He sent early signals of his commitment by building the China Hotel in Guangdong in 1980, well before China opened up.

When putting the satellite for his Star TV into orbit, he chose the Chinese Long March IV rocket rather than European or American launch vehicles. He met Deng Xiaoping in 1986 and has maintained personal contact with the top five figures in central government ever since. He was even consulted on China's posthandover laws for Hong Kong, and he shares business interests with government enterprises such as the China International Trust Investment Corporation and Cosco, a major Chinese shipping company.

The relevance of special relationships extends far beyond the emerging markets of the Far East.[8] Village Roadshow has employed relationships to grow from a small drive-in theater operator to an international entertainment company operating cinemas in Australia, Asia, and Europe, as well as theme parks, radio stations, film and music production, and film and video distribution. Village has active alliances or joint ventures with dozens of companies that have been an integral part of its success (Figure 6.2).

Village's relationship with Greater Union, another local cinema operator, started in 1964 when the two companies joined forces to control the distribution of foreign films in the Australian market. This relationship later evolved into a rollout of multiscreen cinema complexes across Australia. Warner Brothers entered the scene with a film distribution agreement in 1971. Village has married its expertise in cinema operation with Warner Brothers' European cinema sites to accelerate both companies' growth in Europe. At the same time, Village's knowledge of its home market and Warner's theme park expertise have led to the development of Australian theme parks and resorts. The same relationship has also enabled Village to make a foray into retail with a franchise agreement to manage Warner Brothers stores in Australia and New Zealand.

As a family-based company, Village's emphasis on establishing and maintaining long-term special relationships is not surprising. In some cases, cross-ownership is involved, but Village executives mostly find alliances by developing the right chemistry with potential partners. They have a long-standing relationship with Raymond Chow, chairman of Golden Harvest, a Hong Kong–based producer of Chinese language films, and the two companies are partners in a range of joint ventures in cinemas in Asia. Commitment to partners begins at the top. The

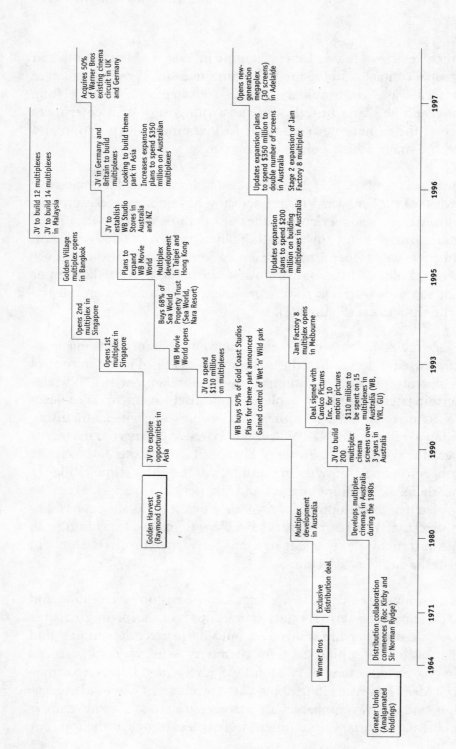

Figure 6.2 Village Roadshow's relationship-based staircases

three leaders of the executive director team, Graham Burke, John Kirby, and Robert Kirby, jointly maintain every key relationship, to the point where they are interchangeable at meetings.

Access-conveying relationships are equally critical for Western companies seeking growth in emerging markets and elsewhere, as Barrick Gold's situation illustrates. Barrick opened its doors in Canada in 1983 under the entrepreneurial leadership of Peter Munk. By 1997, it had become one of the world's largest and most profitable gold-mining companies. But it has met obstacles along the way. Despite Barrick's superior operational skills, investors became concerned in 1993 about the company's lack of options on mines relative to competitors such as Placer Dome and Newmont.

Barrick responded by augmenting its exploration program. But it went a step further: it also played to its strengths in relationships. In 1995, it formed an international advisory board that included former Canadian prime minister Brian Mulroney, former US president George Bush, and former president of the German central bank Karl Otto Pöhl. In assembling this group of heavyweights, Munk was sending a message to investors: we have access to international deals at the highest possible level.

In addition, Barrick formed relationships with many smaller exploration companies operating in Asia, Australia, and Latin America. These companies had innovative ideas, access to exploration acreage, and low overhead, but little money. As such, they complemented Barrick, with its ample capital, substantial mine development, and operational expertise.

Relationships have mattered for as long as people have done business. But recent business history is also littered with cases where the boundary between special relationship and corruption has been crossed. The issue is especially sensitive where the special relationship is with government officials. This makes reliance on special relationships as a capability more complicated than, say, the use of a brand or a distribution network. However, we believe it is possible to derive considerable strategic benefit from relationships without jettisoning ethical values.

From capability to advantage

Successful growth companies invest heavily in scouring the world for new ideas. They track important forces such as demographic trends, technology advances, and regulatory changes. Occasionally, a unique insight will confer enduring advantage, but most opportunities are visible to all competitors at roughly the same time. Even a hidden opportunity is soon exposed to the marketplace by a first mover's early steps, and rapidly duplicated. The value of the original insight soon erodes, and players race to build positional advantage. The winner is the one with the best set of capabilities.

Too zealous an audit of a company's capabilities often leads managers to take a narrow and pessimistic view about its foundations for growth. If tomorrow's activity is dictated by what is done well today, a company will usually find only a limited set of opportunities to grow. In the words of Ghoshal and Bartlett, "core competencies become core rigidities."[9] The essence of the staircase approach, and of much of the literature on core competencies, is that capabilities need to be built. As Hamel and Prahalad wrote, "starting resource positions are a very poor predictor of future industry leadership."[10]

Gaining and keeping positional advantage depend on how well a company assembles the capabilities that a new business requires. Some capabilities are more important than others, and combinations are generally harder to imitate than individual capabilities. The business builder's challenge begins with the need to assemble the capabilities most critical to making money in the business. Lasting competitive advantage comes only when companies assemble difficult-to-imitate combinations of capabilities into bundles.

Controlling critical capabilities early

In the first few steps in a staircase, competitive advantage may not call for superior capabilities in every area of a business. But control of the most important capabilities can determine how much of the value of the staircase will flow to its builder. For every opportunity, it is important to distinguish the capabilities that influence competitive success from those that are merely necessary to play the game.[11] Capabilities that are less critical can be outsourced or controlled by others.

Enron's success in power generation reflects this conviction. As the company built or acquired power plants between 1988 and 1990, it viewed the business in a different way from its utility competitors. It recognized that economic value accrued disproportionately to those who structured the deals, not those who constructed and operated the plants (Figure 6.3). In the early years, Enron was not distinctive at building and operating power stations, but it didn't matter; those skills could be contracted out. Rather, it was good at negotiating long-term fuel supply contracts, electricity sales agreements, construction contracts, financing, and government guarantees – precisely the skills that distinguished successful players from also-rans. By concentrating on these skills, Enron built a strong global position in less than a decade.

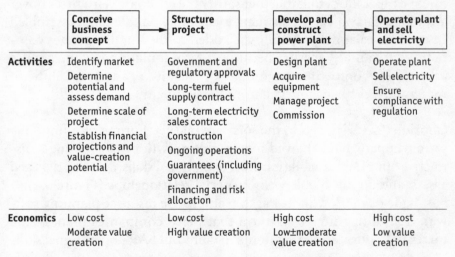

	Conceive business concept	Structure project	Develop and construct power plant	Operate plant and sell electricity
Activities	Identify market	Government and regulatory approvals	Design plant	Operate plant
	Determine potential and assess demand	Long-term fuel supply contract	Acquire equipment	Sell electricity
	Determine scale of project	Long-term electricity sales contract	Manage project	Ensure compliance with regulation
	Establish financial projections and value-creation potential	Construction	Commission	
		Ongoing operations		
		Guarantees (including government)		
		Financing and risk allocation		
Economics	Low cost	Low cost	High cost	High cost
	Moderate value creation	High value creation	Low±moderate value creation	Low value creation

Figure 6.3 Critical capabilities in independent power, circa 1990

This is not an argument for rampant outsourcing. Correctly identifying the critical capabilities early can make or break an entire staircase. In rushing to bring its personal computer to market, IBM outsourced the microprocessor to Intel and the operating system to Microsoft, thus relinquishing two privileged assets critical to the evolution of the computer industry. The market capitalizations of Intel and Microsoft are both now greater than that of IBM.

Bundling capabilities for enduring advantage

Harvard Business School professors David Collis and Cynthia Mont-gomery argue that a capability or resource becomes a source of sustainable competitive advantage only if it passes several tests.[12] First, it must be competitively superior and valuable in the product market. Second, it must be difficult to imitate. Third, it must not be easy to replace by an alternative capability. Fourth, it must be durable. Fifth, it must be difficult to trade. If the capability can walk out the door with an employee, then it is the employee, not the corporation, that will appropriate the value.

Some individual capabilities may pass the tests. A world-class brand, for example, will continue to confer advantage on its owner. But few individual capabilities are unassailable. The key to sustaining competitive advantage on a growth staircase is to build a bundle of distinctive capabilities that together satisfy the criteria. Even a first-mover advantage can vanish if a distinctive capability bundle is not assembled in time. As each new capability is added to the bundle, greater competitive advantage accrues because the combination becomes more difficult for competitors to imitate or substitute, and more difficult for employees to appropriate from the company.

Consider SAP's success in the software market. Europe's leading software company has achieved remarkable growth by assembling a distinctive bundle of capabilities: great operational skills, a set of privileged assets, and an invaluable web of special relationships (Figure 6.4). It has made its mark with its flagship enterprise resource planning software R/3, a distinctive solution that helps companies manage the torrent of information that pours in daily. But SAP's operational skills

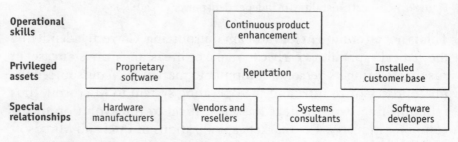

Figure 6.4 SAP's distinctive bundle of capabilities

lie not in the development of radically new technologies, but in continually enhancing and refining its products.

Many companies talk to and learn from customers. SAP achieves constant product improvement by systematically funneling its responses to customer suggestions and requirements into each release of a product. In-depth dialogue with customers and formal meetings with user groups have enabled SAP to convert its customers' specialist knowledge into industry-specific solutions.

Two types of privileged assets contribute to the distinctiveness of SAP's capability bundle: the first is the intellectual property represented by the programming code in R/3 software; the second, the power of SAP's reputation or brand for its 6,000-strong customer base. The commitment of many industry leaders to SAP solutions has helped build momentum toward further growth.

Also at the heart of the growth formula pursued by SAP is a web of complementary relationships. The complexity of its products calls for technical expertise at every stage of implementation. Rather than provide this itself, SAP uses partnerships: with the hardware manufacturers that run its software, with the vendors that sell the product and provide technical support, with the systems consultants that install the product, and with the software developers that provide complementary business- or industry-specific functions. It is in the interests of all of these partners to increase SAP's sales.

While competitors are nipping at SAP's heels, its hard-to-duplicate bundle of skills, assets, and relationships has endowed it with the ability to build and maintain its position as the leading global provider of integrated business software.

In the last two chapters, we have introduced the idea of building a business in a staircase of steps. Thinking step-by-step may make growth less daunting, but building new businesses is still hard for big organizations to do. No matter how much strategic planning they put into the formulation of a business concept – and big companies like to do a lot of planning – they tend to go awry in the execution. Is this because big organizations see execution as inflexible adherence to a plan? Or is it because managing a small, fast-growing venture is incompatible with their size? In the next chapter, we consider what measures a large enterprise can pursue to give a new staircase the best chance of success.

NOTES

1   In "Core competence of the corporation," *Harvard Business Review,* May–June 1990, pp. 79–91, G. Hamel and C. K. Prahalad define a core competency as "the collective learning in the organization, especially how to coordinate diverse production skills and integrate multiple streams of technology." In *Competing for the Future: Breakthrough strategies for seizing control of your industry and creating the markets of tomorrow* (Harvard Business School Press, Boston, Mass., 1994), pp. 199–211, they define it as "a bundle of skills and technologies that enables a company to provide a benefit to customers." A core competency is explicitly defined *not* to be a single technology or skill, a physical asset (such as a factory), or infrastructure (such as a distribution system). For Hamel and Prahalad, not all competitive advantages are core competencies. We agree with their intention of focusing managers' attention on bundles of skills that can endure, and that are difficult for competitors to copy. In practice, however, we see many managers take an unnecessarily restrictive and indeed pessimistic view about the resources at their disposal in pursuit of growth.

2   M. Carter and D. Spina, State Street annual report, 1992.

3   D. J. Collis and C. A. Montgomery, "Competing on resources: Strategy in the 1990s," *Harvard Business Review,* July–August 1995, pp. 118–28.

4   To see that assets and relationships can provide a powerful platform for growth even in the absence of a core competency in the Hamel and Prahalad sense, consider the following example from McKinsey's growth research base.

Many food companies recognize the opportunity for edible oils in China as the spending power of its consumers rises over the coming decades. Yet few will be able to compete effectively with the business established by the Malaysian-based sugar baron Robert Kuok. The Kuok family has two businesses in China: Northseas, based on a plant in Tianjin, and Southseas, based on a plant in Guangdong. The Southseas capability bundle began with a special relationship. Kuok's partner in the venture is the central Grain and Oil Board, the Chinese authority that issues import licences and quotas for edible oils. While competitors rely on expensive or poor-quality local oil seeds, Southseas is able to import much of its needs at lower cost and higher quality. In addition, Kuok's extensive Asian commodities trading capability allows him to purchase and transport imported raw materials more cheaply than others.

Kuok also garners advantage through privileged assets. His Guangdong integrated plant is substantially cheaper to operate than others in China. It includes the largest edible oil refinery and the largest margarine shortening plant in China and a dedicated soybean crushing plant to process imported raw materials. It is located at a deepwater port in a free trade zone with access to Hong Kong–based reexporters. Additional privileged assets include the top brand for bottled oil in China, sales licenses for many provinces, and a salesforce and distribution warehouses across the country.

While this platform does not preempt other players from building substantial positions in China, it is clear that Southseas's capability bundle will give it an advantage in capturing the growth potential of the domestic edible oil market. Contrary to the narrow view of core competencies, much of Southseas's capability platform is based on relationships and assets, not skills.

5 See P. L. Anslinger and T. E. Copeland, "Growth through acquisitions: A fresh look," *Harvard Business Review,* January–February 1996, pp. 126–35.

6 R. Wickham, "Hedging important at American Barrick," excerpt from speech quoted in *American Metal Market,* April 6, 1992, Fairchild Publications, p. 18.

7 For a fascinating analysis of the overseas Chinese business network, see M. Weidenbaum and S. Hughes, *The Bamboo Network* (Martin Kessler Books, New York, 1996). For an excellent summary of relationship strategy in Asia, see Tsun-yan Hsieh, "Prospering through relationships in Asia," *The McKinsey Quarterly,* 1996, Number 4, pp. 4–13.

8 For a discussion of the importance of relationships in the West, see G. Hamel and C. K. Prahalad, *Competing for the Future: Breakthrough strategies for seizing control of your industry and creating the markets of tomorrow* (Harvard Business School Press, Boston, Mass., 1994), pp. 187–93.

9 S. Ghoshal and C. A. Bartlett, *The Individualized Corporation: A fundamentally new approach to management* (HarperBusiness, New York, 1997), p. 284.

10 G. Hamel and C. K. Prahalad, *Competing for the Future: Breakthrough strategies for seizing control of your industry and creating the markets of tomorrow* (Harvard Business School Press, Boston, Mass., 1994), chapter 7, "Strategy as leverage."

11 A. J. Slywotsky and D. J. Morrison, *The Profit Zone: How strategic business design will lead you to tomorrow's profits* (Harvard Business School Press, Boston, Mass., 1997).

12 D. J. Collis and C. A. Montgomery, "Competing on resources: Strategy in the 1990s," *Harvard Business Review,* July–August 1995, pp. 118–28. See also K. Coyne, S. Hall, and P. Clifford, "Is your core competence a mirage?" *The McKinsey Quarterly,* 1997, Number 1, pp. 40–54, and M. A. Peteraf, "The cornerstones of competitive advantage: A resource-based view," *Strategic Management Journal,* March 1993, Number 14, pp. 179–91.

7 Winning through execution

Few large organizations are adept at building staircases. Many lack good ideas. But the notion that a good idea is all it takes to create a valuable business is naïve. If it were true, Visicalc, the original developer of spreadsheet programs, would now be a major force in software, and Xerox would be at the forefront of the personal computer industry it invented. Good ideas are a start, but the majority of new businesses fail because of poor execution, not a flawed concept.[1]

Bad things can happen even to the best ideas for a new business. As we explained in chapter 5, there are two strategic risks to manage: market uncertainty and capability gaps. In addition, new staircases pose organizational challenges. Their exponential growth plays havoc with management processes and systems.

In a large organization, the dominant culture may project a narrow definition of itself that does not include the new business.[2] Processes and systems are usually designed for horizon 1 businesses and can be hostile to the special needs of business-building initiatives in horizons 2 and 3. However, large organizations often incorporate incremental ideas – such as selling more products to existing customers or launching extensions of successful products – into their core businesses quite well because acting on them is relatively straightforward. Horizon 1 ideas tend to be familiar territory, raising fewer skill, marketplace, and organizational issues.

Building a staircase means overcoming both the uncertainty of the marketplace and the resistance, intended or not, of the rest of the organization. The first challenge is addressed by actively adapting the business model – the blueprint that defines how money is to be made – after launch. The second involves protecting the new business from the big organization.

Actively adapting the business model

From 1981 to 1985, General Electric attempted to build what it called the "factory of the future." Jack Welch, a fervent advocate of high-technology opportunities, announced the venture the day after he became chairman, asserting that it would produce $1 billion in annual revenue.

The idea captivated General Electric's senior managers. They envisaged a one-stop shop for industrialists seeking the automated equipment that modern factories would demand. Brimming with confidence, GE's management predicted that in less than a decade, the enterprise would have 20 percent of a projected $25 billion market. It was eager to move fast to beat potential competitors.

But the factory of the future failed to meet expectations. Managers working from over-optimistic financial forecasts did not test the concept thoroughly, assuming customers would find it as exciting as they did. Two years in, the new business had only nine projects, half within GE, half at external companies. Managers attempted to restore confidence with intensive advertising and performance guarantees, but had to rescind them as it became clear that GE could not deliver on its plans. Panic induced heavy cuts, sealing the fate of the venture. Despite the commitment of senior leadership and capital investments in the hundreds of millions of dollars, GE shut down its factory of the future in 1985.

GE's business model turned out to be much less compelling in the marketplace than it was to executives. This is far from rare. Ideally, a business model should provide a clear sense of the market for a product, a convincing reason why a customer would buy it, and a design of the system for delivering it. It should also include projections of time to market and time to profit, financial analyses, a sound assessment of risks, and a plan for marketplace implementation.

No doubt GE addressed all these matters in its business model. But a model can never be more than a best guess, a work in progress. No matter how good it is, there will always be a gap between how a company thinks it should work and how it will have to work to succeed in the marketplace. What turns a good model into a blockbuster business is the willingness to take a few more steps and adapt the model in response to market feedback.

This is what successful entrepreneurs do, but most large organizations fail to do. Unlike many managers in large corporations, entrepreneurs often "cannot easily separate action and analysis."[3] They are not slowed down by formal decision-making processes. They understand that even when there is a detailed concept, the model cannot be set in stone. They are willing to launch the business quickly, but in a measured way, focusing less on planning and more on learning. What works? What doesn't? They learn, fix, learn more, fix again, and so on.

That good business builders are willing to move quickly, fixing as they go, does not mean they are content with shoddy or incomplete business models. On the contrary: they want the best plans possible given the information available. But they recognize uncertainty cannot be resolved without real-world learning. This may seem obvious, but there are plenty of examples in which such learning is neglected because of an almost fanatical commitment to the original model.

We call the process by which companies improve their business models "active adaptation." Builders of successful businesses do not have the luxury of time; they pursue adaptation by means of more, faster, and better-targeted revisions. They subject their business model to market tests even if that means modifying it out of recognition. Instead of passively waiting for learning to happen, they push the pace of learning and the speed of adaptation. This skill more than any other is what makes the premier business builder stand out from the pack.

Perhaps the toughest aspect of active adaptation is that it demands flexibility from managers. It isn't easy to make radical changes to what you believe to be an elegant idea. Champions of new staircases face a paradox: they must be passionate about a concept if they are to endure the arduous business-building process, yet successful active adaptation demands that they set emotion aside and abandon parts of the model as experience dictates. Many new businesses fail because management hangs on to a model for too long, disregarding evidence of flaws or irrelevance. Passion must not be allowed to trump objectivity.

Active adaptation is more than the iterative refinement of an original business model. It frequently involves making fundamental changes in response to market feedback. We call it "active" because it must be proactively managed. The leader of a new business must set milestones to force answers to three critical questions: how best to make the business model work in the marketplace, how far to stretch its growth potential, and how to jump to new staircases.[4]

Making the business model work in the marketplace

Disney's experience in building a chain of retail stores provides an excellent example of active adaptation (Figure 7.1). At the outset, the company had little experience in retailing, apart from its theme parks. An entrepreneurial venture from the start, the Disney Store was launched quickly and at low cost, and modified on the go. The first outlet opened in Glendale, California, in March 1987. It exceeded all expectations by delivering sales per square foot that were three or four times the average for specialist stores.

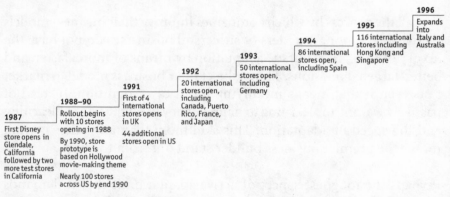

1996
Expands into Italy and Australia

1995
116 international stores including Hong Kong and Singapore

1994
86 international stores open, including Spain

1993
50 international stores open, including Germany

1992
20 international stores open, including Canada, Puerto Rico, France, and Japan

1991
First of 4 international stores opens in UK

44 additional stores open in US

1988–90
Rollout begins with 10 stores opening in 1988

By 1990, store prototype is based on Hollywood movie-making theme

Nearly 100 stores across US by end 1990

1987
First Disney store opens in Glendale, California followed by two more test stores in California

Figure 7.1 Disney Stores' staircase

Over the past decade, Disney has rolled out over 600 stores in the United States and abroad to sell a selection of its 8,000 licensed products. In 1996, the stores contributed 7 percent of total company revenue.

This phenomenal growth story began in 1986, when Steve Burke, Disney's head of business development, held an employee competition to identify business opportunities. The idea most frequently suggested was a chain of shops rather like those in Disney's theme parks. Burke formulated a preliminary business model outlining a plan to put stores selling Disney products into regional shopping centers. Disney executives quickly approved the plan, partly because he requested only $400,000 for development. The onus was now on Burke to prove the concept would work. Michael Eisner recalls, "How long before we opened the first one? About 10 minutes."

The Glendale site was selected not just for its high traffic and attractive environment, but also because it was a short drive from the head office; as Eisner said, "We all can go smell it, feel it, taste it, touch it." When laying out the store, the designers got down on their hands and knees to ensure that the sightlines would work for a three-year-old. Customers duly responded. They also provided detailed feedback about which Disney products the store should carry. The fact that Disney listened and was ready to adjust the product mix offers the first example of active adaptation in this case.

The bottom line of the earliest Disney Stores was impressive. They generated about $2 million in yearly revenue, with pre-tax margins of 15 percent. But Disney was not satisfied. "It took us three or four stores to come up with the idea of putting a large movie screen on the back wall to draw people in," Burke recalled. Documenting the sales figures enabled Disney to negotiate lower rents, since malls usually charge on the basis of a share of a store's sales. Continuing to adapt the model actively to the marketplace while testing its commercial viability, managers saw profits rise by 30 percent by 1989, less than two years after launch.

The Glendale store served as a pilot for Disney. Pilots can facilitate active adaptation, but undertaking one in every aspect of a business model would be expensive and time-consuming. The scope of a pilot should thus be focused as sharply as possible. For "scalable" businesses with small units that can easily be replicated, like the Disney Store, a pilot can be limited to a single outlet. This allows ideas to be tested in a controlled environment where adjustments can be made quickly.

For capital-intensive industries and network-based businesses such as telecommunications and airlines, testing a business model would amount to an immediate rollout or launch; it would be unrealistic to carry out a pilot for a theme park idea, say. In such cases, selected features of the business model could be tested, perhaps through market research.

Stretching the growth potential of the business

Once a business model has been actively adapted with the aid of market feedback, the next challenge is to figure out where else it might be relevant and successful. As we saw in chapter 5, the third stage in a typical staircase entails replicating a business model whose commercial viability has been established. The economic potential of the staircase increases as more and more opportunities for expansion are identified and pursued.

In most cases, the critical driver of value creation will be the productivity of the capital investment. Put simply, the aim should be to reduce the need for capital as much as possible.[5] Not only does capital efficiency improve financial return, but it also preserves capital for use later to hasten the pace of expansion – an important factor when competitors are approaching fast. A capital-efficient business model will make a big contribution to the speed and success of a rollout.

The startup and fixed costs for each Disney Store were relatively high. The company considered other rollout models such as franchising, but rejected them because it wanted to stay close to the customer. The search for alternatives generated several other designs, such as the smaller Disney Corner format for department stores and superstores in certain urban markets. Both kept real estate costs down by avoiding expensive malls.

By 1991, several of Disney's entertainment rivals – Warner Bros., Children's Television Workshop, Ringling Brothers, Barnum & Bailey Circus, and Hanna-Barbera – had begun experimenting with retail formats. The race was on. Having already snapped up many of the best locations, Disney had the advantage.

However, there comes a time when radical modifications to the basic business model must stop. It is difficult to carry on making such changes while rolling out the model at an accelerating pace. Adaptation calls for flexibility and openness to change; rapid rollout demands standardization and predictability. Though management should examine several replication paths, it must commit to one at some point. Further adjustments may still be possible, but attention must be focused on the execution of the rollout plan.

The geographic rollout of Disney Stores has been extremely fast, with a few valuable modifications along the way. Pressured by fast followers, Disney tailored its business models for new markets according to customer preferences. British children prefer Winnie-the-Pooh; the French like Bambi and Thumper; the Japanese love Mickey Mouse. As a result, the merchandise mix carried by stores differs from country to country.

Jumping onto new staircases

The replication of the business model usually yields rich insights about potential staircases; horizon 2 activity tends to generate horizon 3 options in its wake. In turn, each of these options could lead to other opportunities. The leadership challenge is to capture and act on them without distracting the rollout machine from its single-minded focus on execution.

The success of the Disney Stores acted as a springboard for ideas for new retail concepts. In 1990, Disney experimented unsuccessfully with Mickey's Kitchen, a family version of the Hard Rock Café. In 1993 to 1994, it launched the Walt Disney Classic Collection as its first line of animation art (framed cells of original animation from Disney films), and the Walt Disney Gallery retail format. More recently, three other retail ideas have emerged: Club Disney, a family "edutainment" arcade; Disney Quest, a mini theme park; and a concept based on restaurant entertainment linked to ESPN, a sports cable TV network owned by the company.

But at Disney, jumping onto new staircases is not limited to the retail business. It is a way of life for the entire corporation, and explains Disney's remarkable evolution into a media powerhouse. If we look at

Disney's growth, we see the unmistakable pattern of an evolving port-folio of staircases breeding staircases (Figure 7.2).[6]

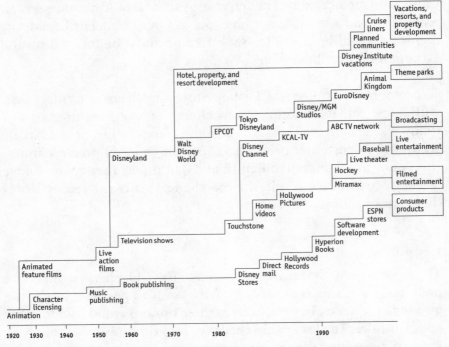

Figure 7.2 Disney's portfolio of staircases

Most people would nominate filmed entertainment as Disney's princi-pal staircase. Over the years, it has developed from its animation roots into motion picture studios, television programming, and, more recently, broadcasting. Animation has also given Disney a way into merchandising. Beginning by licensing characters, Disney entered music and book publishing and then set up its own retail operations.

The early animated films also gave the company an opportunity to build the first theme park, Disneyland, in the 1950s. Its success spawned an international business that is still growing. The theme park staircase has itself acted as the foundation for a successful foray into hotels, resorts, and vacation properties. From there, Disney ventured into developing planned communities – spotlessly clean and secure neigh-borhoods with all amenities – such as Celebration, Florida, just outside Orlando. In 1998, it even entered the cruise line industry.

Protecting a new staircase

Perhaps the only commercial challenge greater than building a new business is building a new business inside a large established organization. Big companies eat their young. Horizon 1 businesses are especially hostile to a new venture when it threatens to cannibalize their base. To disciplined horizon 1 operators, horizon 2 and 3 activities seem chaotic. Their natural temptation is to pin down a new staircase with "good management," using the norms and tools that have proved effective in the core business.[7]

This could be the fastest way to kill a new venture. The culture and management processes critical to maintaining core businesses can be at odds with emerging staircases, which may not survive without firm senior management commitment to meeting their distinct needs.

Shelter and feed the new staircase

Many large companies with strong track records in business creation deliberately protect new staircases by "cocooning" or sheltering them from the corporate body. This creates a small-company environment that fosters urgency, focus, and empathy among employees.

Such was the background to the software product Notes, which is credited with giving the Lotus Development Corporation a new lease on life. That the product exists at all is largely due to then-CEO Jim Manzi's nurturing of Iris Associates, the Lotus-funded development group that created it. Iris operated in a suburban warehouse as an autonomous entity under the direction of Raymond Ozzie, who invented Notes in 1981. Iris succeeded in creating its own entrepreneurial culture. As Lotus president Jeff Papows described it: "The large, bold neon sign that reads 'Iris' at the reception of the facility says it all. It was all about getting four, then six, then eight, and finally 20 extremely smart individuals who truly believed they could change the world.... The sole objective of every single member of the group was to make Notes a success."[8]

According to some executives, Notes was not immediately welcomed by Lotus, then dedicated to pushing its successful 1-2-3 spreadsheet.

Manzi had to step in on several occasions to protect Iris from other Lotus executives and from the board of directors. Had Iris not been cocooned, Notes would not have been there to drive earnings when 1-2-3 ran out of steam. So successful was this approach that IBM, which now owns Lotus, is trying to make it work again. In 1997, IBM and Lotus helped Ozzie found a new Iris-like venture called the Rhythmix Corporation.

The goal of cocooning is to marry the advantages of an independent startup with the possibility of tapping into the capabilities of the core businesses. Maintaining a connection with the larger enterprise rather than being spun off as an independent entity offers several benefits: ready access to cheaper capital, the ability to attract good people, a broad and deep knowledge base, administrative economies of scale, market credibility, and brand recognition.

In the end, the question is not *whether* to cocoon, but where, when, how, and how far. Defining a new staircase's relationship to the broader enterprise is one of the most difficult early decisions for corporate leaders.[9] There are many factors to consider:

- Does the new venture demand more rapid change than the organization is used to?

- How directly is the new staircase likely to compete with (or cannibalize) the existing business?

- How applicable are the organization's operational skills to the new staircase?

- How important is it to create an environment that supports and encourages fresh thinking and counters the organization's traditional biases?

- What will be the process for making decisions about the future of the staircase?

These and other considerations will ultimately determine the extent to which the staircase should be separated from or connected to the larger enterprise. In cases where the new business has similar needs to the existing one and the threat of cannibalization is small, minor cocooning, such as modified reporting requirements, may be adequate.

Structural cocooning was deliberately limited when the Disney Stores were started up. Management established them as a division within the larger consumer products group in order to take advantage of complementary capabilities: the group already focused on merchandising and had a good feel for the target market. The stores would not cannibalize its business; rather, they represented another channel beyond the existing distribution network and catalog businesses. Even suppliers such as toy manufacturer Mattel were not too alarmed because the stores made the merchandising pie bigger. A priority for Disney was to ensure that its customer service culture and values would be perpetuated. Keeping the new business nestled within the organization was a means to that end.

In other cases, it may be important for a new venture to have greater autonomy. As we show in chapter 9, Bombardier's capital group began as the dealership financing arm of its motorized consumer products group. Once its potential had become apparent, the unit was moved out of this group and set up as an independent business with its own president, who reports directly to the chief executive. The move helped to open up fresh opportunities for the new financial services business.

Exempt the new staircase from horizon 1 management systems

The decision to cocoon a new business affects more than just organizational structure. The management systems of a core business may have a profound impact on a fledgling enterprise. Systems that were created to steward a mature business may not serve a new venture with different needs. When new ventures inside large corporations fail, some of the blame may rest with managers too attached to the way they manage core businesses.

We argue in chapter 8 that the assumption that new staircases can be managed in the same way as existing businesses is dangerous. Mechanisms for running a largely predictable horizon 1 operation suit neither the demands of frenetic, fast-growing horizon 2 nor the open-ended nature of horizon 3. What the new business needs is an approach to management that the more risk-averse may find disturbing. The answer is not to overhaul the management systems of the entire corporation, but to exempt the new staircases from potentially damaging elements of corporate policy; in other words, to make exceptions to some of the organization's growth-inhibiting rules.

An established company's primary performance measures may revolve around operational excellence: squeezing out ever-greater volume, quality, and service at declining cost, say. New staircases, by contrast, must create revenue where none yet exists. Profitability may be years away. Holding the leaders of a new staircase accountable for goals they cannot achieve is a sure way to kill the business, and misses the point: if a new staircase is growing well, it should be a net cash consumer. Its goal is not making a profit but meeting project milestones, and ultimately generating high revenue growth. By exempting such a staircase from standard performance measures and giving it a different target, managers can foster growth.[10]

New staircases may need to be granted exemption from orthodox planning and budgeting standards. Relief such as separate reporting requirements can be built into procedures, and fast-track financing can be achieved if ventures are given rapid, direct access to the corporate center. Restrictions on resorting to external sources of finance can be relaxed. Executives may take commitment to the new business to the extreme of allowing managers to make all their own outsourcing and subcontracting decisions, even if they use competitors.

Leeway in human resources systems may also be required. If a large company attempts to build a staircase by using the same people and incentive systems as in its established businesses, frustration will ensue. People with the entrepreneurial skill and energy to build a business may not be attracted to a company with a history of low growth. If standard recruitment, incentive, and performance measurement approaches do not attract them, exceptions must be made. Salary and incentive packages unheard of in the core business may be needed, with the kind of rewards for success that characterize an entrepreneurial startup.

The right leadership is key. The CEO may have to get personally involved in courting and hiring the right kind of leader for the new business. Just as cocooning and physical separation from the core business can foster a different culture, exemption from standard management approaches can reinforce the particular goals and needs of the new business. Together, these measures emphasize a company's commitment to making a new business work, and encourage its people by stressing that they are working on something special.

Building a staircase within a large organization is no small accomplishment. Companies that sustain growth are impressive because they manage to do it again and again. They build multiple staircases in parallel. The cocooning and exemption we describe work well when a company is building only one or two new staircases. But when building businesses becomes a way of life, a different solution is needed: a more systematic approach that calls for a transformation in the way the organization is managed. That is the subject of Part IV.

NOTES

1   A. Bhide, "The questions every entrepreneur must answer," *Harvard Business Review*, November–December 1996, p. 126; "How entrepreneurs craft strategies that work," *Harvard Business Review*, March–April 1994, p. 159.

2   A thought-provoking discussion can be found in M. L. Tushman and C. A. O'Reilly III, "Ambidextrous organizations: Managing evolutionary and revolutionary change," *California Management Review*, Summer 1996, Volume 38, Number 4, pp. 8–30.

3   In the words of A. Bhide, "Many corporations that revere comprehensive analysis develop a refined incapacity for seizing opportunities. Analysis can delay entry until it's too late, or kill ideas by identifying numerous problems." In "How entrepreneurs craft strategies that work," *Harvard Business Review*, March–April 1994, p. 150.

4   For a thoughtful perspective on driving the rhythm of business building, see K. M. Eisenhardt and S. L. Brown, "Time pacing: Competing in markets that won't stand still," *Harvard Business Review*, March 1998, pp. 59–71.

5   A useful discussion of processes that challenge thinking on capital spending is contained in J. Carter, M. van Dijk, and K. Gibson, "Capital investment: How not to build the *Titanic*," *The McKinsey Quarterly*, 1996, Number 4, pp. 146–59.

6   The notion of a constantly evolving portfolio of staircases breeding staircases is akin to J. C. Collins and J. I. Porras's view of a corporation's "purposeful evolution" through "branching and pruning." They note, "The idea is simple: If you add enough branches to a tree...and intelligently prune the dead wood...then you'll likely evolve into a collection of healthy branches well positioned to prosper in an ever-changing environment." *Built to Last: Successful habits of visionary companies* (Century, London, 1994), p. 146.

7   For a fascinating discussion of how good management has caused great firms to fail in the face of disruptive technologies, see C. M. Christensen, *The Innovator's Dilemma: When new technologies cause great firms to fail* (Harvard Business School Press, Boston, Mass., 1997).

8   Interviews by R. Anandan and J. Sinha with Steve Sayre, senior vice-president of Notes marketing, and Jeff Papows, Lotus president, May 1995; "Shaping new markets," O. Sibony and J. Sinha, May 1995, unpublished.

9   For a detailed discussion of the appropriate organizational positioning for new businesses, see Z. Block and I. C. MacMillan, *Corporate Venturing: Creating new businesses within the firm* (Harvard Business School Press, Boston, Mass., 1993), chapters 6, "Locating the venture in the organization," and 8 "Organizing the venture"; and H. W. Chesbrough and D. J. Teece, "When is virtual virtuous?

Organizing for innovation," *Harvard Business Review,* January–February 1996, pp. 65–73.

10 Z. Block and I. C. MacMillan, *Corporate Venturing: Creating new businesses within the firm* (Harvard Business School Press, Boston, Mass., 1993), chapters 5, "Selecting, evaluating, and compensating venture management," 7, and 9 "Controlling the venture."

Part IV

Sustaining growth

To sustain growth, companies must institutionalize the process of business building. In the final part of this book, we suggest how to design this process.

First, we address what may be the most important challenge facing leaders of growth organizations: the successful management of growth initiatives at various phases of maturity. While the demands initiatives make change as they grow, few companies design their management systems to cope with this development. We propose an approach that respects the differences rather than blurring them.

In chapter 9, we describe what role the corporate center can play in encouraging growth through business building. Savvy corporate executives use two approaches: they devolve leadership, and they offer expertise that only the corporate center can economically supply.

If a company relies on one management system across its entire organization, it is making the tacit assumption that all parts of the organization have similar management needs. In fact, this is a dangerous assumption, and helps explain why sustaining growth is so difficult in large corporations, and so rare.

In horizon 3, the object is to explore a new opportunity and gain strategic insight, which comes only when a company takes deliberate steps to secure options for the future. There are few rules, only conversations, research, musings, networking, alliances, small investments, and, with luck, growing conviction about an insight. Consequently, managing horizon 3 feels a bit like diving for sunken treasure.

In horizon 2, the challenge is to take advantage of an insight before competitors do. Time is of the essence. The focus shifts to building the staircase quickly and establishing positional advantage. The pace becomes frenetic as increased risk taking, rapid judgment calls, and larger investments become necessary. In many ways, this business-building process feels like white-water rafting.

Managing horizon 1 is distinctly different from managing the business-building activities of the other horizons. By the time a staircase matures into horizon 1, the initial strategic insight will have been long recognized by competitors, and early positional advantages may well be eroding. Survival depends on superior execution. Great discipline is required in operations, planning, and budgeting to increase predictability and accountability. As a result, managing a horizon 1 business feels rather like coxing a rowing crew.

Only by differentiating their management systems across the three horizons can corporations avoid the barriers to growth that most systems inadvertently perpetuate. If all managers are evaluated purely on the profitability of their businesses – a good measure of horizon 1 performance – they will have little appetite for building horizon 2 enterprises. If some leadership time is not systematically reserved for building fledgling businesses, the needs of the core business will consume all managers' days and nights, and they simply will not have a free moment to build horizons 2 and 3.

The idea of differentiated management systems conflicts with most managers' instincts for uniformity and consistency, and their desire to set standards for the whole organization and stick to them. It is tough news in a world where many businesses define themselves by their management systems: "We're profit focused" or "We nurture innovation."

The challenge in chapter 7 was to manage the development of a single new staircase. We recommended that companies make exceptions to their core management processes so as to protect a new business. But when business building proliferates and becomes a way of life, with more and more new staircases under development, managing by exemption may no longer be sustainable. Instead, it becomes necessary to adopt a more systematic approach to suit the contrasting characteristics of the three horizons. The problem, in short, is to differentiate management systems within a single coherent organizational approach.[1]

We believe three particular areas within management systems have the greatest impact on organizational behavior. First and foremost, talent management is critical in ensuring that the right balance of skills is available to lead businesses and initiatives in each of the three horizons. Second, planning and budgeting systems must enable companies to pursue all three horizons simultaneously by clarifying the appropriate level of investment of resources in each. Finally, performance management systems must create sharp incentives that encourage the right behavior for each horizon.

Talent management

Leaders of growth companies know the value of talent. Alfred Zeien, CEO of Gillette, acknowledged that "the controlling factor in the company's rate of growth is the rate at which we can add talented, globally focused individuals to our management team."[2] Without talented people, the most brilliantly crafted strategies falter and the most inspiring visions lose their sheen. The kind of achievements to which great growth companies aspire call for talented, motivated, energetic people.[3] In a global economy in which competitive advantage depends on securing the right people, the most able are in chronically short supply.

But the belief that there is one ideal profile for talented leaders is as misguided as the notion that one performance metric can apply to all activities. The trick is to find individuals with the right skills, preferences, experience, and knowledge for activities in each horizon (Figure 8.1).

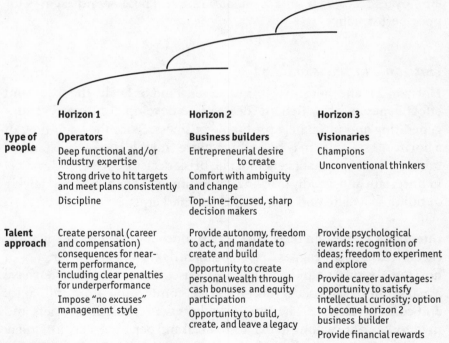

	Horizon 1	**Horizon 2**	**Horizon 3**
Type of people	**Operators**	**Business builders**	**Visionaries**
	Deep functional and/or industry expertise	Entrepreneurial desire to create	Champions
	Strong drive to hit targets and meet plans consistently	Comfort with ambiguity and change	Unconventional thinkers
	Discipline	Top-line–focused, sharp decision makers	
Talent approach	Create personal (career and compensation) consequences for near-term performance, including clear penalties for underperformance	Provide autonomy, freedom to act, and mandate to create and build	Provide psychological rewards: recognition of ideas; freedom to experiment and explore
	Impose "no excuses" management style	Opportunity to create personal wealth through cash bonuses and equity participation	Provide career advantages: opportunity to satisfy intellectual curiosity; option to become horizon 2 business builder
		Opportunity to build, create, and leave a legacy	Provide financial rewards

Figure 8.1 Talent management by horizon

Horizon 1 operators

In horizon 1, mature enterprises must be pushed to their limit. This calls for deep knowledge of the business, along with strong bottom-line discipline and the ability to motivate people in the drive for greater efficiency and continuing (usually incremental) growth. Often, the best horizon 1 leaders are the strong operating managers who will do what it takes to hit their targets. Top performers are critical. They are responsible for the profitability and cash flow that help determine a company's stock price.

To motivate these operators, sharp incentives are vital. Many growth companies use substantial cash bonuses to reward short-term performance. Frito-Lay pays its 100 US zone managers as if they were running their own companies, relying heavily on performance-based cash compensation. Downside measures are equally simple, clear, and consistent. Frito-Lay sales managers who fail to deliver satisfactory results are sent packing, and in annual performance evaluations, about 5 percent of employees receive an "unacceptable" rating. There are no excuses for poor performance.

Horizon 2 business builders

Horizon 2 is another story. Its initiatives stand or fall by the speed and effectiveness with which an idea can be developed into a revenue-generating and ultimately profitable business. Since the beginning of a horizon 2 staircase may be nothing more tangible than a well-formed business concept, managers must be brisk decision makers who excel in uncertain and rapidly growing environments. They must act quickly in building a team and adapting to the marketplace.

Interviews with leading executive search consultants, venture capitalists, executives, and colleagues helped us identify the key characteristics of horizon 2 business builders. They are focused on the top line, often have a marketing or sales background, and feel comfortable amid ambiguity and constant change. They are risk takers who think like owners and investors and are willing to make financial and personal sacrifices today for gains tomorrow. Independent and self-motivated, they have a yearning to create. In short, horizon 2 business builders are like classic entrepreneurs in the world of small to medium-sized businesses.

What does this suggest about the incentives they need to drive their performance? First, given the risk profile of entrepreneurs, a high variable-to-fixed ratio in the total cash compensation package is a must.

Fixed salary alone, even if high, is not sufficient. Second, there should be an opportunity to create personal wealth: uncapped cash bonuses and equity participation are common. Though cash bonuses for making the numbers work well in horizon 1, horizon 2 business builders will often demand a piece of the action as part of their compensation. This gives them a sense of ownership and forces them to act as if their own money were on the line, since it is.

Another marked difference between horizons 1 and 2 lies in the treatment of failure. The "no excuses" style of management that so successfully drives horizon 1 results is seldom appropriate in horizon 2. Building new businesses is riskier than defending an existing one, and some failures must be expected. Not all of these deserve the personal penalties applied in horizon 1. Many growers make exceptions in the case of "good failures": well-executed initiatives that fail because of external factors or market dynamics.

Continuing to punish failures caused by poor execution is necessary to maintain crisp performance accountability. But if top managers want to attract the right people to a venture, these risk takers will need reassurance that their valiant efforts will be rewarded should their ventures fail because of circumstances beyond their control. Some companies even offer contingent career paths to employees who head risky ventures. If theirs folds, they know that another business-building challenge lies waiting for them.

Horizon 3 visionaries

Horizon 3 calls for visionaries. Futures must be imagined, investigated, and elaborated. Horizon 3 needs the kind of person who wants to look beyond conventional wisdom to explore new ideas and opportunities, and who doesn't mind being a lone ranger. To say that horizon 3 visionaries are not motivated by money and wealth creation would be to oversimplify. Still, one of the best incentives for them may be recognition of their ideas.

Successful visionaries may consider the freedom to pursue intellectual curiosity an important part of their incentive package. They often relish a privileged ivory tower position away from the cut and thrust. Some of the legendary hotbeds of innovation, such as Bell Labs and Xerox PARC, have used incentive approaches similar to those of academia, running themselves more like university research departments than businesses. In its heyday, Apple Computer offered sabbaticals to its brightest minds. As intellectual freedom is so valuable to visionaries, the threat of losing it may suffice as a downside measure for poor performance.

Some horizon 3 visionaries may want more than intellectual freedom; they may want a chance to turn their horizon 3 into a horizon 2 business. The opportunity to become an entrepreneur represents a powerful incentive. At Thermo Electron, people who develop a new business with standalone potential are given the opportunity to run it. This approach is a keystone of Thermo's success.

CEO George Hatsopoulos explained: "In this environment, the only thing that counts is building new businesses. You don't get praised for publishing papers – that is MIT's job. What counts here is creating a new business and becoming rich." He continued, "Most technologists we hire have heard of Thermo…they want to be millionaires…[and] we have created 140 millionaires."[4] Theo Melas-Kyriazi, CEO of ThermoSpectra, one of Thermo Electron's second-generation spinoffs, echoed Hatsopoulos: "The spinout strategy is Thermo Electron's winning formula. Imagine what you can achieve when you have 15 CEOs, each with a clear imperative to build his own business."

Great growth companies get a reputation for allowing good people to flourish, and good people consequently knock down their doors to join.

Amassing the right mix of talent

Most people's personality and skills incline them toward one of the horizons, but a great growth leader must be adept at managing across all three. Gary Wendt of GE Capital agrees: "Some people in this world have great ideas, and we have those people around here at GE. You need somebody to think about new crazy stuff. But those people may not be able to motivate a group to get the job done.... At the same time, we have people here that are great operating people.... But these people sometimes – not always but sometimes – don't have the dreaming ability, the visionary ability.... When we have both skills together, that is where we find our managers."[5]

Finding leaders who are suited to and comfortable with the different demands of each horizon is difficult, so companies are forced to make do with a good balance of operators, builders, and visionaries. This balance is especially important in the team at the top. At Disney, the mix of talent in the new management team was critical to the company's turnaround in the mid-1980s. Frank Wells, the chief operating officer, provided the operational and deal-making discipline to turn around the core business; Gary Wilson, then the highest-paid chief financial officer in the United States, developed innovative financing schemes to fuel capital-efficient growth in horizon 2; and CEO Michael Eisner supplied the creative strategy and the vision for growth.

Outside the top team, a company's capacity to sustain growth depends on how well it can balance the three distinct profiles throughout the organization. A company with only operators is unlikely to generate new businesses. A company with too many ideas people and not enough operators is likely to experience flashes of brilliance but no sustained growth. With great operators to maintain and grow the existing enterprises, builders can get on with new businesses.

For companies that are already great growers, their talent pool gives them an advantage. It takes skilled and energetic people to create growth, but growth itself is the best magnet for talent. Companies that are not growing, however, find themselves in a double bind: they need growth skills desperately, but are hard pressed to attract them. So how can they build their talent base?

Over the medium and long term, management development programs can strengthen the ranks, but to kickstart growth, an immediate injection of outside talent is usually required. Especially needed are horizon 2 business builders: people attracted by the challenge of creation who will in time attract other like-minded people.

Planning for growth

Executives dedicate much time to performance planning and budgeting, processes that provide the corporate language to communicate objectives and expectations. Although a single budget has to cover all activities across the three horizons, our view is that it can contain discrete categories, each reflecting agreements on investment activity and performance in the three horizons.

There is widespread dissatisfaction with conventional strategic planning.[6] We believe this is partly due to the mechanical application of "one size fits all" processes to businesses confronting fundamentally different situations. Horizon 1 business planners face strategic choices about positioning and direction from a base of strong capabilities and deep knowledge of industry dynamics. Horizon 3 planning, by contrast, demands that decisions about option creation and experimentation be made from a limited capability base amid great uncertainty about market dynamics.[7] Planning for the three horizons should be separated to avoid the natural tendency for horizon 1 immediacy to overshadow more distant horizon 2 and 3 needs (Figure 8.2).

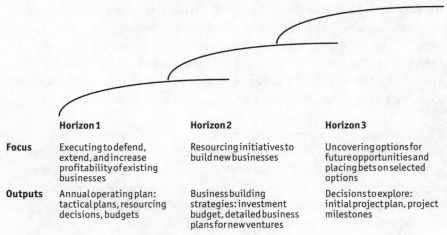

	Horizon 1	Horizon 2	Horizon 3
Focus	Executing to defend, extend, and increase profitability of existing businesses	Resourcing initiatives to build new businesses	Uncovering options for future opportunities and placing bets on selected options
Outputs	Annual operating plan: tactical plans, resourcing decisions, budgets	Business building strategies: investment budget, detailed business plans for new ventures	Decisions to explore: initial project plan, project milestones

Figure 8.2 Planning for growth

Horizon 1 planning

Horizon 1 business or strategic planning is about execution. It focuses on how existing businesses can be defended, extended, and made more profitable. Planning discussions are concerned with improving quality, sales force effectiveness, productivity, asset turnover, and customer satisfaction. The emphasis is on making operations more efficient and serving customers better.

Horizon 1 planning also keeps growth in mind. Growth is usually expected to be incremental, but not always. If horizon 1 planning includes the acquisition of a major competitor, this may radically reshape the industry structure and create dramatic growth opportunities. Horizon 1 planning leads to the annual budget, or profit plan as some companies call it: a commitment to what the immediate returns on past and new investments must be. But the total budget cannot be completed yet. It must also include activities agreed to in the planning for horizons 2 and 3.

Horizon 2 planning

Planning in horizon 2 focuses on business building and the resources this requires. Horizon 2 planning must attempt to capitalize on fresh opportunities; its outputs are the investment and action plans to create new staircases. As a result, it will feature initiatives that carry increased risk – unlike horizon 1 planning, which is usually about minimizing risk. The two processes are incompatible, yet most companies conduct horizon 1 and 2 planning simultaneously. This can be dangerous, because horizon 1 considerations will often dominate.

Good horizon 2 planning forces managers to articulate what they do not know and to work out which assumptions are critical to success. Discussions take on the tone of a business model review, extended over three years or so. Horizon 2 planning requires managers to design capability-building programs; to orchestrate the project management of substantial programs of investment and recruitment; and to design contingency plans. It must not become an exercise in establishing a rigid set of actions, any deviation from which will be seen as failure to execute the plan. The active adaptation described in chapter 7 will certainly result in changes to the business model.

Nevertheless, horizon 2 planning may lead to some kind of budget "set-aside" in which an account must be spent on a specified activity, not transferred to another use. As the chief executive of one growth company said, "Development of new businesses tends to slow down just when it shouldn't. When the idea really begins to pay off, it has the most severe negative impact on the parent business unit's P&L. That's when [business unit leaders] tend to starve it – so they can make their numbers." A set-aside can ensure that horizon 2 is not starved.

Horizon 3 planning

With investments in longer-term growth initiatives identified and resources planned, the annual budget is almost complete. Horizon 3 explorations now need funding. As well as discussing the projects under way, managers need to talk about the more distant future, the evolution of their industry, and the opportunities that might emerge.

These horizon 3 conversations need a separate forum of their own. Outsiders, including academics, futurists, and other specialists, may participate. They can help in the search for analogies, perspectives, and new views of the world to spur ideas and identify promising directions. These discussions will be messy; they will not always produce agreement, or even conclusions. But they are vital. Not all industries are changing at Internet speed, but most are changing faster and more radically than before.

There will be much that is unknown and that cannot be resolved without concrete steps in the marketplace. The output of horizon 3 planning is thus likely to be a commitment to invest in promising options: long-term research, participation in selected industry groups or technology forums, and investment in startups or venture capital funds. This commitment must be firm, reflected in budget categories that cannot be invaded to shore up short-term profits in horizon 1.

Planning for growth across the horizons

Hardly any companies conduct budgeting and planning by horizon as yet, but some are moving in that direction. Emerson Electric, whose growth strategy we described earlier in chapter 3, has taken important steps toward differentiating its business planning processes by creating separate forums for the discussion of core and new businesses. CEO Chuck Knight used to spend about half his time in business planning sessions, but they were so relentlessly focused on productivity improvements that growth initiatives seldom got looked at. So Knight decided to split the planning sessions into two separate meetings. The first focuses on the annual profit plan. It is similar in tone and substance to earlier planning sessions, focuses principally on horizon 1 businesses, and is led by Emerson's chief operating and chief financial officers. Knight himself does not attend.

The second session, which Knight heads, is strictly about growth. Its declared purpose is to create a more receptive atmosphere for growth initiatives. Once these have been identified, evaluated, and approved, they are built into the annual budget. Strategic investment programs for horizon 2 and targeted R&D programs for horizon 3 fund some of the growth initiatives that lie outside the core business.

Performance management

Few dispute that challenging targets are important in motivating performance. Stretch targets get noticed, and they generate the effort and momentum that profitable growth demands. Conventional wisdom has it that aligning targets across and down the organization is the way to get organizational energy and capacity focused on the right goals. This is true enough, but to sustain growth, it is even more important to differentiate performance metrics by horizon.

For simplicity, we will confine our discussion to financially oriented performance measures, but we recognize that the same treatment might apply to a fuller set of performance metrics.[8] Because the financial goals of the activities in each horizon are different, so too should be the way that performance is measured (Figure 8.3).

Horizon 1 metrics

Successful organizations have no trouble understanding what is needed to instill a performance ethic and drive the profitability of a horizon 1 business. The first question is whether a business has earned the right

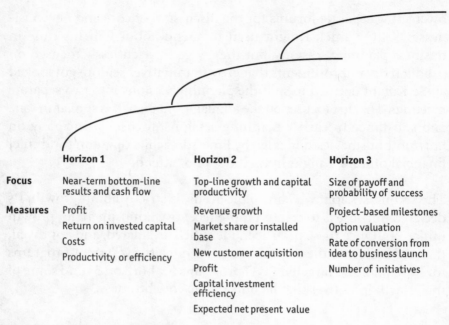

	Horizon 1	**Horizon 2**	**Horizon 3**
Focus	Near-term bottom-line results and cash flow	Top-line growth and capital productivity	Size of payoff and probability of success
Measures	Profit	Revenue growth	Project-based milestones
	Return on invested capital	Market share or installed base	Option valuation
	Costs	New customer acquisition	Rate of conversion from idea to business launch
	Productivity or efficiency	Profit	Number of initiatives
		Capital investment efficiency	
		Expected net present value	

Figure 8.3 Performance measurement

to grow, as we saw in chapter 3. It rarely makes sense to grow unprofitable businesses. Those with performance problems must focus not on top-line growth, but on fixing fundamentals. Most high-performing organizations consider this merely good management, and methods for achieving operational performance improvement are well documented. The financial component of the scorecard can include productivity improvement rates, reductions in unit costs, plant efficiency scores, monthly profit against budget, growth in net income, and return on invested capital.

Horizon 2 metrics

Nothing kills a horizon 2 initiative faster than being managed with horizon 1 performance metrics. The success of an emerging business depends on how quickly it establishes that its product or service is attractive to customers, and how rapidly and effectively it expands. Both experimentation and investment are needed. The aim is not so much achieving profitability as soon as possible, but rather beating competitors to the best market positions.

Geared to profitability at lower growth rates, most horizon 1 metrics are not appropriate for horizon 2 objectives. To impose unnecessarily demanding targets for profit or return on capital on an embryonic business could restrict investment spending precisely when it is most needed. If market position and the development of a viable business model are the key factors for success, it follows that unit sales, revenue growth, gross or operating margin, market share, installed base, and the efficiency of incremental capital investments are more relevant performance metrics for horizon 2 activities. These are the indicators that allow managers to assess a business's potential.

This is not to suggest that horizon 2 should lack profit accountability, but simply that profit expectations should be realistic, and that other measures be applied as primary tests of performance. Even so, in the often chaotic environment of a fast-growing horizon 2 business, selecting the best metrics can be as much art as science.

Horizon 3 metrics

Horizon 3 initiatives have the potential to become viable businesses. They cannot be evaluated by the use of traditional financial measures such as revenue and profit. A manager's job in horizon 3 is to find and plant seeds that will grow into horizon 2 businesses. To measure the performance of such a manager on the basis of today's profits would discourage the very activities that are most valuable in horizon 3: experimentation and development.

Horizon 3 ideally contains a portfolio of options whose value increases as they are developed and refined. The total value of the portfolio depends on the number of options, how much it costs to obtain and maintain them, how likely it is that they will succeed, and how much they might pay off. The measurement challenge for horizon 3 is to determine how to increase the potential payoff and the likelihood of success.

The size of the payoff may be influenced by many factors. Commodity prices determine the value of growth options in natural resources. Regulatory decisions affect the value of options in natural gas, electricity, and long-distance telephony. Standardization increases the value of owning a technology platform.

The likelihood of success also depends on a multitude of factors. Completing a successful clinical trial or gaining regulatory approval for a drug substantially increases the probability that it will reach the market. Achieving project-based milestones such as securing partnerships or contracts, completing successful beta tests or pilots, committing to new infrastructure, or clearing important technology hurdles also increase an option's probability of success.[9] These milestones can become the measures of executive performance and also the triggers to commit subsequent stages of investment.

Differentiating metrics across the horizons

Softbank, a Japanese IT company, offers an example of how performance metrics can be differentiated across the three horizons. Founded as a software distributor by entrepreneur Masayoshi Son in 1981, Softbank enjoyed more than a decade of successful growth, reaching a market capitalization of $9 billion in 1997 with compound annual growth of 28 percent in sales and 87 percent in net income between 1986 and 1996.

In its horizon 1 businesses, software distribution and PC magazine publishing in Japan, Softbank has introduced daily profit and loss reporting to ensure a performance-driven bottom-line focus. Recognizing that the Internet threatened to make its distribution business obsolete, the company has focused on building an impressive portfolio of horizon 2 and 3 businesses.

Acquired in the mid-1990s, Softbank's largest horizon 2 businesses are Ziff-Davis computer magazine publishing and Comdex computer trade shows. The company has introduced metrics and targets to drive globalization and top-line growth in both. In publishing, the goal is to increase the number of titles from 150 in 1996 to 1,000 by 2005 and to achieve tenfold revenue growth in 10 years. In the trade show business, the target is to increase the number of annual events from 55 to 300.

In horizon 3, Softbank has focused on securing options at strategic points on the Internet. It has invested more than $70 million in some 30 companies, among them Yahoo!, Cisco Systems, CyberCash, United States Web, On Live!, and Palace, and plans to increase its stake to $600 million in over 100 companies. With options at almost every important intersection of Internet activity, including hardware, software, content provision, funds transfer, and virtual communities, Softbank aims to cover its bets no matter how the Internet should evolve. There are no immediate expectations of profit; rather, the performance metric is share of future profits. Specifically, Softbank aims to have 30 percent of its profits "Internet-generated" within five years, and 50 percent in 10 years.

Softbank can boast rich business creation activity in all three horizons. The goals for each are clear, as are the specific results sought. If any business were neglected, the effect would be noticed long before the pipeline stopped flowing.

In our research, we were struck by the number of companies that did not want details of their management systems to be made public. In some cases, they were even more secretive about their systems than about their strategies. Such sensitivity suggests how much value they place on these systems.

Yet as far as we know, no company, not even those on our list of sustained growers, is using distinct management systems for each horizon. There are no best-practice cases. We believe this is the main reason why sustained growth is so rare, and why some of the companies we mention in this book, notwithstanding their past record of growth, have begun to falter.

Companies that differentiate management systems by horizon may develop an enduring competitive advantage. The three management systems we discuss in this chapter are not the only ones that can be effectively deployed across the three horizons, but they do, we believe, have a disproportionate impact on individual and organizational behavior.

In chapter 1, we said that the central challenge in sustaining growth is to build and manage a continuous pipeline of business creation. Ultimately, this is possible only if companies adopt distinct management systems for each of the three horizons.

NOTES

1   Several scholars have argued the need for an organizational culture that is capable of handling multiple challenges. M. L. Tushman and C. A. O'Reilly III offer their concept of the "ambidextrous organization – one capable of simultaneously pursuing both incremental and discontinuous innovation" in "Ambidextrous organizations: Managing evolutionary and revolutionary change," *California Management Review*, Summer 1996, Volume 38, Number 4, pp. 8–30.

   J. C. Collins and J. I. Porras identify a fundamental characteristic of visionary companies as their ability to "stimulate progress while preserving the core" and reject the "tyranny of the 'or' in favor of the genius of the 'and.'" *Built to Last: Successful habits of visionary companies* (Century, London, 1994).

   S. Ghoshal and C. A. Bartlett describe the need to manage "the sweet and the sour" simultaneously: "Continuous self-renewal is built on the tension that develops between two symbiotic forces – the need for ongoing improvement in operational performance as provided by continuous rationalization, and the need for growth and expansion as generated by continuous revitalization." *The Individualized Corporation: A fundamentally new approach to management* (HarperBusiness, New York, 1997), pp. 134–7.

2   Gillette 1995 annual report, p. 17.

3   For an engaging discussion of leadership development, see N. M. Tichy with E. Cohen, *The Leadership Engine: How winning companies build leaders at every level* (HarperBusiness, New York, 1997).

4   Interviews by S. Coley, R. Anandan, and R. Foster with George N. Hatsopoulos and Theo Melas-Kyriazi, August 1995.

5   C. B. Wendel, *The New Financiers* (Irwin, Chicago, 1996), pp. 320–25.

6   See, for example, H. Mintzberg, *The Rise and Fall of Strategic Planning: Reconceiving roles for planning, plans, planners* (Free Press, New York, 1994), and A. Campbell and M. Alexander, "What's wrong with strategy?" *Harvard Business Review*, November–December 1997, pp. 42–51.

7   A. Campbell and M. Alexander, "What's wrong with strategy?" *Harvard Business Review*, November–December 1997, p. 44.

8   The metrics for measuring the health of an organization go beyond the financial to include measures such as customer satisfaction, organizational learning, and employee satisfaction. The seminal work in this area is R. S. Kaplan and D. P. Norton, *The Balanced Scorecard* (Harvard Business School Press, Boston, Mass., 1996).

9   See the discussion of performance evaluation and venture control in Z. Block and I. C. MacMillan, *Corporate Venturing: Creating new businesses within the firm* (Harvard Business School Press, Boston, Mass., 1993), chapter 9.

"Our dream, and our plan, well over a decade ago, was simple," recalled Jack Welch, describing how General Electric organized to sustain growth. "We set out to shape a global enterprise that preserved the classic big-company advantages, while eliminating the classic big-company drawbacks. What we wanted to build was a hybrid, an enterprise with the reach and resources of a big company – the body of a big company – but the thirst to learn, the compulsion to share, and the bias for action – the soul – of a small company."[1]

How to balance the advantages of scale against those of smallness is a classic organizational dilemma, but it has particular relevance for growth companies. More and more executives and organizational theorists are heralding disaggregation as a hallmark of the corporation of the future.[2] Rather than simply expanding the executive team, sustained growers push leadership down into the organization, creating many small growth communities. The benefits are clear to see. Making a large number of people responsible for growth relieves the pressure on senior executives, and creating more units increases the corporation's exposure to the outside world and new ideas.

Having small units also confers strategic benefits such as focus and agility. Mimicking the speed and responsiveness of startups, small units overcome some of the disadvantages of being connected to a mammoth enterprise. And working in small units gives people a greater sense of purpose, ownership, and control. This is why we often refer to them as communities. They help to avoid the organizational ossification that can occur when an individual works as one of nameless thousands.

"While there is a price that we pay for decentralization," said Ralph Larsen, CEO of Johnson & Johnson, "I think it is the magic that allows us to continue to grow and prosper because people feel a deep sense of responsibility and ownership for the businesses they are running."[3]

Still, the advantages of smallness must be weighed up against those of greater size. Several areas exist where the benefits of scale must be pursued. The corporate center is best placed to offer shared services such as merger and acquisition skills. It must also ensure that the small communities are connected and encourage the sharing of ideas and the capture of synergies. To make it possible to realize these benefits of scale, the best chief executives develop inspiring visions to motivate and unite their organizations.

Creating small communities

Our sample of successful growth companies shows a striking consistency in the importance attached to devolving leadership by creating small communities. But there is less consensus about how to achieve this devolution. The solutions adopted fall into three broad categories.

Some companies create independent operating companies or business units connected to the hierarchical corporate structure. A second approach is to divide business units or operating companies into entrepreneurial communities of project teams. The more radical third option entails spinning out subsidiaries to create a network of partly owned public companies that are directly exposed to the incentives and disciplines of the financial markets.

Independent operating companies

A simple way to create small communities is to split an organization into independent operating companies. Illinois Tool Works, a $4 billion manufacturer of specialist industrial products, is so committed to the concept of small communities that it has broken itself up into 250 independent operating units. "The secret is proper size," said former CEO John Nichols. "Size solves a lot of problems. It depends upon the business but we start to look at a unit when it climbs into the range of 100 to 150 people. We measure by people, not sales."[4] Such disaggregation creates numerous points of growth leadership.

GE Capital also divides itself into small units, with 27 operating businesses ranging from aircraft leasing to consumer credit cards. Group

CEO Gary Wendt explained the power of distributed leadership: "People take up the bit when you give it to them. It is such a difference to operate this company as a series of small companies as opposed to one big company. The one thing that separates us from the others in the financial services industry would be that this company is really a series of small companies…we are a rinky-dink three-ball finance company – I want the people in my business who do credit life insurance in Europe to think of themselves as small, nimble, fast-moving businesses."[5]

Small-group environments based on teams

Not all businesses can be sensibly disaggregated into separate operating companies or business units. This is particularly true of network-based businesses or those with large manufacturing plants. But even in these environments, growth leadership can be devolved to teams and project groups to simulate the feel of a small community and create a sense of personal ownership. Sophisticated companies recognize the power of teams and use them to achieve advances in business performance. Indeed, what distinguishes many of the sustained growers we studied is the extent to which they use teams.

Kyocera is a Japanese corporation that manufactures some 5,000 products from ceramics to electronic equipment and optical instruments. In all its activities, it makes a concerted effort to devolve growth leadership through a flexible organizational structure. It breaks itself into the smallest possible units and gives each its own profit and loss responsibility. These "amoeba" units, each comprising from three to 50 people, act like independent companies with their own internal and external customers, suppliers, and markets. Each amoeba – usually a sales or manufacturing unit – is responsible for strategic planning, personnel management and training, pricing, operational and capital budgeting, and process and product innovation.

The idea is to create miniature businesses with leaders who have authority and autonomy in financial management. In 1994, there were over 1,000 amoebas in Kyocera's Japanese operations alone. This decentralized structure has helped the company adapt quickly to change.

"Amoeba management has allowed Kyocera to preserve the vitality of a small business, despite having grown into a substantially large business," said Hideki Ishida, general manager of the financial and accounting department. "In order to promote internal flexibility, an amoeba allows its member to practice high levels of freedom within the organization. All the members are given a chance to prove their ability by having to manage their own job rather than depending upon someone else's supervision. They have the opportunity to exploit their potential to create and manage themselves. In this respect, the amoeba organization is oriented toward the individual rather than a collective or hierarchical system."[6]

Spinouts

Spinouts may have even greater potential to unleash the power of devolved growth leadership. In a spinout, a corporation not only creates an independent unit, but establishes it as a separate company with some public shareholding. (Such spinouts or equity carveouts, in which the parent company retains a majority shareholding, differ from spinoffs, which are sold 100 percent to the market.) The senior management team enjoys the excitement and, with luck, the financial and emotional rewards of running an independent public company. At the same time, the corporation, as the majority shareholder, can enjoy the benefits of keeping the unit connected to the larger enterprise. Many organizations have used this approach to good effect.[7]

The Thermo Electron Corporation has pioneered the use of spinouts to keep creating new businesses. Often referred to as the "perpetual idea machine," it competes in a broad range of technology-based industries from analytical instruments and biomedical products to paper recycling equipment and clean-fuel power plants.

Founder George Hatsopoulos described the spinout rationale thus: "By combining the entrepreneurial atmosphere of a startup venture with the financial and managerial strengths of a well-established company, we have created a new kind of corporate enterprise – one that is uniquely capable of sustained growth in today's rapidly changing world."[8]

Spinouts typically follow the same pattern. First, a new technology is acquired or developed internally. It is improved over a couple of years, and related businesses are added either by acquisition or by transfer from within Thermo Electron. Finally, the business is spun out, with a minority share of common stock bought by private investors. In time, the spinout issues 10 to 25 percent of its shares in an initial public offering.

Before it can be spun out, a business must meet three criteria. It must have a credible business plan for rapid growth. Thermo Electron's senior team scrutinizes spinout plans, making sure that growth opportunities exist and that the intended strategies can capture them. Second, the business must have a solid management team capable of handling the market pressures of a publicly traded company. Third, the financial market must be receptive. If investors are flocking to blue-chip companies and shying away from riskier high-technology ventures, the spinout may have to wait.

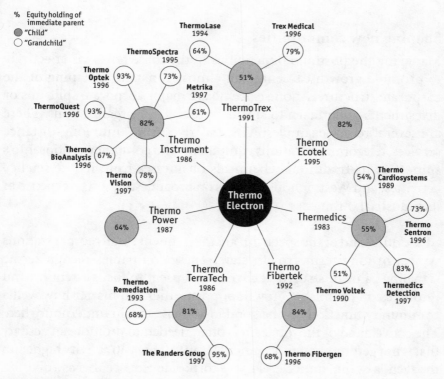

Figure 9.1 Spinouts from Thermo Electron

In every case, Thermo Electron retains majority ownership of between 51 and 95 percent. At the end of 1996, it had seven first-generation spinouts, or children, each operating in a different industry. The first spinout back in 1983, Thermedics, manufactures air particle detection systems and biomedical products. The second generation of spinouts – the grandchildren such as Thermo Cardiosystems and Thermedics Detection – operate within the technology field of their parent. By the end of 1997, Thermo Electron had added 15 grandchildren, making a total of 22 spinouts (Figure 9.1).

The company's record speaks for itself. From 1986 to 1996, sales grew at a compound annual rate of 24 percent, and net income at 30 percent. Total return to shareholders increased by 23 percent a year. The company's total capitalization (including the equity stakes in the spinouts) soared from $350 million in 1986 to $10 billion in 1996, a compound annual increase of 40 percent.

Shaping new communities

Managing the portfolio of activities in the three horizons effectively to promote growth can entail an almost constant reshaping of the corporate structure. At one extreme are major corporate split-ups or divestments undertaken to create more focused organizations. There are several recent examples: AT&T's "trivestiture" into long-distance services, telecommunications equipment, and computers; Monsanto's spinoff of its traditional chemicals businesses from its life science activities; and Westinghouse's focus on broadcasting at the expense of its industrial businesses.

At the other end of the spectrum are the frequent small reorganizations typical of long-term growth stars. These companies recognize the signaling value of structural change and use it to focus attention and resources on promising growth opportunities. No matter how well a community functions, some good ideas may remain undernourished. The active hand of the top team is often needed to promote an activity that is not getting enough attention. It can put such an activity higher up the agenda by moving it closer to the corporate center, either as a division or group in its own right or as a new unit within an existing business.

Many of the best growth opportunities may lie in the no-man's-land between business units, needing the capabilities of several but moving in the principal strategic direction of none. Identifying these opportunities and assembling the capabilities to exploit them are the responsibility of the corporate center, which alone has the necessary perspective and objectivity. Creating a new unit to focus squarely on an opportunity will increase its chances of success.

As we saw in chapter 8, Bombardier has followed this approach with notable success. In the 1970s, when snowmobile dealers were finding it difficult to obtain financing, it created a separate capital group. Banks and finance companies had no way of assessing the resale value of snowmobiles, so the new unit began developing expertise in that area by acting as a wholesale financier to its dealers. The unit now has 4,500 dealers and 400 manufacturers on its books, and has branched into several other kinds of financing, such as the manufactured housing mortgage business.

Bombardier's services group had similar origins. "We already carried out some service activities," said CEO Laurent Beaudoin, "but they were integrated into the existing groups. They didn't have the profile and support to grow. We decided to take them out and create a dedicated group that could gradually build a role for itself."[9] The services group provides long-term maintenance and support for Bombardier's aerospace and transportation customers, and has found innovative ways to grow the business. Building on its reputation for training military and civilian pilots, it started the NATO flight training school in Canada and is setting up maintenance centers in North America for owners of Bombardier's regional aircraft.

"Recreating and reshaping Bombardier is a continuous process," said Dr. Yvan Allaire, Bombardier's executive vice-president for strategy and corporate affairs. Indeed, in early 1998, Bombardier announced the formation of a sixth business group at the corporate level. Responsible for growth in emerging markets, it will consolidate and reinforce efforts previously undertaken by the three principal businesses of aerospace, transportation, and motorized consumer products.

Connecting communities

The move to smaller communities raises questions about the value of the corporate entity. "We have deliberately chosen a minimalist model," Bombardier's Beaudoin acknowledged. "We would rather lose some synergy across the groups than hamper decision making and entrepreneurialism within them." Most sustained growers share this viewpoint. They may also agree with a second observation from Beaudoin. "If and when there is a strong need for shaping," he said, "the corporate center will intervene, and often I will get personally involved."

There are two big reasons for promoting connectivity within the enterprise. First, economies of scale justify some shared services. Second, the perpetual need to build new staircases demands that different communities freely share ideas, capabilities, and people. For this to happen, the center must nurture internal networks between individuals and communities.

Connecting to the center

Economies of scale are the justification for shared services. At many growers, the corporate center is responsible for developing and supplying the growth-enabling skills we described in chapter 6. Many of these skills are widely available from professional service providers in banking, the law, and accounting. But the companies we studied prefer to build up a small team of qualified people in-house and provide expertise from the center to the units. Owning the expertise encourages the operating units to pursue opportunities such as acquisitions more frequently than they otherwise would, as well as increasing the responsiveness and cost-effectiveness of service provision to multiple communities.

Our research indicates that about three-quarters of the companies that sustain high growth and high shareholder returns make acquisition a critical component of their growth strategies. They frequently acquire other companies – often up to five a year – to further the development of their growth staircases.

Thermo Electron has relied heavily on acquisitions in its growth formula; since 1980, it has completed over a hundred. Between 1986 and 1996, new companies and technologies accounted for more than two-thirds of its revenue growth. For the most part, Thermo's acquisitions have involved buying and improving turnaround candidates, but it also uses acquisitions to obtain capabilities. When a spinout starts to get serious about an acquisition, the vast experience and resources of the corporate center come into play. It provides deal-making and financing skills and has employed novel financial instruments in the US capital market to ensure successful public offerings.

Connecting to other communities

Individual communities are better equipped to identify and exploit growth opportunities if they have access to each other's capabilities and knowledge. "At Disney, it is our conviction that synergy can be the single most important contributor to profit and growth in a creatively driven company," said Michael Eisner. "It is simply this: when you embrace a new idea, a new business, a new product, a new film or TV show, whatever – you have to make sure that everyone throughout the company knows about it early enough so that every segment of the business can promote or exploit its potential in every other possible market, product, context."[10]

Consider Disney's animated film *The Lion King*. By 1997, not only was it the second-highest-grossing film of all time and the highest-grossing animated film ever at $1.5 billion, but it had also created opportunities to sell merchandise worth more than $1 billion. It led to a sequel called *Simba's Pride* for distribution through home video, and an opportunity for syndication on television networks. The soundtrack from the movie was 1994's best-selling album in the United States, and was followed by another release, *Rhythm of the Pride Lands*. The Lion King character was used in Disney's theme parks and resorts, and a street show was performed at Disneyland. The film has also been transformed into an award-winning Broadway show and has spawned a new theme park, Animal Kingdom, which opened in 1998 in Orlando, Florida.

Such synergies can be realized only if ideas are readily shared across an enterprise. For the corporate center, the trick is to ensure there is sufficient coordination to achieve these benefits, but without eroding the value of devolved leadership.

Consider Seven-Eleven Japan, which has an extraordinary commitment to making connections across its 7,000-plus stores. Some organizations might bring together their field managers once or twice a year to transfer best practice; it assembles more than 1,000 of its field counselors (district managers who oversee up to 10 stores) from across the country every Tuesday in Tokyo. Senior leadership addresses the group about company-wide strategic issues, not in vague terms, but using concrete examples from the stores. A meeting to discuss new product and merchandising issues follows before the group breaks up into smaller zone and district meetings.

These meetings often translate into immediate results. One field counselor noticed that women were the main buyers of *Men's Nonno* magazine, and shared this observation with his peers. After analysis confirmed it, Seven-Eleven moved the magazine from the middle of the men's counter to the border between the men's and women's counters. Sales soared.

Inspiring the organization

Maintaining the organizational conviction and momentum to grow can be a daunting task for leaders at any level. How can the corporate center hope to inspire a set of small communities to stay hungry for growth? In chapter 3, we described the importance of raising the bar to signal the resolve to grow. Great growers often make a point of setting what many would consider to be unreasonable financial targets and pushing accountability for them down the organization. Top- and bottom-line annual growth targets of 12 to 20 percent per year are common, even in markets that are growing in line with GDP.

Growth-oriented corporate centers set high targets for two reasons. First, they get noticed. They must be ambitious enough to seize the organization's attention, but not so overwhelming that managers become cynical. In 1995, the $4.2 billion Taiwanese PC manufacturer Acer Computer set a target that it terms "4,000 in 2000": it aims to reach

NT$400 billion ($14.5 billion or 4,000 Chinese *yi*) in revenue by the year 2000.

Second, stretch targets encourage people to be more imaginative. If a target strikes them as out of the ordinary, people will realize that their usual strategies, products, and markets will not take them far enough. To earn the growth it is seeking, the company will need to reinvent itself.

All the same, quantitative targets are blunt instruments. Few people can be inspired year after year through exhortations to achieve abstract numerical results for the benefit of faceless shareholders. It is hardly surprising, then, that the guiding principles of great growth companies usually transcend financial targets to include qualitative aspirations that give people a clear sense of purpose.

Ghoshal and Bartlett put it well: "Strategies can engender strong, enduring emotional attachments only when embedded in a broader organizational purpose. Today, the corporate leader's great challenge is to create a sense of meaning within the company, which its members can identify, in which they share a feeling of pride, and to which they are willing to commit themselves."[11]

The Australia-based entertainment company Village Roadshow has revised its aspirations at least three times in the past four decades to sustain its sense of purpose. In the 1960s, when its core horizon 1 business was limited to drive-in cinemas in Melbourne, the company's aspiration was to become a leading national film exhibitor. Founder Roc Kirby declared, "I had a clear dedication for Village to achieve a commanding cinema circuit throughout Australia."[12]

By the late 1980s, the company had achieved its goal, leading managing director Graham Burke to articulate an even higher aspiration: "Village Roadshow's objective is, very simply, to be the best entertainment company in Australia and the Pacific Basin." To push for expansion, Village started horizon 2 businesses such as home video, radio, and theme parks, and pursued cinema deals in Asia and Europe with its joint venture partners.

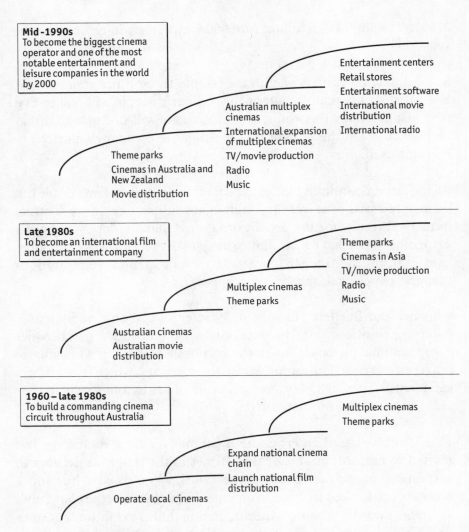

Mid-1990s
To become the biggest cinema operator and one of the most notable entertainment and leisure companies in the world by 2000

Theme parks
Cinemas in Australia and New Zealand
Movie distribution

Australian multiplex cinemas
International expansion of multiplex cinemas
TV/movie production
Radio
Music

Entertainment centers
Retail stores
Entertainment software
International movie distribution
International radio

Late 1980s
To become an international film and entertainment company

Australian cinemas
Australian movie distribution

Multiplex cinemas
Theme parks

Theme parks
Cinemas in Asia
TV/movie production
Radio
Music

1960 – late 1980s
To build a commanding cinema circuit throughout Australia

Operate local cinemas

Expand national cinema chain
Launch national film distribution

Multiplex cinemas
Theme parks

Figure 9.2 Village Roadshow's evolving aspirations

In 1995, Roc Kirby upped the ante again. "My vision now is for Village Roadshow to become an overall world entertainment entity." Graham Burke added, "In five years, I believe this little Melbourne-based company will be the biggest exhibitor by far in the world. I don't say that lightly because all of the plans are in place. The sites are real, they're there, it's happening. Our partnerships are all in place. It's just a matter of making it happen and keeping that energy up to it."[13] Village plans to go from 400 screens in 1995 to 3,000 screens worldwide by 2000.

Reflecting on the company's journey, Roc Kirby said, "I see from the small beginning of Village Roadshow to this present day that not one of the 40-odd years since the company's inception has been without continuity of growth." The evolution of Village's aspirations has contributed to this growth legacy. As each new goal comes within reach, Village redefines the market it is in, inspiring its people to reach new heights (Figure 9.2).

The most powerful and enduring corporate purposes speak to stakeholders at three levels. At the most basic, they must reflect the need to meet profitability targets in order to ensure continuing access to capital, and hence a company's very survival. At the next level, they must hold out to employees the prospect of self-actualization through playing on a winning team, through personal achievement, and through personal growth. At the highest level, the corporate purpose should include the possibility, in some small way at least, of making the world a better place.[14]

When an inspiring purpose is linked to strong values and energetic leadership, the impact on growth can be dramatic. Hindustan Lever, the dominant consumer goods company on the Indian subcontinent, provides an example. The *Far Eastern Economic Review* cited it as the most admired company in India in 1995, 1996, and 1997. An energetic senior leadership group drives the company's passion to succeed. "You really need to articulate a vision and will it to happen," said the chairman, Keki Dadiseth.[15]

Hindustan Lever wants to push its success in the Indian consumer goods sector still further. However, when we asked its senior executives what really motivated them, their answers went far beyond the language of an annual report. They said they wanted to work for the country's most innovative marketer and best developer of management talent, with the highest standards of ethical corporate behavior, for the benefit of India. They were inspired by the opportunities and challenges of marketing a wide range of consumer products across the immense diversity of India, and by the international dimension that comes from Unilever's involvement.

Some managers may see the altruism in these responses as inconsistent with commercial survival in an unforgiving competitive world. But studies of long-lived companies provide evidence that noble purpose and wealth creation can not only coexist, but be mutually reinforcing.[16] Johnson & Johnson has a goal of "alleviating pain and disease," and vows to put customers, employees, and society before shareholders. Kyocera's management seeks "to provide opportunities for the material and intellectual growth of all our employees, and through our joint effort, contribute to the advancement of society and mankind."[17]

The alchemy of growth offers more than mere financial rewards. Just as alchemy sought to transform the everyday into the exalted, growth can transform employees' working lives. Work can become more exciting, more purposeful, and more fulfilling when employees are pursuing the common goal of growth. The effects ripple out as growth benefits society through job creation. Growing enterprises can help alleviate one of our gravest social problems: chronic high unemployment.

Through this modern-day alchemy, businesspeople who lead successful growth efforts leave their mark on the world. Given the social benefits this brings, it is disappointing that so few managers become growth alchemists – and that society so often criticizes, rather than celebrates, the exceptional leaders who master that difficult art. Popular stories about growth leaders frequently dwell on the greed and excessive compensation of a few prominent individuals. What of the unsung heroes who through their leadership have created many jobs for others?

We believe that every leader has the potential to be a growth alchemist in his or her team, department, business unit, or corporation. We hope that this book will, in some small way, inspire and equip more business-people to respond to the noble purpose that we have called the alchemy of growth.

NOTES

1 General Electric annual report, 1995.

2 See, for example, J. D. Day and J. C. Wendler, "The new economics of organization," *The McKinsey Quarterly,* 1998, Number 1, pp. 4–32.

3 R. Foster, interview with Ralph Larsen, August 1995.

4 Quoted in D. Young, "Illinois Tool still fastened to keep-it-simple formula," *Chicago Tribune,* April 26, 1993.

5 Quoted in C. B. Wendel, *The New Financiers* (Irwin, Chicago, 1996), pp. 320–25.

6 H. Ishida, "Amoeba management at Kyocera Corporation," *Human Systems Management,* 1994, Volume 13, Number 3, pp. 183–95.

7 P. Anslinger, D. Carey, K. Fink, and C. Gagnon, "Equity carve-outs: A new spin on the corporate structure," *The McKinsey Quarterly,* 1997, Number 1, pp. 165–72.

8 S. Coley, R. Anandan, and R. Foster, interview with George N. Hatsopoulos, August 1995. As this book went to press, Thermo Electron announced a proposed reorganization that is expected to reduce the number of its majority-owned public subsidiaries.

9 M. A. Baghai, S. C. Coley, R. H. Farmer, and H. Sarrazin, "The growth philosophy of Bombardier," *The McKinsey Quarterly,* 1997, Number 2, pp. 4–29.

10 Speech to Executive Club of Chicago, April 19, 1996.

11 S. Ghoshal and C. A. Bartlett, *The Individualized Corporation: A fundamentally new approach to management* (HarperBusiness, New York, 1997), pp. 307–8.

12 Village Roadshow 1995 annual report. Other quotations are taken from the 1990 and 1997 annual reports.

13 Quoted in I. Porter, "Village Roadshow shoots for top billing," *Australian Financial Review,* October 12, 1995, p.23.

14 The ideas in this paragraph were derived from conversations with Richard Barrett.

15 D. White and A. Quay, interview with Keki Dadiseth, May 1996.

16 Four empirical studies of long-lasting companies demonstrate that success over long periods is correlated with noble purpose: J. C. Collins and J. I. Porras, *Built to Last: Successful habits of visionary companies* (Century, London, 1994), chapter 3, "More than profits"; S. Ghoshal and C. A. Bartlett, *The Individualized Corporation: A fundamentally new approach to management* (HarperBusiness, New York, 1997), pp. 307–8; James Burke interviewed in T. R. Horton, *What Works for Me: 16 CEOs talk about their careers and commitments* (Random House, New York, 1986), pp. 15–35; and A. De Geus, *The Living Company: Growth, learning and longevity in business* (Nicholas Brearley, London, 1997), prologue, pp. 7–19.

17 K. Inamori, *A Passion for Success: Practical, inspirational, and spiritual insights from Japan's leading entrepreneur* (McGraw-Hill, New York, 1995), p. 63.

Appendix: Research base and case studies

The thinking behind this book is based on many sources of information and expertise. Chief among them is the experience drawn from more than 600 growth-related engagements in which McKinsey consultants have served clients around the world.

We have drawn heavily on comprehensive research undertaken by our team into 30 of the world's great growers. Some of these companies are already renowned for their growth skills; others are less well known. We deliberately chose to examine companies that were not under the media and academic spotlight, and to depart as far as possible from the usual emphasis on American enterprises. We interviewed more than 300 senior and middle managers from client and other companies, and tested our concepts and frameworks with them.

Our research was supplemented with information from annual reports and other corporate publications; filings with regulatory authorities; magazine and newspaper articles; and speeches by senior executives. It was also informed by a review of management and academic literature on growth strategies and organizational approaches.

Our selection criteria were as follows:

- To be included, companies must demonstrate a considerable period of sustained revenue growth at a level above the average for their industry, and also exhibit sustained growth in earnings and returns to shareholders.

- Comprehensive information about the companies must be available, and there must be a possibility of interviewing their executives.

- The set of cases must reflect a wide range of geographies and industries.

We analyzed corporate research databases to find companies with exceptional sales and shareholder returns relative to competitors. In some cases, we relaxed our selection criteria to include companies that offered learning opportunities and helped us obtain the geographic range we sought. Taiwan's Acer, for instance, was studied over a relatively short period (1990–96), while most companies in the sample show a 10- to 15-year record of successful growth.

The 30 companies we selected come from Asia, Australia, Europe, and North America, and represent a cross-section of industries. With average annual sales growth of 23 percent and average annual total returns to shareholders of 29 percent over the review period, these were not only great growers but also great value creators.

The great growers

Table 1 lists the 30 companies we studied; the period during which they were evaluated; their industry; their home country; and their compound annual growth rate (CAGR) in sales, net income (NI), and total return to shareholders (TRS) for the period. Details of these cases can be found immediately after this introduction.

Table 1 30 great growers

Company	Case period	Primary industry	Home country	Sales CAGR %	NI CAGR %	TRS CAGR %
Acer	1990–96	Computer equipment	Taiwan	29	90	12
Arvind Mills	1986–96	Textiles and apparel	India	22	38	22[1]
Barrick Gold	1983–96	Goldmining	Canada	71	31	31
Bertelsmann	1986–96	Entertainment	Germany	11	15	N/A[2]
Bombardier	1986–96	Transportation equipment	Canada	22	24	42
Coca-Cola Amatil	1980–96	Beverages	Australia	26[3]	11	31
ConAgra	1980–96	Food	USA	20	22	30
CRH	1970–96	Building materials	Ireland	20	22	21
Walt Disney	1980–96	Entertainment	USA	21	15	22
Enron	1987–96	Energy	USA	10	30	23
Federal Signal	1986–96	Industrial equipment	USA	12	18	25
Frito-Lay	1980–96	Snack foods	USA	11	13	24[4]
GE Capital Services	1986–96	Financial services	USA	19	19	22[5]
Gillette	1980–96	Consumer goods	USA	9	14	31
Hindustan Lever[6]	1986–96	Consumer goods	India	25	29	64
Hutchison Whampoa	1986–96	Diversified conglomerate	Hong Kong	17	19	32
Jefferson Smurfit Group	1986–96	Paper and publishing	Ireland	9	17	22
Johnson & Johnson	1980–96	Consumer and health care	USA	10	13	21
Kyocera	1986–96	Electronic components	Japan	10	10	6
Lend Lease	1980–96	Financial services	Australia	8	18	24
Nokia[7]	1986–96	Telecom equipment	Finland	13	33	44
SAP	1988–96	Software and IT services	Germany	41	37	51
Sara Lee	1980–96	Consumer goods	USA	8	13	26
Charles Schwab	1987–96	Financial services	USA	19	28	35
Seven-Eleven Japan	1981–96	Convenience stores	Japan	16	22	23
Softbank[8]	1986–96	Computer products and services	Japan	92	146	29
State Street	1980–96	Financial services	USA	14	18	35
Tejas Gas[9]	1988–96	Energy	USA	33	23	23
Thermo Electron	1980–96	Scientific equipment	USA	19	23	20
Village Roadshow	1988–96	Entertainment	Australia	67	52	39
Average				**23**	**28**	**29**

1 1990–96.
2 Not publicly traded.
3 Sales figures are for CCA's beverage division (1985–96).
4 Frito-Lay is a non-traded subsidiary of PepsiCo Inc.; TRS figures refer to parent company results.
5 GE Capital Services is a non-traded subsidiary of the General Electric Company; TRS figures refer to parent company results.
6 Sales and net income period 1987–96; TRS period 1990–96.
7 TRS period 1988–96.
8 Sales, net income, and TRS period 1994–96 because Softbank was not listed publicly until 1994.
9 TRS period 1989–96.

The growth "kickstarters"

As well as studying these 30 companies in depth, we also examined companies that had taken successful steps to kickstart growth – that is, to move from a starting point of slow or nonexistent growth to a sustained pattern of revenue growth. Our research focused on the specific management actions that were used to launch a company's growth trajectory.

We started with the more than 1,300 publicly traded US companies that had revenues of over US $1 billion in 1996. We then looked for companies that had entered a growth "inflection period" in which a flat or minimal annual sales growth rate was followed by sustained sales growth. The increase in the sales growth rate had to be at least double, and it had to have driven substantial growth in net income and returns to shareholders.

To increase our chances of obtaining detailed background information and access to executives, we looked at recent inflection cases dating from the late 1980s to the mid-1990s. We added Nokia, a company

Table 2 Nine kickstarters

Company	Primary industry	Home country	Years	Sales CAGR %	NI CAGR %	TRS CAGR %
Compaq Computer	Computer equipment	USA	1986–92	37	31	39
			1992–96	45	58	46
Walt Disney	Entertainment	USA	1980–84	16	–8	10
			1984–96	22	23	28
Emerson Electric	Electrical equipment	USA	1985–94	7	8	15
			1994–96	14	14	28
Gillette	Consumer goods	USA	1980–85	1	5	30
			1985–96	14	18	32
Lear Corporation	Automotive systems	USA	1989–92	2	–41	N/A
			1994–96	41	59	31
Nokia	Telecom equipment	Finland	1988–91	5	3	–9
			1991–96	21	71	91
Reynolds & Reynolds	Business forms and systems	USA	1988–91	–0.1	–5	38
			1991–96	13	21	43
Warnaco	Apparel	USA	1986–90	–2	21	N/A
			1991–96	14	37[1]	18
Wells Fargo	Banking	USA	1990–95	–2	8	30
			1995–96	62	4	27

1 Excludes one-time restructuring charges.

from our case studies that had experienced a turnaround in revenue growth, and Wells Fargo, a retail bank that had refocused on growth (Table 2). Full details of these cases follow this introduction.

The business builders

Most of the 30 great growers and nine growth kickstarters we studied built substantial new businesses. In addition to these two groups, we examined several other companies that had attempted to build new businesses. Not all were successful. We were interested in how companies had progressed from the idea phase to the development of a robust business case and on to launch and the subsequent replication of the business model. Table 3 lists the companies we examined in this category.

Table 3 Business builders

Company	New business	Home country
AT&T	Universal Card and Medis	USA
Walt Disney	Disney Stores	USA
Enron	Gas trading and power generation	USA
General Electric	Factory of the future	USA
Samsung	Semiconductors	South Korea
Sears	Home Central	USA
Virgin	Airline, cola, financial services	UK
Williams	WilTel, Vyvx, ChoiceSeat	USA

Acer   1990–96

Company overview

Founded in 1976 by Stan Shih as the Multitech International Corporation, Acer was created to focus on the development and commercialization of the microprocessor for the Taiwan domestic market. It now manufactures and sells a full range of desktop and notebook PCs, peripheral equipment, and software, not only for the Taiwan market but worldwide. The case research focused on the period following Acer's big international push and introduction of major PC product innovations.

Consolidated revenue in 1997 for Acer was NT$60.7 billion (US $2.2 billion). Acer has become Taiwan's largest brand-name exporter, the world's eighth-largest PC company, and the number 1 PC brand in the Middle East, Southeast Asia, Africa, and South America. It operates in 44 countries, exports to over 100, and employs 23,000 people.

Highlights

Earning the right to grow in Taiwan: Setting out to achieve domestic dominance, Acer concentrated principally on developing the local computer market in Taiwan. It pushed PC sales into ordinary households, factories, and small companies. It was one of the first companies to develop Chinese-language software, which helped it secure a dominant position in the local market.

Product innovation: In the late 1980s and early 1990s, Acer unveiled and marketed several product innovations. Its ChipUp technology was the first single-chip 386 to 486 CPU upgrade available in the market in 1991. The introduction of the first 64-bit RISC-based desktop PC followed in 1992.

Value delivery system: In 1985, the company set up Acerland, Taiwan's first and largest franchised computer retail chain, with more than 100 stores nationwide. Overseas, Acer instituted a McDonald's-style manufacturing network, combining low-cost Asia-based production, consistent quality, and a respected brand. Components are made and assembled in Taiwan to produce a high-quality, low-cost PC sold under the Acer brand name and distributed through local affiliates.

Geographic expansion and spinouts: Building on its domestic success, Acer entered other markets in 1988 by acquiring related businesses,

Growth credentials

NT$1 = US $0.0363, December 31, 1996

Total sales
NT$ billion

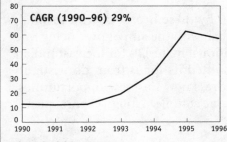

CAGR (1990–96) 29%

Net income
NT$ billion

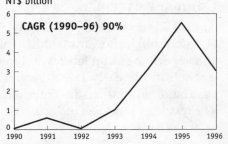

CAGR (1990–96) 90%

Shareholder returns
Value of NT$1 invested

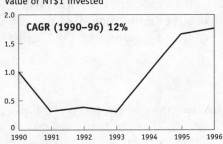

CAGR (1990–96) 12%

Market capitalization
NT$ billion

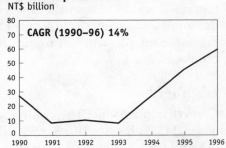

CAGR (1990–96) 14%

Source: Annual reports; Datastream

building joint ventures, and forming alliances in the United States, Mexico, the Netherlands, and Germany. This expansion has been fueled by a global federation of autonomous companies jointly owned by Acer and local investors and operated by local management. In line with Shih's "global reach, local touch" philosophy, Acer takes minority shareholdings in local manufacturing and distribution joint ventures, leveraging its partner's knowledge (and investment capital) while retaining control of design and brand management. More recently, Acer has begun to spin out parts of its shareholding in manufacturing and distribution subsidiaries to increase autonomy and incentives for these companies. Shih's goal is to have "21 in 21": 21 publicly listed Acer companies by the twenty-first century.

Arvind Mills   1986–96

Company overview

Arvind Mills was established in 1930 by three brothers, Khasturbhai, Narottambhai, and Chimanbhai Lalbhai, with the aim of producing fine and superfine cotton fabrics and traditional materials for the vast Indian market. In the early 1980s, Arvind shifted its focus from domestic to international markets in order to address new business opportunities. The textiles it produces include high-value cotton shirtings, export-quality yarn, voiles, and denim.

In 1997, revenue reached 9.28 billion rupees – a large sum for the Indian market. Arvind is the world's biggest denim exporter and third-biggest denim manufacturer. In India, it is the biggest denim manufacturer, the biggest garment manufacturer in the branded segment, and the biggest retailer of jeans.

Highlights

Growth aspirations: The company focuses on growth from the CEO down. Managing director Sanjay Lalbhai said, "The company has grown in denim from 3 million metres to 120 million metres in 10 years and our explosive growth continues." A two-fold expansion in the textile business is expected to make Arvind a US $1 billion company by the turn of the century. It aspires to become the world's biggest denim manufacturer in the coming decade.

Product innovation: Arvind Mills entered the high-value shirtings and denim segment in response to the emergence of small, inexpensive powerlooms and the liberalization of the Indian market. In 1986, the company established its first denim plant, with a capacity of 3.6 million meters per year. The plant was expanded to 14 million meters between 1987 and 1991, and its present capacity is 120 million meters.

Arvind has consistently stayed a step ahead of the competition in Indian denim production. It was the first manufacturer of jeans in India, the first to achieve efficient scale in manufacturing, and the first to enter the massive low-price segment with Ruf and Tuf, a ready-to-stitch pack of denim, rivets, label, and zip. Its rope dyeing unit at Naroda (Ahmedabad) is the biggest rope plant in the world, with capacity of 40 million meters

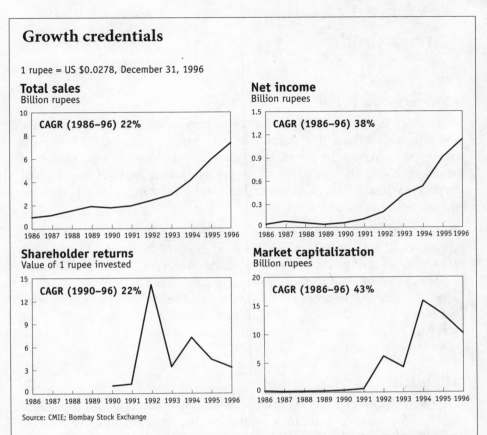

Growth credentials

1 rupee = US $0.0278, December 31, 1996

Total sales
Billion rupees

CAGR (1986–96) 22%

Net income
Billion rupees

CAGR (1986–96) 38%

Shareholder returns
Value of 1 rupee invested

CAGR (1990–96) 22%

Market capitalization
Billion rupees

CAGR (1986–96) 43%

Source: CMIE; Bombay Stock Exchange

per year. Arvind currently produces 70 percent of India's denim. Its product innovation embraces new products such as jute and colored denim and yarn-dyed indigo shirtings.

Going global: Arvind began to export denim in 1988. As part of the move toward globalization, it established strategic alliances and collaborations with world leaders, including US companies Arrow (Cluen Peabody), Lee (VF Corporation), and Knitfabrics (Alamac). It established sales offices in key centers such as New York, London, and Hong Kong, and is now present in 70 countries worldwide. It has also purchased and upgraded a denim plant in Mauritius, which has special trading status with the European Union.

Barrick Gold   1983–96

Company overview

Barrick is in goldmining exploration, development, and operations. Initially called Canadian Barrick, it began operations in 1983 when it acquired an interest in two small mining companies in Alaska. A series of small-scale acquisitions in North America followed. By 1985, Barrick had built a small portfolio of mines and the operating capabilities needed for domestic expansion.

Revenue in 1996 totalled C$1.8 billion (US $1.3 billion), making Barrick the second-biggest gold producer in the world. With the lowest cost structure of any gold producer in North America, it also became the world's most profitable goldmining company. Even as gold prices fell in 1997, Barrick was divesting its higher-cost mines to position itself better for continued profitable growth. Together with a sophisticated hedging strategy, this resulted in a 33 percent increase in 1998 first-quarter profits over the previous year.

Highlights

Operational excellence: Barrick developed a systematic and replicable method for acquiring and turning around underperforming assets. After acquiring a new mine, Barrick installs new management and a generous incentive program to spread its culture. Staff rationalization and the introduction of efficient technology follow to increase productivity. Barrick is renowned for its lean, high-technology approach to operations. It uses the largest autoclaves in the industry, for example, and employs satellite-based global positioning systems to track and direct trucks in its open-cast mines. It also sets a "blitz" team to work to unlock additional potential from reserves and transfer best practices from existing Barrick mines. These practices have allowed Barrick to create additional value from its acquisitions and mining operations.

Growth-enabling competencies: Barrick revolutionized the goldmining industry by introducing creative financing techniques such as gold loans, warrants, and options to finance acquisitions and development. It has also developed the most extensive gold hedging strategy in the industry.

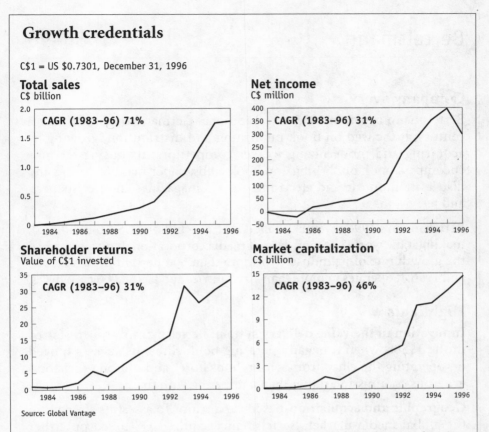

Growth credentials

C$1 = US $0.7301, December 31, 1996

Total sales
C$ billion

CAGR (1983–96) 71%

Net income
C$ million

CAGR (1983–96) 31%

Shareholder returns
Value of C$1 invested

CAGR (1983–96) 31%

Market capitalization
C$ billion

CAGR (1983–96) 46%

Source: Global Vantage

Running out of steam: As 1993 approached, Barrick found its stock price discounted relative to that of other gold producers because of its exclusive focus on North America. The market perceived it as having limited options for future growth. In response, the company began an international expansion program. Barrick now conducts exploration, development, and mining activities in North America, Chile, Indonesia, China, and West Africa, and has extensive relationships with junior exploration companies in these areas. As the market was made aware of Barrick's growth opportunities and plans, its stock took a sharp turn upward.

Bertelsmann   1986–96

Company overview

Bertelsmann began in 1835 as a traditional German bookbinder. For a century, it focused on book publishing and distribution, growing by acquiring and modernizing weaker competitors. Its businesses now encompass book publishing and book clubs, paper manufacturing and distribution, music and electronic media, magazines and newspapers, and television.

Bertelsmann's 1996 revenue totalled DM 21.5 billion (US $14.0 billion), making it the world's second-largest media corporation. It outperformed the growth rate of its industry by more than 500 percent between 1986 and 1996. It operates in more than 40 countries and has 58,000 employees.

Highlights

Innovation in the value delivery system: Bertelsmann's growth started in the 1950s, when it began operating book clubs. Its success hinged on operating the clubs from within bookstores and offering the stores generous commission rather than competing with them.

Geographic and acquisition-based expansion: To assert its strength in the global media market, Bertelsmann acquired US-based publisher Doubleday and record company RCA in 1986. The acquisition of Random House in 1998 made Bertelsmann the world's largest book publisher. These big acquisitions aside, much of Bertelsmann's growth has come from its acquisition of small and medium-sized companies in related fields in over 40 countries. These are managed in a decentralized structure of more than 400 profit centers.

New competitive arenas: In 1980, Bertelsmann entered Germany's television market by launching a general entertainment channel, RTL. During the 1990s, it has shown a keen interest in new media and is forming international alliances to develop new markets. It has entered multimedia through a joint venture with America Online to build online services in Europe. The venture served more than a million customers in Germany alone by early 1998. Bertelsmann has also acquired a 50 percent stake in Berlin-based Pixelpark, a multimedia company providing Internet services.

Growth credentials*

DM 1 = US $0.6499, December 31, 1996

Total sales
DM billion

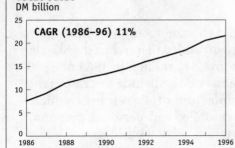

Net income
DM million

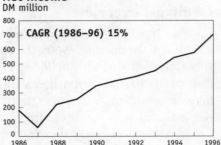

* As Bertelsmann is a private company, data on shareholder returns and market capitalization are not available.
Source: Global Vantage

In late 1998, Bertelsmann agreed to acquire 50 percent of Barnes and Noble's online book division for $200 million.

Bombardier   1986–96

Company overview

Bombardier Inc. was founded in 1942 as a manufacturer of snow-going equipment. In the mid-1960s, the company added to its range the Ski-Doo snowmobile, which propelled sales from C$10 million in 1963 to C$200 million in 1970. Bombardier's businesses now include aircraft manufacturing and maintenance, the manufacture of mass transit vehicles, recreational vehicles, including snowmobiles and personal watercraft, financial services, and other transportation-related businesses.

With 1996 revenue of C$8 billion (US $5.8 billion), Bombardier is now the world's largest manufacturer of regional jets, the third-largest manufacturer of civilian aircraft, the largest manufacturer of personal watercraft and jet boats, and the second-largest player in snowmobiles. In mass transit systems, it is number 1 in North America and number 4 in Europe. It operates manufacturing plants in nine countries and employs 40,000 people.

Highlights

Step-outs into new competitive arenas: In the aftermath of the 1973 energy crisis, which damaged sales of its Ski-Doo, Bombardier sought to develop new product lines such as trams and electric subway cars. Winning major subway contracts in Montreal and New York gave it the financial flexibility to extend its product line further. During the 1970s, it started offering inventory financing to dealers.

In the 1980s, Bombardier entered the aerospace industry through its purchase of Canadair. Manufacturing business jets and 50- and 70-seat regional jets propelled Bombardier into the global big league of aircraft manufacturers. The company built its success internally as well as through acquisitions (including Short Brothers, Learjet, and de Havilland) to become the number 3 commercial aircraft maker in the world.

The pursuit of opportunities continues in the 1990s. The company is market-testing a neighborhood electric vehicle, an electric-powered buggy designed to transport people and light cargo within gated communities. Bombardier's capital financing group entered businesses including railcar leasing, mortgages for manufactured housing, and international inventory

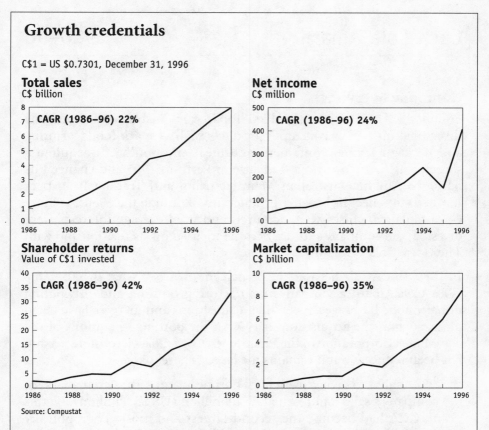

Growth credentials

C$1 = US $0.7301, December 31, 1996

Total sales
C$ billion

CAGR (1986–96) 22%

Net income
C$ million

CAGR (1986–96) 24%

Shareholder returns
Value of C$1 invested

CAGR (1986–96) 42%

Market capitalization
C$ billion

CAGR (1986–96) 35%

Source: Compustat

financing. Its services group plans to expand its aircraft maintenance programs to regional airlines. In addition, the company is in partnership with the Canadian Air Force and NATO to manage the NATO flight training school in Canada. In the mid-1990s, Bombardier made business jets more affordable by introducing a time-share ownership program.

Coca-Cola Amatil   1980–96

Company overview

Founded in 1927 as British Allied Tobacco in Australia, the company diversified into other consumer products such as snack foods, printing and packaging, fiber containers, and meat and poultry. It acquired a share of its first Coca-Cola franchise in Perth in 1965 and changed its name to Amatil (Australian Manufacturing and Trading Industries Limited) to reflect its broader product mix. Through the 1980s, as more Coca-Cola franchises were acquired and nonbeverage interests were divested, the company's future became focused on its relationship with The Coca-Cola Company.

In 1989, Coca-Cola became the 60 percent owner of what then became Coca-Cola Amatil: a company manufacturing, bottling, and distributing nonalcoholic beverages. As further acquisitions and mergers have taken place, such as the acquisition in 1997 of the bottling operations of the San Miguel Corporation of the Philippines, Coca-Cola's level of ownership has been reduced, but it remains the largest shareholder.

By 1997, thanks to high growth in its European and Australasian markets, the company's sales had reached A$4.8 billion (US $3.8 billion). By this point, CCA had become the second-largest and most geographically dispersed Coca-Cola bottler in the world.

Highlights

Focus on beverages: Although CCA had achieved reasonable success and become a strong player in Australia in a broad range of consumer products, the growth strategy developed in 1984 focused exclusively on beverages. As a result, the tobacco, poultry, and printing businesses were sold off, and were followed in 1990 by the divestment of the snack food business. From a diversified Australia-based consumer products company, CCA became a global beverage provider.

Geographic expansion: CCA began its international expansion by acquiring two Austrian franchises in 1982. As it improved its international operating model, it slowly began to expand with further franchises in Australia, New Zealand, and Austria. Between 1989 and 1990, it purchased the remaining significant Australian and New Zealand Coca-Cola

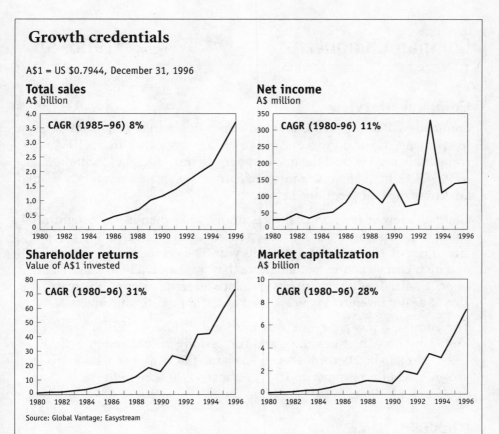

Growth credentials

A$1 = US $0.7944, December 31, 1996

Total sales
A$ billion

CAGR (1985–96) 8%

Net income
A$ million

CAGR (1980–96) 11%

Shareholder returns
Value of A$1 invested

CAGR (1980–96) 31%

Market capitalization
A$ billion

CAGR (1980–96) 28%

Source: Global Vantage; Easystream

franchises, as well as two more franchises in Austria. Recognizing the value of consolidating neighboring franchises and building credibility with The Coca-Cola Company, CCA embarked on rapid expansion in Asia and Eastern Europe. By 1997, it had become the sole or principal Coke franchisee in Australia, New Zealand, Indonesia, the Philippines, Papua New Guinea, Hungary, the Czech Republic, Slovakia, Belarus, Slovenia, the Ukraine, Poland, Romania, Croatia, Switzerland, and Austria.

Restructuring: In early 1998, the company was restructured. Its European interests were spun off into a separate public company, Coca-Cola Beverages, leaving CCA to focus on the Asia Pacific region. While this move marked a recognition of the difficulties of managing such geographically dispersed operations, it also emphasized the substantial growth potential of both regions and enabled sufficient resources and attention to be allocated to each.

Compaq Computer   1986–96

Company overview

Founded in 1983 by Rod Canion and four other engineers from Texas
Instruments, Compaq was one of the earliest entrants into the IBM PC
compatible market, and the first company to introduce a PC with Intel's
80386 CPU. In 1986, it rose into the *Fortune* 500 list more quickly than
any company had ever done before.

Compaq grew at phenomenal rates until 1990, when it was caught off
guard by cheap clones that ate into its market share. Sales fell by 9 percent
after a rise of 25 percent the previous year. The company was the victim
of a high cost structure and a culture that was not ready to handle cost
or price cuts. In addition, an over-reliance on trade promotion created a
glut of dealer inventory, which stifled orders for existing products.

The company was ready for a turnaround. Eckhard Pfeiffer replaced
Rod Canion as chief executive and successfully kickstarted growth. By
1994, Compaq had become the world's largest PC supplier, with a strong
presence in both consumer and business markets. It achieved 1996 revenue
of US $18.1 billion.

Highlights

Earning the right to grow: Pfeiffer moved immediately to improve the
company's cost structure, reducing the workforce by 14 percent, slashing
overhead per unit by 63 percent, and cutting dealer margins. These drastic
measures allowed the company to regain its former profitability. Having
pledged to make Compaq the top PC company in the world by 1996,
Pfeiffer reached his goal early, in 1994.

Kickstarting growth: To return the company to its former growth rate,
Pfeiffer undertook several initiatives. Compaq entered new markets and
speeded up new product development. In 1992, prices on low-end PCs
were reduced by between 10 and 35 percent to compete with the clones.
Between 1991 and 1996, Compaq introduced such new products as file
and print servers, low-end business PCs, consumer PCs, database and
application servers, mid-range servers, NT professional workstations, and
super-servers. At the same time, a broad reengineering of its
manufacturing and distribution systems reduced unit costs.

Growth credentials

Total sales
US $ billion

CAGR (1986–92) 37%
CAGR (1992–96) 45%

Net income
US $ million

CAGR (1986–92) 31%
CAGR (1992–96) 58%

Shareholder returns
Value of US $1 invested

CAGR (1986–92) 39%
CAGR (1992–96) 46%

Market capitalization
US $ billion

CAGR (1986–92) 40%
CAGR (1992–96) 51%

Source: Compustat

Geographic expansion: As well as entering new customer segments, Compaq expanded its geographic presence with moves first in Western Europe and later in Japan, Latin America, Eastern Europe, and the Asia Pacific region.

Industry consolidation: In 1997, Compaq completed the acquisition of Tandem, a manufacturer of high-end servers. In June 1998, it acquired Digital Equipment Corporation to strengthen its position in the mini-computer and computer services markets.

ConAgra   1980–96

Company overview

ConAgra was founded in 1919 as a collection of four grain-milling companies in Nebraska. For much of its early history, it concentrated on grain and feed commodities. It now produces a wide range of products in the food inputs and ingredients, grocery, and refrigerated food categories, and is known as "the food-chain company" for the breadth of its offering.

ConAgra has become the second-largest food company in the United States, with 1996 revenue of US $24 billion. It has also been the fastest-growing packaged goods company in the United States, using acquisitions to accelerate its growth.

Highlights

New competitive arenas: During the 1960s, in response to declining profits from its flour mills, ConAgra diversified for the first time by moving into the poultry business. In 1980, to offset the cyclicality of its commodity businesses, it acquired Banquet Foods, a producer of branded prepared foods. Between 1982 and 1990, the company entered the prepared seafood, red meat, and frozen foods sectors, assembling a stable of some of the best-known brands in the United States. In the early 1990s, ConAgra cemented its position in the food industry by acquiring Beatrice and Golden Valley Microwave. Between 1979 and 1995, it had completed more than 140 acquisitions in total.

Product innovation: In addition to acquisition, ConAgra has also been adept at organic growth. In 1989, after four years of research and development, it introduced its own brand of frozen meals, Healthy Choice. The brand has been extended across numerous product categories and generates over $1 billion in sales. ConAgra seeks to renew and extend its product line continuously; it introduced 114 new products in 1993 alone.

Organizing for growth: ConAgra has built a decentralized entrepreneurial culture. Each of its more than 100 businesses are managed as independent operating companies. Most are run by mini–chief executives who are given the incentive to run their business as if they owned it. Supporting this culture are stretch targets of 14 percent earnings growth

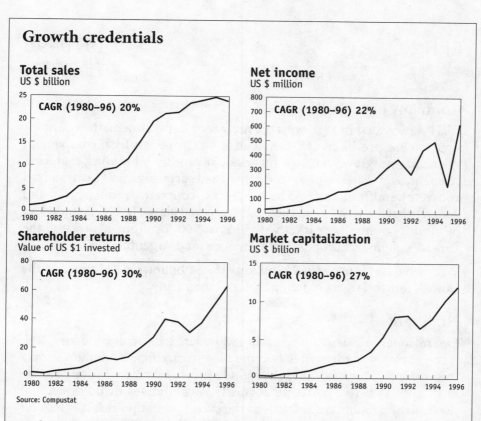

Growth credentials

Total sales
US $ billion

CAGR (1980–96) 20%

Net income
US $ million

CAGR (1980–96) 22%

Shareholder returns
Value of US $1 invested

CAGR (1980–96) 30%

Market capitalization
US $ billion

CAGR (1980–96) 27%

Source: Compustat

and 20 percent return on equity per year. These targets have been met consistently for 16 years.

CRH   1970–96

Company overview

CRH was created in 1970 with the merger of Irish Cement, the country's first cement producer, and the Roadstone Group, an Irish company in the sand and gravel haulage business. It produces building materials (cement, aggregates, asphalt and other road surfacings, and ready-mixed concrete) and building products (precast concrete products, clay and concrete bricks, pavers and tiles, and tempered glass). It has expanded far beyond its domestic market with almost 900 locations in Ireland, the United Kingdom, Europe, North America, and Argentina.

With 1996 revenue of IR£2.4 billion (US $4 billion), CRH ranks as the world's fourth-largest building materials company.

Highlights

Operational excellence: The early 1980s were a difficult time for CRH. A severe recession forced it to become a low-cost, efficient operator simply to survive. This earned CRH the right to grow and made it adopt a long-term approach to evaluating acquisition candidates through cyclical downturns, reaping the rewards as the cycle moves upward. Its focus on performance has been a major factor in CRH's growth.

Geographic expansion: To reduce its dependence on the small and cyclical Irish construction industry, CRH set out in the mid-1970s to generate two-thirds of its earnings outside its home market. This strategy took it to the United States, where it acquired Amcor, a manufacturer of concrete products, in 1978. More acquisitions followed, and by 1983, CRH's US holding company, the Oldcastle Group, had 20 plants in nine states. By 1996, CRH's US business was worth $1.6 billion and accounted for 40 percent of total sales.

Small-scale acquisitions: Since the mid-1980s, CRH has pursued a strategy of identifying and exploiting opportunities for small-scale acquisitions to accelerate its US and European expansion. Since 1994, it has sought to find high-growth markets in developing regions. These efforts led to investments in Argentina and Poland between 1994 and 1996.

Stretch targets: When CRH set a growth target of doubling its earnings per share every five years, few people thought it could be done. That goal

Growth credentials

IR£1 = US $1.6920, December 31, 1996

Total sales
IR£ billion

CAGR (1970–96) 20%

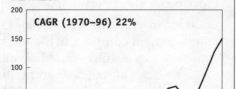

Net income
IR£ million

CAGR (1970–96) 22%

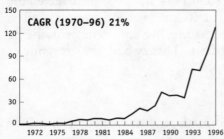

Shareholder returns
Value of IR£1 invested

CAGR (1970–96) 21%

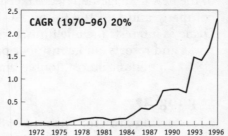

Market capitalization
IR£ billion

CAGR (1970–96) 20%

Source: Global Vantage

is now seen as a minimum hurdle: the company has been growing profits by over 30 percent a year, and sales by 20 percent. Finance director Harry Sheridan said, "You don't know what people can do until they're stretched. You have to keep giving them stuff that you think they can't do, and they must be doing the same to people below them."

Walt Disney   1980–96

Company overview

Founded in 1923, the Walt Disney Company has become the best-known entertainment company in the world. Under its founder's leadership, the company successfully started up and developed businesses that formed the beginnings of staircases accounting for 90 percent of today's portfolio. But after Walt Disney's death in 1966, the company slumped as the fast-changing world of giant television networks and big-budget Hollywood blockbusters passed it by.

A turnaround engineered by incoming CEO Michael Eisner and the rest of the new management team recruited in 1984 and 1985 resurrected the company and laid the foundation for its subsequent growth. Today, Disney's interests include films, broadcasting, live entertainment, theme parks and resorts, and consumer products. Disney had 1997 revenue of US $22.5 billion, almost double that of 1995.

Highlights

Kickstarting growth: The mid-1980s management shakeup proved the turning point for Disney. The new management team of Michael Eisner, Frank Wells, Jeffrey Katzenberg, and Gary Wilson overhauled each major business, reducing the dependence on theme parks and generating cash to reduce debt and fuel new growth initiatives. They also ensured the company pursued initiatives in all three horizons:

• Horizon 1. At its existing theme parks, Disney raised admission prices by 45 percent and introduced new attractions. It also opened new theme parks in the United States and overseas.

• Horizon 2. At the film studios, kickstarting the cash flow involved unleashing the privileged assets of Disney's archive by re-releasing classics such as *Snow White* on video. Innovative financial structuring generated the money to make new movies, including animations with characters that have developed into consumer products. Disney's films have also spawned a new live entertainment business, with former animation feature *Beauty and the Beast* debuting on Broadway, and the Anaheim Mighty Ducks of the National Hockey League carrying on from the *Mighty Ducks* feature.

Growth credentials

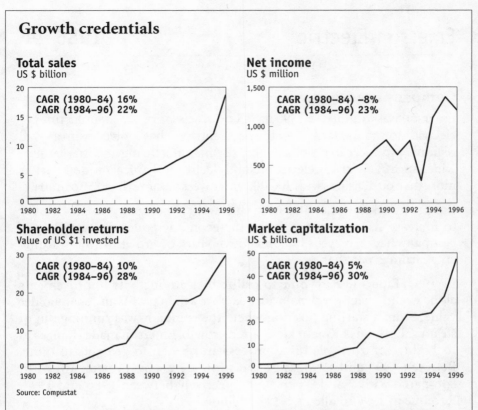

Total sales
US $ billion

CAGR (1980–84) 16%
CAGR (1984–96) 22%

Net income
US $ million

CAGR (1980–84) –8%
CAGR (1984–96) 23%

Shareholder returns
Value of US $1 invested

CAGR (1980–84) 10%
CAGR (1984–96) 28%

Market capitalization
US $ billion

CAGR (1980–84) 5%
CAGR (1984–96) 30%

Source: Compustat

- Horizon 3. Within its consumer products business, Disney has experimented with new distribution concepts. One of its most successful new businesses is the Disney Stores chain. In its first 10 years, 636 outlets were opened. The business accounted for 7 percent of total sales in 1996. Other businesses, such as Disney Interactive and Disney Online, have been started to exploit new technologies.

Organizing for growth: Key in Disney's successful turnaround was the creation of a performance-oriented entrepreneurial culture. Many new people were brought into the organization, and some 400 were dismissed. Incentive compensation plans were expanded and linked to shareholder value creation. CEO Eisner's aspirations unite everyone in the organization in the same goal: "to create shareholder value by continuing to be the world's premier entertainment company from a creative, strategic, and financial standpoint."

Emerson Electric   1985–96

Company overview

Emerson was founded in 1890 in St. Louis, Missouri, as a manufacturer of electric motors and fans. Over the past century, it has evolved from a small regional producer to a global enterprise manufacturing and marketing a wide range of electrical, electronic, and electromechanical products. It has more than 60 divisions with 100,000 employees in more than 150 countries.

Emerson is known as the best-run cyclical company for its ability to increase its profits even when the economy is down. By 1994, the company had achieved 38 consecutive years of growth in net income and earnings per share.

By 1993, Emerson had come to realize that productivity improvements alone would no longer sustain adequate growth in profits and shareholder value. From a starting position where the company was running out of steam, CEO Chuck Knight kickstarted growth. Emerson made changes to its highly regarded planning process and began to grow its top line. Between 1994 and 1996, sales and profits grew by 14 percent a year, compared with 7 and 9 percent respectively between 1985 and 1994. Revenue in 1997 totalled US $12.3 billion.

Highlights

Resolving to grow: To continue Emerson's enviable record of profit growth, Knight refocused the company on top-line growth. But the strengths that had driven "consistent profits consistently" – an operations culture that emphasized the need to meet profit targets – were a barrier to the new order. Knight sent a powerful message to senior management when he split the annual planning conference into a profitability review and a growth conference, presiding over the latter but not even attending the former.

Divesting distracting businesses: Although Emerson had previously earned the right to grow with its operational excellence, it still had to prune its portfolio of distracting nongrowth businesses. It rationalized its operations by spinning off defense, consumer branded power tools, and other unrelated businesses while absorbing restructuring charges of $329 million.

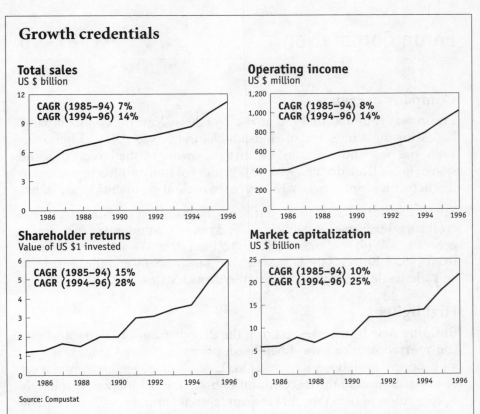

Growth credentials

Total sales
US $ billion

CAGR (1985–94) 7%
CAGR (1994–96) 14%

Operating income
US $ million

CAGR (1985–94) 8%
CAGR (1994–96) 14%

Shareholder returns
Value of US $1 invested

CAGR (1985–94) 15%
CAGR (1994–96) 28%

Market capitalization
US $ billion

CAGR (1985–94) 10%
CAGR (1994–96) 25%

Source: Compustat

Differentiated management systems: Emerson has experienced a big shift in personnel resources. The number of employees assigned to growth projects leaped from 300 in 1994 to 2,200 in 1996, while the headcount in horizon 1 core businesses fell by 20 percent between 1995 and 1997. New recruits are joining faster than ever as gaps in the capabilities required for growth are filled. Incentive systems have been revised so that top-line growth may account for as much as 55 percent of the total bonus for horizon 2 and 3 businesses and initiatives. In Emerson's strategic investment program, managers are given short-term relief from meeting target profit margins if a growth business is being developed.

Enron Corporation   1987–96

Company overview

Enron was founded in 1930 as the Northern Natural Gas Company. Following the acquisition of Houston Natural Gas for US $2.3 billion in 1985, the new entity, Enron, became the owner of the largest pipeline system in the United States, with 38,000 miles of transmission pipes. Today, this network supplies nearly 18 percent of natural gas in the United States.

Enron has demonstrated an outstanding ability to redefine itself and create new businesses, notably in gas and power trading and private power generation. With revenue of US $13.3 billion in 1996 – a 45 percent jump from 1995 – Enron is the largest natural gas company and the largest gas and wholesale electricity trader in the United States.

Highlights

Building new businesses: During the deregulation of US natural gas, transportation access was liberalized, prices were freed from controls, and supply regulations were relaxed. Enron's managers perceived a set of opportunities in the discontinuities buffeting the market, and developed a vision of being the first major player in natural gas. The company saw a need for greater security of price and supply on the part of local gas distribution companies and electricity generators. This led to the innovative Enron Gas Bank and to gas forward curve products that allowed the company to pool gas reserves of different time maturities and finance physical positions with less risk while offering risk-managed contracts to end users.

Similarly, Enron identified an unmet need on the production side of the market, where independent producers of modest size were unable to gain access to finance to fund further development and production activities. In response, it formed Enron Finance Corporation and established innovative prepayment contracts.

These products and services led Enron Gas Services to move into a clearer intermediary role, acting as a risk manager for customers on both sides of the market and trading actively in physical and financial gas with suppliers, customers, and other intermediaries. A range of branded and

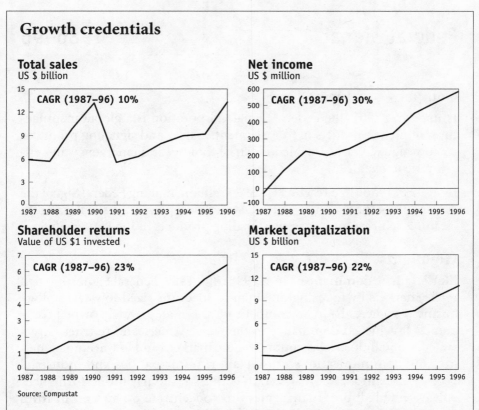

Growth credentials

Total sales
US $ billion

CAGR (1987–96) 10%

1987 1988 1989 1990 1991 1992 1993 1994 1995 1996

Net income
US $ million

CAGR (1987–96) 30%

1987 1988 1989 1990 1991 1992 1993 1994 1995 1996

Shareholder returns
Value of US $1 invested

CAGR (1987–96) 23%

1987 1988 1989 1990 1991 1992 1993 1994 1995 1996

Market capitalization
US $ billion

CAGR (1987–96) 22%

1987 1988 1989 1990 1991 1992 1993 1994 1995 1996

Source: Compustat

customized risk management products and services followed. Enron became the leading force in the development of forward and derivative markets for gas.

This expertise has been transferred into new markets such as liquid fuels and wholesale electricity, where Enron is the largest trader. It has also built a business in independent power production globally, and has recently entered the electricity retailing and water utility businesses.

Federal Signal   1986–96

Company overview

Founded in 1901, the Federal Signal Corporation is a global manufacturer of niche products in four segments: safety and signaling products,
custom signage, consumable industrial tooling, and emergency and environmental vehicles.

By 1997, revenue had reached US $925 million, making Federal Signal the
top manufacturer of fire trucks, street sweepers, industrial vacuum
cleaning vehicles, and warning signaling products in the United States.

Highlights

Market niche dominance: From 1985 until 1992, Federal Signal pursued
niche markets by focusing on small to medium-sized low-technology
businesses where the main competitors are small privately owned companies. It achieved dominance in the North American fire truck, street
sweeper, and industrial vacuum cleaning markets, and in warning, signaling, and communications products for municipalities and industrial
users. A decentralized organization with a strong "pay for performance"
culture enabled local management to concentrate on and profit from
operational excellence and market dominance.

Acquisition capability: Federal Signal's expertise in mergers and acquisitions has enabled it to make up to three purchases a year in the United
States and abroad. The company stays in the acquisition deal flow
by actively courting small privately owned companies with less than
$50 million in sales. It targets strong players in the United States that can
benefit from its large dealer network or provide an entry into a new
market. In the international arena, Federal Signal targets direct
competitors, often market leaders, to enter new markets.

Geographic expansion: Since 1992, US market share has grown from
30 to 50 percent in many businesses. Federal Signal has shifted its expansion strategy from the United States to the rest of the world, and pursues
it largely through acquisitions. After a Spanish sign manufacturer was
acquired in 1992, for instance, it was used as a springboard to penetrate
other European markets. In total, Federal's international acquisitions and
entries into joint ventures or alliances numbered over a dozen between

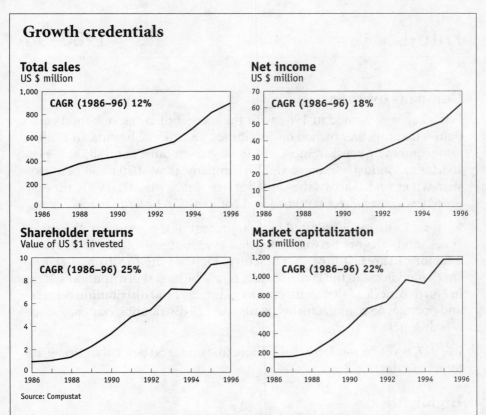

Growth credentials

Total sales
US $ million

CAGR (1986–96) 12%

Net income
US $ million

CAGR (1986–96) 18%

Shareholder returns
Value of US $1 invested

CAGR (1986–96) 25%

Market capitalization
US $ million

CAGR (1986–96) 22%

Source: Compustat

1990 and 1995, increasing the proportion of its international sales from 10 percent of the total in 1987 to 23 percent in 1995.

Frito-Lay   1980–96

Company overview

Frito-Lay was formed in 1961 with the merger of two snack food companies that together owned or distributed 18 regional brands. In 1965, it was acquired by PepsiCo Inc. Until 1984, growth came naturally as the US snack food industry expanded. The company grew at 20 to 30 percent a year as it extended across the United States. But by the mid-1980s, the easy growth was over. Sales flattened and competition became fierce.

Even so, Frito-Lay accounted for 100 percent of the growth of the entire snack food category between 1990 and 1995, outgrowing the industry by a factor of three. It now manufactures eight of the top 10 best-selling snack food items in the United States. It has the largest distribution system in North America (48 manufacturing plants and 190 distribution centers) and operates 65 manufacturing plants and 725 distribution centers outside North America.

In 1997, revenue was US $10.4 billion, just under 50 percent of PepsiCo's total net sales.

Highlights

Product innovation: Beginning in the early 1990s, Frito-Lay made strenuous attempts to extend existing product lines and introduce new brands and categories. Existing products (including Fritos Scoops and Baked Lay's, extensions of the original Fritos and Lay's products, respectively) accounted for 40 percent of sales growth from 1985 to 1995. Low-fat and fat-free products have also become a major group within the Fritos line. New products accounted for 20 percent of growth in the same period, and included Tostitos, Sun Chips, and Grandma's Cookies.

Sales force effectiveness: Frito-Lay has the largest store-door sales force in North America. A hundred or so zone managers make the marketing and sales decisions for $40 to $50 million ventures. Each has tough targets on revenue, operating profit, and market share, and strong incentives to achieve and exceed them. As in the Pepsi organization, the environment is a demanding one: people "grow or go."

International replication: The remaining 40 percent of revenue growth between 1985 and 1995 came from the successful launch of US brands in

Growth credentials

Total sales
US $ billion

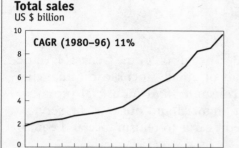

CAGR (1980–96) 11%

Operating income
US $ billion

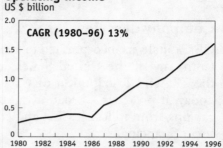

CAGR (1980–96) 13%

Shareholder returns (PepsiCo)
Value of US $1 invested

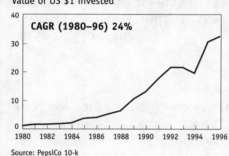

CAGR (1980–96) 24%

Market capitalization (PepsiCo)
US $ billion

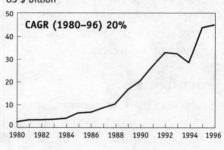

CAGR (1980–96) 20%

Source: PepsiCo 10-k

overseas markets, often with the help of an acquisition or joint venture partner. International business now represents 33 percent of total sales.

GE Capital Services   1986–96

Company overview

GE Capital was incorporated in 1943 as a division of the General Electric Company of the United States, and originally focused on financing the sale and distribution of GE's consumer and industrial products. Today, it provides a broad array of financial and outsourcing services ranging from railcar leasing and credit cards to reinsurance and equipment financing.

In 1997, GE Capital's revenue was US $39.3 billion and its total assets US $255.4 billion. It accounted for 44 percent of GE's total revenue and 84 percent of its assets. In the same year, GE Capital's operating income increased by 9.2 percent while all other GE divisions dropped by an average of 3.6 percent.

Highlights

Step-outs into new competitive arenas: Not surprisingly for a company whose mission is to be number 1 or 2 in every market, GE Capital's businesses are among the largest in their categories in the world. GE Fleet Services, owner of Avis Lease Europe, is the world's largest fleet management company. Genstar Container is the largest player in the leasing of shipping and intermodal containers. GE Retailer Financial Services is the largest supplier and manager of private-label credit cards.

Growth-enabling competencies: Key to GE Capital's growth is its acquisition skill. The company finds acquisitions the quickest and cheapest way to pursue growth opportunities. It is adept at identifying candidates, structuring and negotiating deals, and executing acquisitions. It spent more than $3 billion a year on acquisitions in the three years up to 1995. Its efforts are supported by a privileged asset that its competitors do not enjoy: its relationship with its parent. GE's economic clout, triple-A credit rating, and established international operations have eased the way for both the financing of growth-oriented acquisitions and entry into new geographic markets.

Geographic expansion: Much of the company's growth comes from globalization. It has acquired strong niche players worldwide that already have or can assume a dominant role in their market. During 1994 to 1995,

Growth credentials

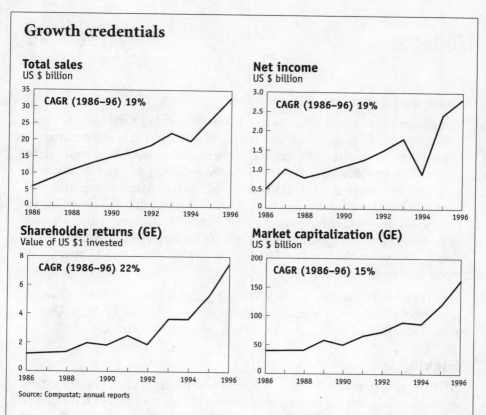

Total sales
US $ billion

CAGR (1986–96) 19%

Net income
US $ billion

CAGR (1986–96) 19%

Shareholder returns (GE)
Value of US $1 invested

CAGR (1986–96) 22%

Market capitalization (GE)
US $ billion

CAGR (1986–96) 15%

Source: Compustat; annual reports

while US revenue grew at only 15.7 percent, European revenue grew by
64.5 percent, and Asian by 83.2 percent.

Gillette   1980–96

Company overview

The company was started in Boston in 1901 to market King Gillette's new invention: safety razors with disposable blades. By 1920, the company's US market share already exceeded 80 percent, with sales of more than 120 million blades a year. By the 1930s, Gillette had 44 branch offices in locations including Baghdad, Manila, and Buenos Aires, a forerunner of the global distribution network it has today. Although best known for its razors and blades (Sensor, Sensor Excel, MACH2), Gillette is also a leader in batteries (Duracell), dental care (Oral-B), toiletries (Right Guard, White Rain), stationery (Parker Pen, PaperMate, Waterman, Liquid Paper), and small appliances (Braun).

Gillette's 1997 revenue was US $10.1 billion. It derives more than 70 percent of its revenue and earnings from 200 countries outside the United States, and manufactures its products in almost 30 countries.

Highlights

Kickstarting growth: Following a price war brought about by the introduction of disposable razors, margins on blades and razors fell sharply between 1980 and 1985, and revenue stalled. In 1986, Gillette embarked on a restructuring program after narrowly avoiding a hostile takeover. Initiatives included tightening operations to maximize near-term earnings, divesting distracting or underperforming businesses, and revitalizing the core business. Despite these efforts, another takeover attempt was launched in 1988. While Gillette management again prevailed, the company had to raise its debt to critical levels, wiping out its entire shareholder equity.

Shortly after, 1989 marked a rebirth with the "Gillette – the best a man can get" advertising campaign and the launch of the phenomenally successful Sensor razor line. This served as a springboard for a number of blockbuster products, including the Gillette Series for Men, Sensor for Women, and Sensor Excel. Between 1985 and 1996, following the period of kickstarting growth, sales grew by over 14 percent a year, and profits by over 18 percent.

Product innovation: One of America's premier corporate innovators, Gillette has taken a pharmaceutical company's approach to product devel-

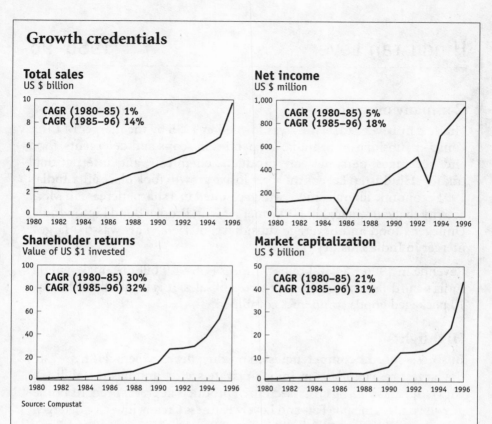

Growth credentials

Total sales
US $ billion

CAGR (1980–85) 1%
CAGR (1985–96) 14%

Net income
US $ million

CAGR (1980–85) 5%
CAGR (1985–96) 18%

Shareholder returns
Value of US $1 invested

CAGR (1980–85) 30%
CAGR (1985–96) 32%

Market capitalization
US $ billion

CAGR (1980–85) 21%
CAGR (1985–96) 31%

Source: Compustat

opment. It invests in research to secure patentable breakthroughs in product and process technology. It strikes a balance between harvesting profits from existing products, driving the growth of the new releases that will be tomorrow's core products, and investing in the products of the future. Gillette's target is for 40 percent of sales to come from products introduced in the past five years.

In April 1998, Gillette announced the new MACH3, a three-blade razor emerging from six years of research and more than $1 billion in development costs. It planned to spend $430 million on advertising in the first year. One innovation is that the thin blades are coated with a microscopic layer of carbon in a process borrowed from the semiconductor industry to make the blades three times harder than steel.

Hindustan Lever   1986–96

Company overview

Hindustan Lever Ltd. (HLL) was formed in 1956 by the merger of three Unilever subsidiaries in India. It operates in soaps and detergents, food and beverages, personal care products, chemicals, and international trading. Hindustan Lever's most explosive growth took place after India's 1991 economic liberalization, which resulted in a sharp increase in M&A activity that culminated in HLL's merger with Brooke Bond Lipton India, Unilever's food and beverage subsidiary, in 1996. This was the largest merger in India's history.

Revenue in 1996 was 71.3 billion rupees (US $1.9 billion), making HLL India's third-largest company in terms of sales. It is bigger than the next 10 packaged goods companies combined.

Highlights

Business-specific competencies: In product development, HLL operates the largest research labs in India's private sector, and has the ability to churn out an amazing cross-section of products at great speed. Its home-grown winners include Fair and Lovely Fairness Cream, low-cost detergent Wheel, and Rin detergent bar.

HLL is also the most admired marketer in India. Its rural marketing is a model of how to tap emerging third world consumerism. It uses vans equipped with audio and video equipment that travel through country villages putting on entertaining shows that demonstrate how to use products such as toilet soap and laundry detergent.

Privileged assets: HLL owns 13 of India's top 60 brands. They provide a platform for a rich array of new products and product extensions. The company has a vast distribution network covering the entire country, even the small rural villages that are difficult to reach by vehicle. HLL uses more than 3,000 distributors to supply more than a million retailers in 80,000 villages. Such scope gives it a matchless ability to commercialize new products at modest incremental cost.

Special relationships: As an affiliate of Unilever, which owns 51 percent of the company, HLL gains access to a stable of world-leading brands, marketing knowhow, the latest R&D expertise, and the benefit of swapping

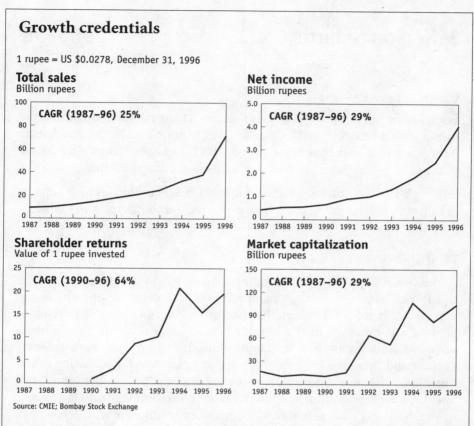

Growth credentials

1 rupee = US $0.0278, December 31, 1996

Total sales
Billion rupees

CAGR (1987–96) 25%

Net income
Billion rupees

CAGR (1987–96) 29%

Shareholder returns
Value of 1 rupee invested

CAGR (1990–96) 64%

Market capitalization
Billion rupees

CAGR (1987–96) 29%

Source: CMIE; Bombay Stock Exchange

managers to broaden their experience. In addition, HLL has enjoyed consistently good relations with the Indian government, despite its status as a multinational in a nationalistic environment.

Growth-enabling competencies: HLL is recognized as having perhaps India's most systematic M&A expertise. It has put together a string of more than a dozen acquisitions and alliances to establish or strengthen its leadership in multiple arenas, including beverages, tomato-based products, and ice cream.

Bundle of capabilities: This capability platform allows HLL to continue introducing incremental extensions of its horizon 1 businesses in soap and detergent and chemicals; to drive growth in its horizon 2 businesses such as personal products; and to build horizon 3 options in frozen food and branded staples that should become massive businesses in time.

Jefferson Smurfit Group   1986–96

Company overview

Founded in Ireland in 1934 as a box-making factory, Jefferson Smurfit is now a global company with operations in Europe and North and South America and a small presence in Asia. Its businesses span paper-based packaging, printing and publishing, and electronic publishing.

Smurfit's 1997 revenue was IR£2.6 billion (US $4.4 billion). The company is Europe's largest corrugated board producer and operates the world's largest network for waste paper reclamation.

Highlights

Acquisition capability: Since its first major acquisitions in Ireland in the 1960s, Jefferson Smurfit has made acquisitions its main vehicle for expansion. It scours the world for attractive candidates that it purchases at the right moment in the industry cycle. Once a company has been acquired, Smurfit applies its operational skills to improve performance rapidly, and then uses the new company as a platform for acquiring other businesses that are geographically or vertically adjacent. Between 1984 and 1994, Jefferson Smurfit acquired or formed joint ventures, alliances, or partnerships with a total of 40 companies around the world.

US expansion: Smurfit began to expand into the United States in 1974 with the acquisition of Time Industries, followed by Diamond International and the Alton Box Board Company. In 1983, it floated 22 percent of its US subsidiary. Three years later, it, acquired 50 percent of the Container Corporation of America.

The US operation, the Jefferson Smurfit Corporation (JSC), was restructured in 1989, providing Jefferson Smurfit Group with $1 billion in cash to invest in growth opportunities. JSC, now 78 percent owned by Smurfit, reports separately; its results, which accounted for almost two-thirds of sales and profits in 1988, are no longer consolidated with the Group, accounting for the dip in sales in 1990. Still, the Group's results have far outstripped those of its industry.

European, Latin American, and Asian expansion: Having firmly established itself in the United States, Smurfit switched the focus of its expansion to Latin America and Europe. It added a newsprint and a fine

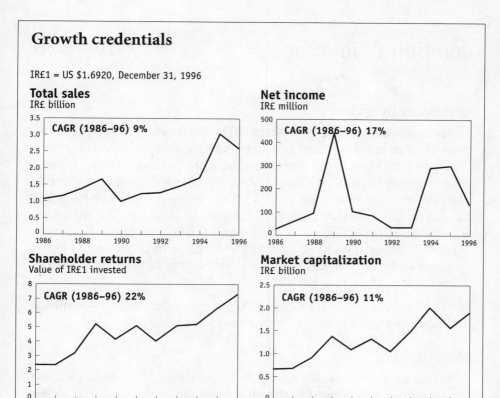

Growth credentials

IR£1 = US $1.6920, December 31, 1996

Total sales
IR£ billion

CAGR (1986–96) 9%

Net income
IR£ million

CAGR (1986–96) 17%

Shareholder returns
Value of IR£1 invested

CAGR (1986–96) 22%

Market capitalization
IR£ billion

CAGR (1986–96) 11%

Source: Global Vantage

print manufacturer to its portfolio, and by 1995 had become Europe's third-largest paper producer in terms of market capitalization. Its expansion into Latin America began with an acquisition in Venezuela, followed by others in Colombia, Mexico, and Argentina. More recently, it has formed joint ventures in China and Singapore to establish a foothold in Asia.

Johnson & Johnson   1980–96

Company overview

Johnson & Johnson (J & J) was founded by the Johnson brothers in 1886 as a manufacturer of wound dressings. Now the world's largest and most diversified maker of health care products, it operates in three sectors: consumer products (with brands such as Reach toothbrushes and Band-Aid plasters), professional products (ranging from surgical instruments to joint replacements), and pharmaceuticals (including Ergamisol cancer treatment, Hismanal antihistamine, and Ortho-Novum oral contraceptives). It continues to expand its product line through an ambitious research and development program and through acquisitions; it made more than 30 of these in the 1990s.

J&J's 1996 revenue was US $21.6 billion. It manufactures in 48 countries and markets products in 158, with a workforce of 89,000.

Highlights

New business creation: Thanks to the aspirations of its managers and the growth expectations of its shareholders, Johnson & Johnson faces the constant challenge of finding the next big idea, and has consequently entered many new competitive arenas. The 1977 acquisition of Extracorporeal Medical Specialties led it into dialysis, while the 1980 acquisition of Iolab, a maker of ocular lenses, took it into eye care and opthalmics. The Lifescan acquisition in 1986 allowed it to become a major player in the field of glucose monitoring devices. In each chosen area, J&J pursues an ambitious set of initiatives to build leading-edge applications that can be distributed through its global sales network under its trusted brands.

Identifying opportunities: J&J's growth path is distinguished by the pace of its new product development and commercialization. Dozens of vice-presidents of licensing and acquisition drive J&J's continuous pursuit of new business ideas to fill its three horizons. They spend most of their time on the road looking for ideas, which they then screen for feasibility and fit. They look to the venture capital community, research institutes, think tanks, competitors, and entrepreneurs for the latest technologies and applications. As soon as they spot a promising idea, they hasten to secure the rights and negotiate the best deal for bringing the new product into the J&J fold.

Growth credentials

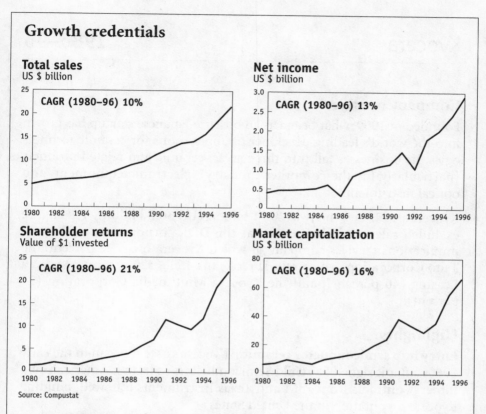

Total sales
US $ billion
CAGR (1980–96) 10%

Net income
US $ billion
CAGR (1980–96) 13%

Shareholder returns
Value of $1 invested
CAGR (1980–96) 21%

Market capitalization
US $ billion
CAGR (1980–96) 16%

Source: Compustat

Organizing for growth: J&J has built a decentralized and entrepreneurial environment of more than 160 independent operating companies. The autonomy of the separate businesses is highly valued. As CEO Ralph Larsen said, "We have hundreds of very talented people around the world working very hard to develop businesses; the last thing they need is someone at headquarters telling them what to do."

Kyocera 1986–96

Company overview

Founded in 1959, what began as an obscure Japanese startup has grown into the world's leading developer of applications for ceramic technologies. Its businesses fall into three areas: ceramic and related products (particularly for the computer industry), electronic equipment, and optical instruments.

Kyocera's 1997 revenue was ¥714 billion (US $6.2 billion). This figure excluded sales in affiliates such as the DDI Corporation, a telecommunications services company of which Kyocera owns 22 percent; the Taito Corporation, which sells karaoke machines (20 percent); Kyocera Leasing (40 percent); and the Kyocera Multimedia Corporation (23 percent).

Highlights

Entry into semiconductor ceramics: Kyocera's ascent began in the early 1960s, after it signed Fairchild Semiconductors as its first American customer. Contracts from IBM and Texas Instruments followed, building Kyocera's reputation in the United States.

In the early 1980s, Fairchild sold its unprofitable ceramics production plant to Kyocera. The new owner, anticipating a microchip boom, expanded capacity, while its main competitors, Coors Porcelain and Alcoa, hesitated. When demand for microchips picked up, Kyocera gained business from Intel, National Semiconductor, and Advanced Micro Devices. Growing with its existing customers and adding new ones, Kyocera became the world's leading producer of integrated circuit ceramic packages in the mid-1980s.

Capability assembly: Kyocera made a number of acquisitions that allowed it to leverage its ceramic technology capabilities into other applications. The acquisition of a band radio maker in 1979 gave it a foothold in technology for telecommunications equipment. Similarly, acquiring a calculator maker enabled it to develop expertise in computer manufacture, and snapping up an undervalued electrical connector manufacturer in 1989 gave it access to European markets and electronic components technology.

Growth credentials

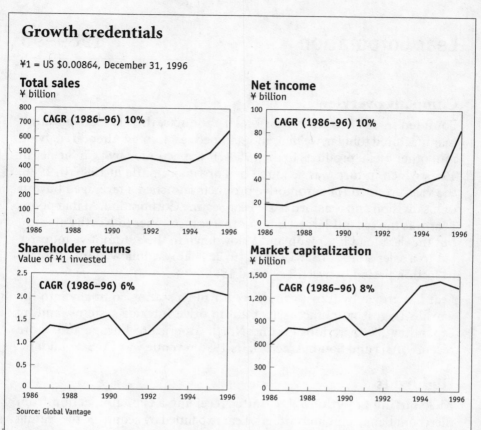

¥1 = US $0.00864, December 31, 1996

Total sales
¥ billion

CAGR (1986–96) 10%

Net income
¥ billion

CAGR (1986–96) 10%

Shareholder returns
Value of ¥1 invested

CAGR (1986–96) 6%

Market capitalization
¥ billion

CAGR (1986–96) 8%

Source: Global Vantage

Leadership: An intriguing factor in Kyocera's growth has been the vision and charismatic leadership of its founder, Kazuo Inamori, whose management philosophy is put forward in his book *A Passion for Success*. (Passion stands for profit, ambition, sincerity, strength, innovation, optimism, and never give up.)

Lear Corporation 1989–96

Company overview

Founded in 1917 as American Metal Products, the Lear Corporation manufactured tubular, welded, and stamped seat frames. After diversifying into other metal products in the 1950s, it was acquired by Lear Siegler in 1966, which in turn was acquired by Forstmann Little in 1986. In 1988, the vice-president of automotive products launched a leveraged buyout of his division and renamed it the Lear Seating Corporation. At that point, Lear was the second-largest automotive seat supplier in North America, but the debt load it took on and a slowdown in the automotive industry led to a sales slump from 1989 to 1992. That was followed by a growth inflection period between 1992 and 1994.

Lear has grown by transforming itself from a seating company into the world's largest manufacturer of automotive interior systems, and by expanding its operations beyond North America to Europe and, more recently, Asia and South America. Its 1996 revenue was US $6.2 billion.

Highlights

Kickstarting growth: In 1990, after receiving a capital injection from merchant bank Lehman Brothers, Lear expanded by acquiring the seating operations of auto companies such as Saab (1991), Volvo (1992), Ford North America (1993), and Fiat (1994). It made a particularly successful stride into the European market by consolidating seating operations there. In 1994, it completed an initial public offering worth an estimated $735 million.

Step-outs to other systems: Building on its reputation for operational excellence, Lear began to enter other automotive interior businesses in 1995. A key step was its acquisition of Automotive Industries, which specialized in overhead systems and door and interior trim. The acquisitions of Masland (floor and acoustics) and Borealis (instrument panels) followed in 1996, with Empetek (plastic molded trim) in 1997. In recognition of its broader remit, the company was renamed the Lear Corporation that year.

Geographic expansion: In addition to its seating operations in Europe, Lear has now opened plants in India, Thailand, Brazil, and Argentina

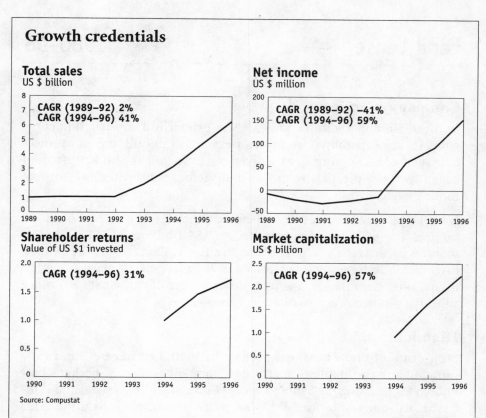

Growth credentials

Total sales
US $ billion

CAGR (1989–92) 2%
CAGR (1994–96) 41%

Net income
US $ million

CAGR (1989–92) –41%
CAGR (1994–96) 59%

Shareholder returns
Value of US $1 invested

CAGR (1994–96) 31%

Market capitalization
US $ billion

CAGR (1994–96) 57%

Source: Compustat

(1996), and China (1997). To reflect its focus on international markets, the company reorganized itself into North American and international operations.

Lend Lease   1980–96

Company overview

In the 1950s and 1960s, Lend Lease was primarily a construction company. Its key capability was superior execution in building and project management, allowing it to deliver on time and on budget. It then began to develop expertise in risk management and real estate mutual funds management.

Lend Lease now operates in property, financial, real estate, and capital services. Its 1997 operating revenue was A\$2.1 billion (US \$1.7 billion), making it Australia's largest corporate funds manager in the pooled diversified funds sector. It has also achieved a 21 percent market share in total funds under management in Australia, and has grown its insurance subsidiary to become the country's second largest.

Highlights

Step-outs into new business arenas: In 1970, Lend Lease was a fast-growing and profitable property development company, perhaps best known for building the Sydney Opera House. A logical vertical and skill-based step-out was to establish a property investment institution. This became Australia's first public property trust and paved the way for ventures into the finance industry.

As the property market softened in the 1980s, Lend Lease pursued further opportunities in the finance sector by purchasing an Australian life insurance company, MLC. By acquiring several more life insurers and strenuously pursuing organic growth, it made MLC the number 2 fund management company in the country.

Lend Lease has also diversified into other new businesses, such as IT services and infrastructure investment.

Geographic expansion: Lend Lease is rapidly expanding its businesses around the world. Assets outside Australia amounted to just 5 percent in 1993, but had reached 34 percent by 1997. The recent acquisition of ERE, the largest manager of investment real estate in the United States, led to the formation of Lend Lease's first two global businesses: Real Estate Investment Services, based in New York, and COMPASS Management & Leasing, a facilities management company based in Atlanta with operations

Growth credentials

A$1 = US $0.7944, December 31, 1996

Total sales
A$ billion

CAGR (1980–96) 8%

(chart: Total sales, A$ billion, 1980–1996, y-axis 0 to 2.0)

Net income
A$ million

CAGR (1980–96) 18%

(chart: Net income, A$ million, 1980–1996, y-axis 0 to 350)

Shareholder returns
Value of A$1 invested

CAGR (1980–96) 24%

(chart: Shareholder returns, value of A$1 invested, 1980–1996, y-axis 0 to 35)

Market capitalization
A$ billion

CAGR (1980–96) 21%

(chart: Market capitalization, A$ billion, 1980–1996, y-axis 0 to 6)

Source: Global Vantage; Easystream

in North and South America, Asia, Europe, and Australia. COMPASS manages over 160 million square feet of space for corporate customers such as General Motors, AT&T, and Bell South.

Lend Lease is also undertaking major international property development projects, such as the multibillion-dollar Bluewater project in the United Kingdom.

Li Ka-shing/Hutchison Whampoa   1986–96

Company overview

Entrepreneur Li Ka-shing's rise from poverty to become one of the wealthiest people in the world is the stuff of legend. Li's empire has grown steadily since the 1950s, when he quit his job at a Hong Kong plastics company to start his own plastic flowers business, Cheung Kong. As the 1950s ended, he moved into commercial property development, which became the springboard for his future success. Gradually amassing holdings of land and buildings, he was one of the biggest landlords in Hong Kong by the early 1970s.

Today his interests include property development, container terminals, telecommunications, hotels, retail, energy, concrete and cement, and financial services. One of his three principal publicly traded companies, Hutchison Whampoa, had 1997 revenue of HK$44.6 billion (US $5.8 billion).

Highlights

Expansive mindset and new arenas: Between 1976 and 1985, Li Ka-shing entered international property development and real estate by purchasing interests in numerous hotels, land sites, and commercial real estate properties in China and North America. At the same time, he acquired a 28 percent interest in Hutchison Whampoa, a trading company with diversified interests that included container terminals in Hong Kong. In 1985, he took over Hong Kong Electric from the Jardine Group for HK$3 billion to become the largest energy producer on the island. Another acquisition of this period was Watson's retail stores.

From 1986 on, Li Ka-shing continued to extend his empire by starting new ventures and acquiring businesses. Examples include a telecommunications acquisition in 1986; Canada's Husky Oil in 1987; an investment management subsidiary, CEF, in 1988; a mobile telephone and paging concern in 1989; and numerous property development projects around the world in the 1990s. Other notable ventures were the StarTV satellite television network in Asia, a Hong Kong brokerage company, and a 75 percent stake in a British port.

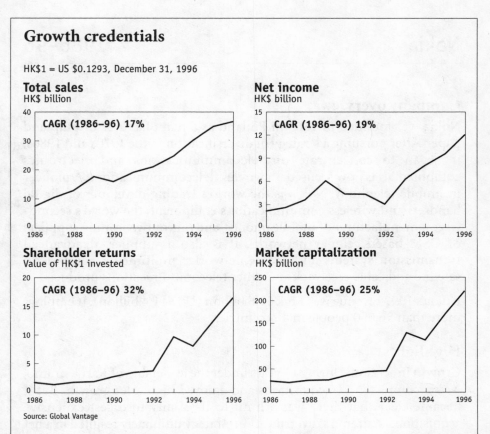

Growth credentials

HK$1 = US $0.1293, December 31, 1996

Total sales
HK$ billion

CAGR (1986–96) 17%

Net income
HK$ billion

CAGR (1986–96) 19%

Shareholder returns
Value of HK$1 invested

CAGR (1986–96) 32%

Market capitalization
HK$ billion

CAGR (1986–96) 25%

Source: Global Vantage

Three horizons in infrastructure businesses: Li currently owns almost half of Hutchison Whampoa, which has built dominant and defendable positions in rapidly growing infrastructure businesses such as telecom, property, container terminals, and retail. In each of these, he uses his consummate deal-making, financing, and relationship skills to pursue three horizons of growth. In container ports, for example, the horizon 1 business consists of a dominant share of Hong Kong's container terminals; horizon 2 is about building growth engines in fast-growing Chinese ports such as Shanghai; and horizon 3 is to do with securing positions in smaller emerging Chinese ports such as the Pearl River delta ports.

Nokia   1986–96

Company overview

Nokia was founded in 1865 in Finland as a manufacturer of pulp and paper. After pursuing a strategy of diversification in the 1970s and 1980s, it began to concentrate on telecommunications and electronics equipment. It is now focused on wireless telecommunications. A pioneer in mobile telephony, Nokia is the world's leading developer of digital handsets and wireless communications equipment, the world's second-largest manufacturer of mobile phones, and one of two leading suppliers of GSM-based cellular networks. It is also a supplier of advanced transmission systems and access networks, multimedia equipment, satellite and cable receivers, and other telecommunications products.

Nokia's 1997 revenue was Fmk 52.6 billion (US $11.4 billion). It employs more than 36,000 people in 45 countries.

Highlights

Growth inflection: During 11 years under the leadership of Kari Kairamo, Nokia completed 21 acquisitions and enjoyed high sales growth. But it became clear that there was a limit to its ability to digest expensive acquisitions. Kairamo's diversification strategy ultimately resulted in a net loss of Fmk 273 million in 1989. Contributing factors included saturated markets and hence fierce price competition in consumer electronics and computers; losses in Nokia's traditional low-growth divisions; under-performance in newly acquired companies; the economic recession; and the collapse of trade with the Soviet Union following political changes.

Beginning in 1992, new CEO Jorma Ollila successfully refocused the company on the telecommunications sector, and it launched its first GSM portable phone. Nokia disposed of noncore businesses, rationalized all its divisions, and boosted operational performance and asset utilization in the remaining businesses. To kickstart growth, it formed partnerships with several global technology leaders and launched a w orldwide drive for expansion.

Geographic expansion: In 1994, Nokia became the first Finnish company to be listed on the New York Stock Exchange. Early telecommunications deregulation in Scandinavia gave its companies a head start in developing

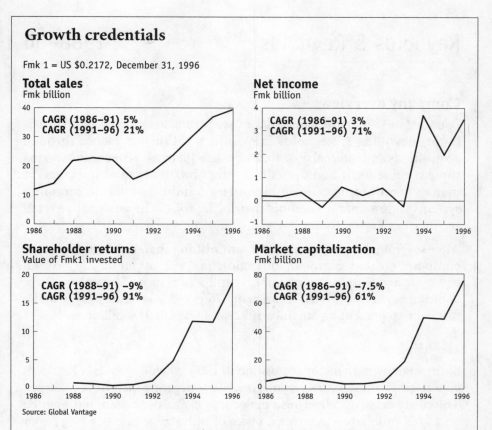

Growth credentials

Fmk 1 = US $0.2172, December 31, 1996

Total sales
Fmk billion

CAGR (1986–91) 5%
CAGR (1991–96) 21%

Net income
Fmk billion

CAGR (1986–91) 3%
CAGR (1991–96) 71%

Shareholder returns
Value of Fmk1 invested

CAGR (1988–91) –9%
CAGR (1991–96) 91%

Market capitalization
Fmk billion

CAGR (1986–91) –7.5%
CAGR (1991–96) 61%

Source: Global Vantage

cellular technology applications. Nokia has gone on to take its telecommunications equipment business around the world, earning more than 90 percent of its sales and profits outside Finland. It has emerged as the market leader in many international markets where companies such as Motorola had a considerable positional advantage.

Reynolds & Reynolds   1988–96

Company overview

Founded in 1866 in the United States as a forms manufacturer and distributor, Reynolds & Reynolds grew into a national presence through acquisitions and internal growth. By the late 1980s, with operations across three continents, it had diversified into a broad range of information management products, from high-margin industry-specific computer systems to low-margin computer printing rolls. The automotive retail sector was a key customer.

After several years of flat sales and diminishing shareholder returns, the company created a growth inflection in 1992 by embarking on an energetic acquisition campaign. It is still a provider of business forms, computer systems, and trade financing. Reynolds's revenue has grown by just over 16 percent a year since 1992, and was US $1.4 billion in 1997.

Highlights

Slump: Following a major acquisition in 1986, when Reynolds & Reynolds experienced its last year of record revenue, operating income fell sharply. The costly delay in delivering a major new car dealer system represented an added problem. Moreover, a series of industry shocks – rising paper prices, fiercer competition in business forms, consolidation among auto dealerships, and changes in printing technology – conspired to bring the company's growth to a grinding halt.

Earning the right to grow: In 1989, at the height of Reynolds & Reynolds's performance crisis, David Holmes replaced Terry Carter as chief executive officer. He initiated a number of programs aimed at earning back the right to grow. The company rationalized its operations, divested unprofitable and distracting businesses, and regained the confidence of investors despite continuing poor business and adverse market conditions by emphasizing its growth aspirations.

Kickstarting growth: By 1990, the company had focused on growth. Its new strategy was to choose a few critical customer segments and build market leadership positions in them by offering a deeper set of products. In each business area, operational performance was substantially improved. At the same time, the search began for small to medium-sized

Growth credentials

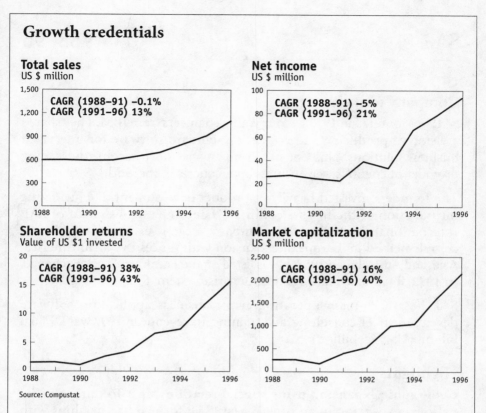

Total sales
US $ million

CAGR (1988–91) –0.1%
CAGR (1991–96) 13%

Net income
US $ million

CAGR (1988–91) –5%
CAGR (1991–96) 21%

Shareholder returns
Value of US $1 invested

CAGR (1988–91) 38%
CAGR (1991–96) 43%

Market capitalization
US $ million

CAGR (1988–91) 16%
CAGR (1991–96) 40%

Source: Compustat

companies operating in the new target markets that could be acquired. In all, Reynolds completed more than 24 acquisitions to strengthen its position in automotive, health care, and general business. It also launched a new management consulting service for auto dealers.

SAP   1988–96

Company overview

SAP was founded in 1972 by four young engineers from IBM. They shared a vision of producing and marketing standard software for integrated business solutions. This German company has since become the leading provider of client/server business applications in the world.

The founders invested heavily in product development. Following the introduction of the R/2 system in 1979 and the establishment of SAP International in 1984, the company began to grow rapidly. It complemented its European expansion with offices in North America, Asia, and Australia. In 1988, it was listed on the Frankfurt Stock Exchange. In 1992, it launched its flagship enterprise system, R/3.

SAP has three main operating arms: business application software development, IT consulting, and training. Its revenue in 1997 was DM 6.0 billion (US $3.9 billion).

Highlights

Geographic expansion using special relationships: To pursue international expansion in an orderly way, SAP formed partnerships with numerous hardware and software development companies and global and local consulting firms. In 1996, it began cooperating with Microsoft to define industry standards for conducting business on the Internet. SAP now generates 67 percent of its revenue outside Germany. Between 1991 and 1995, US revenue overtook that from the home market and grew at more than 85 percent a year, compared with Germany's 22 percent.

New market segments: SAP widened its market focus from process and manufacturing industries to retailing, banking, telecommunications, and the public sector. It began to focus more sharply on the mid-market customer by authorizing small vendors to sell and service its software. Where the larger multinational corporate customers are concerned, SAP's geographic expansion has tended to follow their own.

Product innovation: SAP is developing its products both on a functional basis (in the broad categories of planning, procurement and distribution, finance, plant operations, and management) and for specific industry needs (more recently, banking, retail, and public utilities).

Growth credentials

DM 1 = US $0.6499, December 31, 1996

Total sales
DM billion

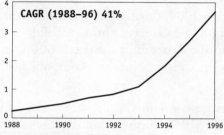

CAGR (1988–96) 41%

Net income
DM million

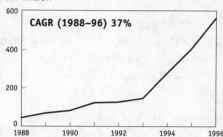

CAGR (1988–96) 37%

Shareholder returns
Value of DM 1 invested

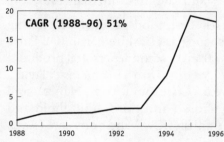

CAGR (1988–96) 51%

Market capitalization
DM billion

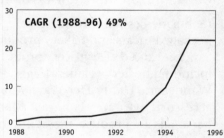

CAGR (1988–96) 49%

Source: Global Vantage

Sara Lee   1980–96

Company overview

From its beginnings as C. D. Kenney in 1939, through its growth in the grocery and food business as Consolidated Grocers and Consolidated Foods and its diversification into nonfood products in the 1960s and 1970s, to its current guise as the Sara Lee Corporation, this company has repeatedly reinvented itself.

Today, Sara Lee is one of the world's largest and most successful packaged goods companies. With 1997 sales of US $19.7 billion, it manufactures and markets branded products from baked goods to hosiery throughout the world, with operations in 40 countries and sales in more than 140.

Its businesses fall into three categories: first, food products, including packaged meats and bakery products (such as Hillshire Farm, Ball Park, Sara Lee) and coffee grocery products (Bravo); second, personal products, including hosiery (Hanes, L'eggs, Pretty Polly, Dim), intimates (Playtex, Wonderbra, Hanes Her Way), knitwear (Champion, Dim, Hanes), and accessories (Coach, Isotoner, Mark Cross); and third, household and personal care products including shoe polish (Kiwi) and body care (Aqua Velvet, Brylcream).

Highlights

Brand leadership: For the past 20 years, Sara Lee has pursued a strategy of building highly profitable leadership positions in consumer packaged goods markets. It specializes in branded nondurable, nonfashion, repeat purchase products. In most of the categories in which it competes, there had been no previous brand leader; indeed, these categories were thought by many to be unbrandable. CEO John Bryan said, "I think it makes sense that building in a somewhat contrarian manner should be a good source of creating value, for there are usually greater rewards by being the first to do something."

Capabilities: Four key skills stand out at Sara Lee. First, it has a good batting average in strategy: in acquiring and divesting businesses and selecting opportunities to invest in growth. Second, it is adept at organizing into autonomous profit centers and recruiting and motivating managers to build businesses. Third, it has distinctive experience in

Growth credentials

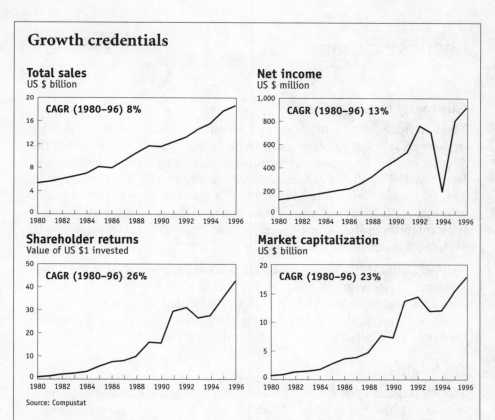

Total sales
US $ billion

CAGR (1980–96) 8%

Net income
US $ million

CAGR (1980–96) 13%

Shareholder returns
Value of US $1 invested

CAGR (1980–96) 26%

Market capitalization
US $ billion

CAGR (1980–96) 23%

Source: Compustat

marketing products through multiple channels of distribution. Fourth, it is able to apply brand management to categories without a history of brand development.

Acquisition skill: Evidence of Sara Lee's core growth-enabling skill – finding and securing acquisitions – comes in the more than 80 acquisitions completed since 1981, and over 150 since 1960. While the pace of acquisition has slowed in recent years, 50 percent of revenue growth between 1984 and 1994 came from acquired companies and brands. Sara Lee has also divested more than 55 businesses since 1981. In total, 90 percent of the businesses that existed in 1975 have been sold.

Charles Schwab   1987–96

Company overview

The Charles Schwab Corporation was founded in 1971 as a full-service brokerage. It began to offer discount brokerage services in 1975 after the Securities and Exchange Commission abolished fixed commissions. Between 1983 and 1987, Schwab was a subsidiary of BankAmerica. Its growth took off after a leveraged buyout and subsequent initial public offering in 1987. Today, Schwab is a diversified financial services company with interests in discount brokerage, asset management, mutual funds, and, most recently, life insurance.

In 1997, Schwab had revenue of US $2.3 billion based on 4.8 million active accounts with US $354 billion in customer assets. It is the largest discount broker in the United States and United Kingdom, the third-largest mutual funds supplier in the United States, and the largest online broker in the United States, with 1.2 million accounts.

Highlights

Stretch targets: Schwab not only uses stretch targets to manage its growth, but also it publishes them in its annual report and regularly exceeds them. Its long-term annual goals of 20 percent revenue growth, 20 percent return on equity, and 10 percent after-tax profit margin were surpassed in 1997 with results of 24, 27, and 12.8 percent respectively.

Business reinvention: Schwab's early entry into discount brokering launched a long series of new business creation. The damage it suffered after the 1987 stock market crash was the catalyst that drove it to diversify into new services to increase its noncommission revenue. Over the next few years, it launched its own money market, equity, and bond funds. In 1992, it began marketing its successful Mutual Fund OneSource retail program, extending it to institutional investors in 1994. A year later, Schwab introduced AdvisorSource for customers requiring investment advice. This enabled it to establish relationships with independent financial advisers who would direct new customer assets under the Schwab umbrella – and pay it a percentage of their fees for the privilege.

Not content to focus exclusively on its brokerage and mutual funds businesses, Schwab relaunched its employee retirement plan business in

Growth credentials

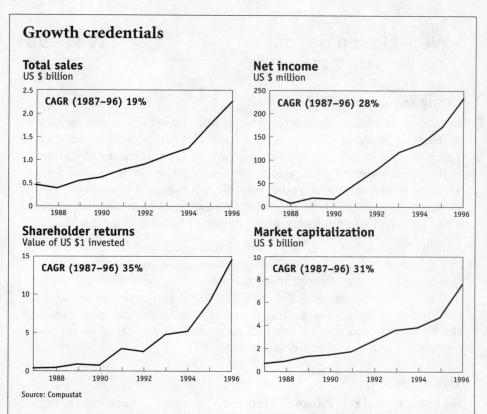

Total sales
US $ billion

CAGR (1987–96) 19%

Net income
US $ million

CAGR (1987–96) 28%

Shareholder returns
Value of US $1 invested

CAGR (1987–96) 35%

Market capitalization
US $ billion

CAGR (1987–96) 31%

Source: Compustat

1992, focused on the US 401(k) deferred tax provisions, and began a pilot life insurance program in 1996.

Business system: Schwab has repeatedly upgraded its IT infrastructure to provide improved service to customers or enable new products and services. It introduced Telebroker, a 24-hour trading service operating through call centers, in 1989, and PC trading in 1990–91. In 1996, it launched an Internet-based trading service, establishing a lead in this market.

Geographic expansion: In 1995, Schwab acquired ShareLink Investment Services, the largest UK discount broker, and is using it as a platform to enter the European market. It has also opened an Asia Pacific services center and a Latin American center, and offices in Hong Kong, Puerto Rico, and the Cayman Islands. It continues to increase its penetration of the United States with more than 270 offices.

Seven-Eleven Japan   1981–96

Company overview

In 1973, Ito-Yokado, one of the five biggest retailers in Japan, formed a partnership with the US-based Southland Corporation to introduce the Seven-Eleven convenience store concept to Japan. The newly formed Seven-Eleven Japan Corporation was wholly owned by Ito-Yokado, with an agreement from Southland to provide management knowhow. Seven-Eleven Japan grew rapidly, and when Southland went into bankruptcy in 1990, it was able to rescue the ailing company, taking a 70 percent share.

Seven-Eleven Japan operates over 7,000 owned and franchised stores in Japan and Hawaii. Its 1996 total chain sales revenue was ¥1.5 trillion (US $13.0 billion), of which the company receives a percentage in franchise and other fee revenues; Southland's 11,000 stores across the world contributed another US $7.0 billion. Seven-Eleven Japan was recently voted the number 1 company for corporate excellence by 1,000 other Japanese companies in a Nikkei Shimbun survey.

Highlights

Business model replication: Seven-Eleven Japan has been expanding at an average rate of a new store a day for the past 15 years: a roster of 800 stores in 1980 became over 6,000 in 1996. This growth occurred at a time when retail outlets in Japan were declining, and was made possible through the conversion of many troubled "mom and pop" stores. The company has captured one-third of the convenience store market in Japan, and is well ahead of its closest rival, Lawsons.

Merchandising: A key factor in the company's success has been its merchandising systems, which are designed to cope quickly with changes in consumer preferences. The company's sales per square foot of retail space substantially exceed those of its competitors. Its franchisees make it the largest single seller of magazines in Japan and the top food retailer, with almost US $11 billion in annual sales, of which its US $4 billion from take-out food surpasses McDonald's showing in Japan. It is also the largest single channel for beer sales in the country.

Store systems: One of Seven-Eleven Japan's advantages has been its ability to track individual products. Its *Tanpin kanri* (item by item) system

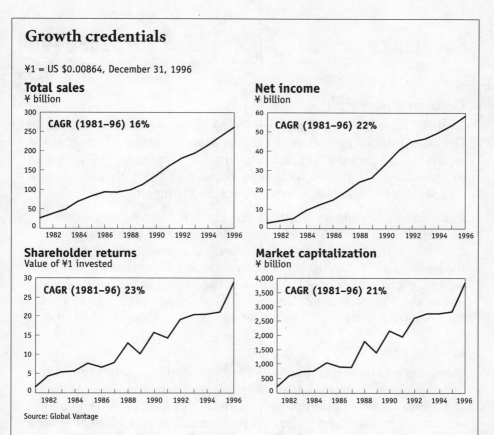

Growth credentials

¥1 = US $0.00864, December 31, 1996

Total sales
¥ billion

CAGR (1981–96) 16%

Net income
¥ billion

CAGR (1981–96) 22%

Shareholder returns
Value of ¥1 invested

CAGR (1981–96) 23%

Market capitalization
¥ billion

CAGR (1981–96) 21%

Source: Global Vantage

ensures that each store carries the best mix of products by tracking every product sold. The system also tracks the time of each sale and the gender and approximate age of the customer. Each store makes its own business decisions on merchandising, ordering, logistics, and inventory. With an average of three deliveries per store per day, store operators can change their product mix and introduce fresh food every few hours.

Softbank   1986–96

Company overview

Softbank started out at a trade fair, selling software from a rented booth. On its first day of operation in 1981, its founder, Masayoshi Son, stood on a crate and announced to his two part-time employees, "We are going to make US $100 million within five years and US $500 million within 10 years. One day, we will be a US $10 billion company."

From modest beginnings, Softbank has expanded into various computer-related fields, including software distribution, publishing, trade exhibitions, multimedia, and PC hardware manufacturing. It dominates the Japanese software distribution market with a 50 percent share. It is the world's largest publisher of PC magazines and organizer of trade fairs, and one of the biggest Internet advertisers. Son has not yet achieved his US $10 billion goal, but 1996 revenue totalled ¥171 billion (US $1.5 billion).

Highlights

Step-outs into related arenas: In 1989, after becoming a dominant whole-sale software distributor and a major PC magazine publisher, Softbank moved into a new arena, network solutions. An acquisition, and a joint venture with Novell and a German provider, allowed Softbank to take a leading role in formulating networking standards in Japan.

Softbank acquired a trade show business from Ziff-Davis Publishing in 1991, supplementing it by purchasing Comdex, the world's largest computer and technology trade show, in 1995. These acquisitions not only added profitable and growing businesses to Softbank's portfolio, but allowed it to stay on the cutting edge of technology, especially in relation to the Internet. Softbank has invested in a multitude of Internet-related companies, including Yahoo!.

Softbank eventually bought Ziff-Davis Publishing in 1995 for US $2.1 billion, as well as acquiring several smaller PC magazine publishers. It has recently purchased an 80 percent share in Kingston Technology, a US-based manufacturer of memory boards.

Three horizons: The Japanese market rewarded Softbank with a price-to-earnings ratio exceeding 100 in March 1996. This plummeted to about 50 in 1997–98 even as profitability soared, with 1997 net income up by

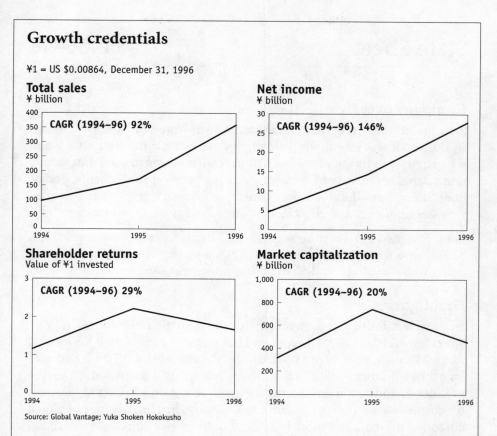

Growth credentials

¥1 = US $0.00864, December 31, 1996

Total sales
¥ billion

CAGR (1994–96) 92%

Net income
¥ billion

CAGR (1994–96) 146%

Shareholder returns
Value of ¥1 invested

CAGR (1994–96) 29%

Market capitalization
¥ billion

CAGR (1994–96) 20%

Source: Global Vantage; Yuka Shoken Hokokusho

57 percent on 1996. Notwithstanding its recent stock performance, Softbank remains a good example of a company with three balanced horizons.

State Street   1980–96

Company overview

State Street traces its origins to the founding of Union Bank in 1792. Based in Boston, it was essentially a small regional bank until the 1970s, when it began to turn its attention away from retail banking toward the custody and related servicing of financial assets for pension fund clients. Today, State Street spans the globe, providing a full range of products and services for asset managers as well as being a large fund manager in its own right.

State Street's 1997 revenue was US $2.3 billion, and its total assets US $35.4 billion. With customers in over 80 countries, it had $3.9 trillion in assets under custody, and $390 billion under management.

Highlights

Expansive mindset: State Street entered the mutual fund business in 1924, when it was chosen as safekeeper and transfer agent by the first US mutual fund, Massachusetts Investors Trust. By the end of the 1970s, it had sold its affiliated community banks. It gradually built a reputation as the premier custody company, becoming involved not only in custody services for corporate and public pension funds but also in a broad range of global custody, defined-contribution fund administration, and financial statement administration services.

IT capability platform: One of the capabilities that allowed State Street to enter the asset servicing business was its strength in information technology. It leverages customer information in a way that allows it to cross-sell products and services successfully. Capitalizing on this capability, State Street was a pioneer in the development of international index funds in the early 1980s. Later in the decade, it started offering a full range of customized investment strategies, as well as foreign exchange and currency risk management.

Geographic expansion: In the late 1970s and early 1980s, an increasing number of US customers wanted to invest in foreign markets, so State Street began to take over custody of overseas assets. The 1980s also saw the expansion of its global institutional investor services business. Today, international businesses account for almost 25 percent of fee revenue and

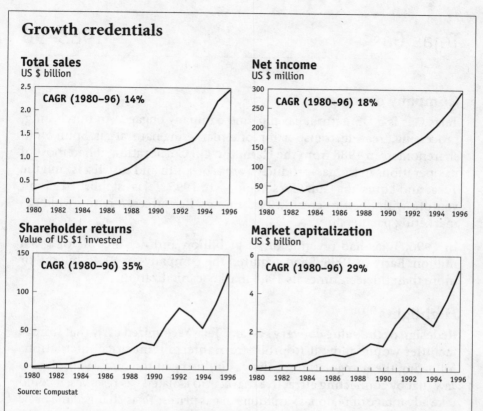

Growth credentials

Total sales
US $ billion

CAGR (1980–96) 14%

Net income
US $ million

CAGR (1980–96) 18%

Shareholder returns
Value of US $1 invested

CAGR (1980–96) 35%

Market capitalization
US $ billion

CAGR (1980–96) 29%

Source: Compustat

profits, a figure that CEO Marshall Carter hopes to increase to as much as 40 percent before 2000.

Tejas Gas   1988–96

Company overview

Tejas Gas is a US natural gas pipeline company engaged in purchasing, processing, treating, transporting, and marketing natural gas. Spun off to shareholders in 1988 from the Hamilton Oil Corporation, it had most of its operations in the gas-producing areas of south and east Texas, and the Texas and Louisiana Gulf Coast regions. In 1995, Tejas established a joint venture with Shell to create Coral Energy Resources, a nationwide gas marketing partnership.

In 1996, Tejas had revenue of $2.11 billion and net income of $43.4 million. Early in 1998, Shell acquired the company for $1.45 billion, or more than thirteen times its 1988 market capitalization.

Highlights

Redesign of the value delivery system: Tejas recognized early that storage facilities would allow it to profit from intermittent price fluctuations following the deregulation of the gas industry in the mid-1980s. It also saw that by connecting attractive markets to isolated gas reserves, it could take advantage of regional variations in gas prices. Tejas changed the basic gather/transport/deliver role of the pipeline operator by adding network and storage functions. It captured value by using its pipeline network with nearly 300 interconnections to move gas from cheaper producers to attractive markets, and its storage facilities to buy gas cheaply and supply it later. The combination of network and storage also provided a reliable outlet for producers and dependable supplies for consumers.

Privileged assets: Tejas started with a thin transmission network in two southern states. Between 1988 and 1996, it spent hundreds of millions of dollars on acquiring strategic assets. By consolidating these assets, it established a network covering Louisiana, Oklahoma, and Texas that allowed it to capture scale advantages and exploit arbitrage opportunities. This made it an attractive partner for Shell.

Growth aspirations and targets: To signal its commitment to growth, Tejas linked employee compensation to steep earnings targets. Its aim was to raise earnings per share by 20 percent a year and achieve at least 10 percent annual growth in earnings before interest, taxes, depreciation,

Growth credentials

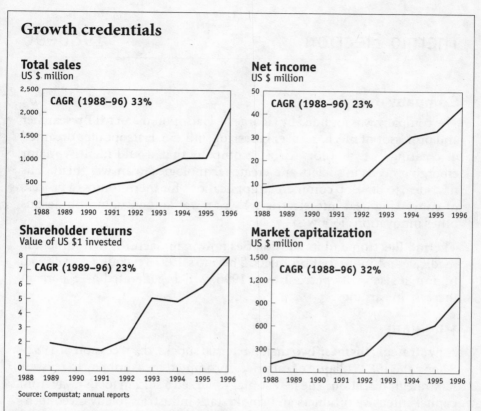

Total sales
US $ million

CAGR (1988–96) 33%

Net income
US $ million

CAGR (1988–96) 23%

Shareholder returns
Value of US $1 invested

CAGR (1989–96) 23%

Market capitalization
US $ million

CAGR (1988–96) 32%

Source: Compustat; annual reports

and amortization. Between 1988 and 1996, revenues increased from $221 million to $2.1 billion at a compound rate of 33 percent, while market capitalization increased a similar 32 percent a year from $107 million to $979 million.

Thermo Electron   1980–96

Company overview

The company was founded by George N. Hatsopoulos, an MIT researcher and professor of mechanical engineering, in 1956. Hatsopoulos dreamed of creating "a technology-driven company that would identify major emerging needs in society and create technologies to answer them." His first idea, to develop commercial applications for thermionics (a process of converting heat into electricity) was never launched, but numerous other innovations followed.

Thermo Electron and its subsidiaries now manufacture environmental, medical, and industrial products. Thermo's 1997 revenue was US $3.6 billion, a rise of 24 percent over 1996, which generated a 25 percent increase in earnings.

Highlights

New strategic themes: Two major external shocks, the recession of 1981–82 and the 1982 collapse of oil prices, prompted the company to reassess its strategic direction. The new strategy marked a shift in focus away from capital-intensive products and smokestack industries to advanced technology, medicine, and the environment.

Product innovation: Thermo Electron began to invest heavily in research and development projects involving technology-intensive businesses, and through both internal development and acquisitions built a reputation as the "perpetual idea machine." Innovative products include ThermoLase's SoftLight hair removal system, Thermo Cardiosystems's left ventricle assist system, and Thermo Power's ThermoLyte propane lighting products.

Spinouts: To fund the development of its heart-assist technology, Thermo spun out its Thermedics division in 1983, with an offering of 80,000 shares to a private capital firm and subsequently 700,000 shares in a public offering. Since then, it has used the spinout strategy more than a dozen times to reap the benefits of small entrepreneurial enterprises while retaining the advantages of large, stable companies. Being able to keep key employees is one: the spinout structure rewards innovators by giving them ownership of a company that will commercialize their technology. Spinouts also eliminate the bureaucracy that can impede

Growth credentials

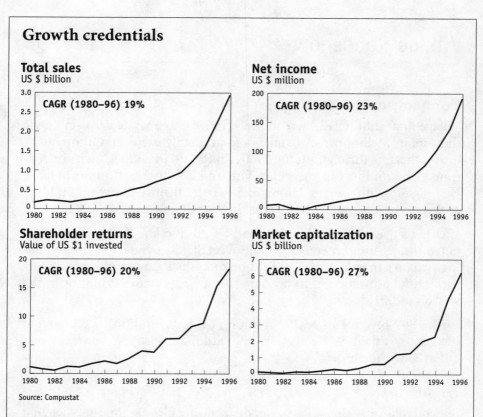

Total sales
US $ billion

CAGR (1980–96) 19%

Net income
US $ million

CAGR (1980–96) 23%

Shareholder returns
Value of US $1 invested

CAGR (1980–96) 20%

Market capitalization
US $ billion

CAGR (1980–96) 27%

Source: Compustat

decision making and stifle innovation at big conglomerates. Thermo Electron's track record of bringing technologies from the lab to the marketplace and rewarding employees with options serves as an incentive for researchers to take their ideas to management.

Village Roadshow   1988–96

Company overview

Village Roadshow (VRL) was founded in 1954 to operate drive-in movie theaters in Melbourne, Australia, and gradually expanded into regular movie theaters throughout the 1960s. In the 1970s and 1980s, it concentrated on building an Australian film and TV distribution business in partnership with Greater Union and Warner Brothers, and on building multiplex cinemas across Australia. It was publicly listed in 1988.

VRL has since expanded into film and TV production, theme parks, radio networks, leisure centers, records, and retail. Since the mid-1990s, it has focused on a massive global expansion of its distinctive multiplex cinema format. Its aspiration is to become the largest cinema exhibitor in the world by 2001.

With 1997 revenue of A$393 million (US $312 million), a 32 percent increase over the 1996 figure, Village Roadshow is Australia's most eminent entertainment company.

Highlights

Special relationships: VRL began distributing films in the 1960s when it formed its first major alliance with Greater Union to create Roadshow Distribution. Today, the company is the Australian distributor for Warner Brothers, Disney (including Touchstone and Buena Vista), and several independent studios. Its partnership with Warner Bros. involves joint ventures in Australian theme parks, retail outlets, and film distribution, as well as international cinemas. In 1997, Village completed the purchase of 50 percent of Warner Bros.' multiplex circuits in the United Kingdom and Germany. The deal strengthened its operations in Greece and Hungary and involved commitments to develop new operations in Italy, Switzerland, France, Austria, and the Czech Republic.

Expansive mindset: From its base in film exhibition and distribution, VRL has become a much more diverse entertainment company. It entered film production for television and cinema in 1990, and is now a major player in Australia.

In 1991, Village Roadshow expanded into theme parks, and currently operates three of the most successful in Australia. In addition, it acquired

Growth credentials

A$1 = US $0.7944, December 31, 1996

Total sales
A$ million

CAGR (1988–96) 67%

400
350
300
250
200
150
100
50
0

1987 1988 1989 1990 1991 1992 1993 1994 1995 1996

Net income
A$ million

CAGR (1988–96) 52%

70
60
50
40
30
20
10
0

1987 1988 1989 1990 1991 1992 1993 1994 1995 1996

Shareholder returns
Value of A$1 invested

CAGR (1989–96) 39%

12
10
8
6
4
2
0

1987 1988 1989 1990 1991 1992 1993 1994 1995 1996

Market capitalization
A$ million

CAGR (1988–96) 51%

1,200
1,000
800
600
400
200
0

1987 1988 1989 1990 1991 1992 1993 1994 1995 1996

Source: Global Vantage; Easystream

part ownership of a national FM radio network in 1993, and bought it outright in 1997. The network commands massive audiences among 19- to 39-year-olds and is the largest FM network outside the United States. VRL is also entering virtual reality indoor theme parks, interactive software, and records, as well as venturing into retail in a joint enterprise with Warner Bros. Studio Stores.

Capital productivity: To reduce the capital required to support its global multiplex expansion, VRL has spun off its real estate holdings into a property trust, focusing its capital and talent on building and operating cinemas.

Shared leadership: VRL is headed by a triumvirate who share leadership responsibilities and rotate the title of CEO every year.

Warnaco   1986–96

Company overview

Founded in 1874, Warnaco became a US market leader in intimate apparel by developing a broad range of bras and related products for sale in better department stores nationwide. During the 1950s and 1960s, it made numerous acquisitions, transforming itself into a diversified apparel manufacturer.

The 1970s saw the first of several business setbacks. Following a change in management, sales began to flatten in the 1980s as a result of excessive cost cutting. In 1986, Andrew Galef and Linda Wachner led a leveraged buyout and started to implement ideas to kickstart growth.

Today, Warnaco is a supplier of women's intimate apparel and menswear. The company aspires to become the "Coca-Cola of the bra business." Revenue in 1996 was US $1.1 billion.

Highlights

Leadership: It is unlikely that the turnaround at Warnaco would have been so successful without Linda Wachner. A vice-president of Warnaco in the 1970s, she joined Max Factor in 1978 and engineered a turnaround from a loss of US $16 million to a profit of US $5 million in two years. When she attempted a leveraged buyout of Max Factor, she was beaten out by US food company Beatrice. She then sought to take over Revlon, but lost to Ronald Perlman. After targeting Warnaco because of its underperformance, she succeeded in taking it over.

Earning the right to grow: The new management team initiated several programs to rationalize business operations and divested a number of businesses, cutting the company's divisions from 15 to just three: intimate apparel, menswear, and retail stores. In addition, extensive cost cutting increased profits and cash flow to service the US $500 million debt from the buyout. The new Warnaco made fundamental strategic choices and focused on intimate apparel as its key growth engine.

Brand management: Having restored profitability, the company went public in 1991. Throughout the 1990s, it continued to grow by licensing the manufacture and marketing of such brands as Calvin Klein, Fruit of

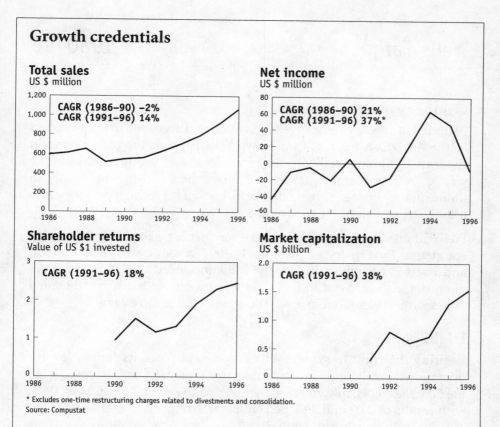

Growth credentials

Total sales
US $ million

CAGR (1986–90) −2%
CAGR (1991–96) 14%

Net income
US $ million

CAGR (1986–90) 21%
CAGR (1991–96) 37%*

Shareholder returns
Value of US $1 invested

CAGR (1991–96) 18%

Market capitalization
US $ billion

CAGR (1991–96) 38%

* Excludes one-time restructuring charges related to divestments and consolidation.
Source: Compustat

the Loom, Lejaby, and Marilyn Monroe. Brands that were no longer profitable were judiciously pruned.

Geographic expansion: Warnaco actively pursued a globalization strategy, establishing production and sales operations in Europe, South America, and Asia.

Wells Fargo   1980–96

Company overview

Founded in 1852 by Henry Wells and William Fargo, two of the founders of the American Express Company, Wells Fargo is the oldest bank in California. It grew steadily by acquiring local and regional banks in the west of America, but by 1995 had retrenched and operated only in California. A super-regional retail bank known for its high performance, it took steps to kickstart growth in 1995–96.

Wells doubled its assets after its first-ever hostile takeover, of Californian competitor First Interstate Bancorp. In 1997, revenue was US $6.7 billion and assets $97.5 billion. In June 1998, it announced a $34 billion merger of equals with Norwest to form the seventh-largest bank in the United States with $191 billion in assets, doubling its size once again.

Highlights

Earning the right to grow: Wells Fargo has earned its reputation for operational excellence. Largely thanks to its intense focus on costs, it led the 50 largest US banks in return on assets and return on equity in 1995, with results of 2.03 and 29.7 percent respectively.

Running out of steam: The bank came to realize that annual cost cutting could not be sustained, and that future shareholder value creation would have to be driven by top-line growth.

Kickstarting growth: The appointment of Paul Hazen as chairman and CEO and William Zuendt as president and COO in January 1995 set the stage for new aspirations. They hired more senior managers from the outside, raised investment in new technologies, shifted the retail network from traditional bank branches to supermarket minibranches and kiosks, and expanded small-business lending nationwide. But there was more to come.

The hostile takeover of First Interstate Bancorp, completed in April 1996, was a clear sign that things had changed at Wells. While it was still struggling to digest its acquisition, it moved to merge with Norwest to create an even stronger competitor with complementary capabilities and broader geographic coverage in the United States.

Growth credentials

Total sales
US $ billion

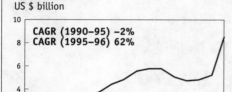

CAGR (1990–95) –2%
CAGR (1995–96) 62%

Net income
US $ million

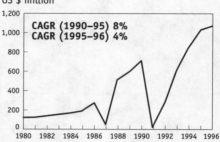

CAGR (1990–95) 8%
CAGR (1995–96) 4%

Shareholder returns
Value of US $1 invested

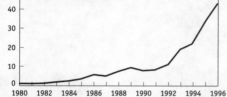

CAGR (1990–95) 30%
CAGR (1995–96) 27%

Market capitalization
US $ billion

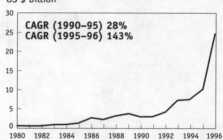

CAGR (1990–95) 28%
CAGR (1995–96) 143%

Source: Compustat

Bibliography

Z. Achi, A. Doman, O. Sibony, J. Sinha, and S. Witt, "The paradox of fast-growth tigers," *The McKinsey Quarterly*, 1995 Number 3, pp. 4–17.

I. Adizes, *Corporate Lifecycles: How and why corporations grow and die and what to do about it* (Prentice Hall, Englewood Cliffs, New Jersey, 1989).

K. Andrews, *The Concept of Corporate Strategy* (Richard D. Irwin, Burr Ridge, Ill., 1971).

P. Anslinger, D. Carey, K. Fink, and C. Gagnon, "Equity carve-outs: A new spin on the corporate structure," *The McKinsey Quarterly*, 1997 Number 1, pp. 165–72.

P. L. Anslinger and T. E. Copeland, "Growth through acquisitions: A fresh look," *Harvard Business Review*, January–February 1996, pp. 126–35.

W. B. Arthur, "Competing technologies, increasing returns, and lock-in by historical events," *The Economic Journal*, March 1989, Number 99, pp. 116–31.

C. Baden-Fuller and J. Stopford, *Rejuvenating the Mature Business: The competitive challenge* (Routledge, London, second edition, 1996).

M. A. Baghai, S. C. Coley, R. H. Farmer, and H. Sarrazin, "The growth philosophy of Bombardier," *The McKinsey Quarterly*, 1997 Number 2, pp. 4–29.

M. Baghai, S. C. Coley, and D. White, "Staircases to growth," *The McKinsey Quarterly*, 1996 Number 4, pp. 38–61.

J. Bain, *Barriers to New Competition* (Harvard University Press, Cambridge, Mass., 1956).

C. Y. Baldwin and K. B. Clark, "Capital-budgeting systems and capabilities investments in US companies after the Second World War," *Business History Review,* Spring 1994, Number 68, pp. 73–109.

A. Bhide, "How entrepreneurs craft strategies that work," *Harvard Business Review,* March–April 1994, pp. 150–61.

A. Bhide, "The questions every entrepreneur must answer," *Harvard Business Review,* November–December 1996, pp. 120–30.

J. Bleeke and D. Ernst (eds), *Collaborating to Compete: Using strategic alliances and acquisitions in the global marketplace* (John Wiley, New York, 1993).

Z. Block and I. C. MacMillan, *Corporate Venturing: Creating new businesses within the firm* (Harvard Business School Press, Boston, Mass., 1993).

H. K. Bowen, K. B. Clark, C. A. Holloway, and S. G. Wheelwright, "Development projects: The engine of renewal," *Harvard Business Review,* September–October 1994, pp. 110–20.

M. Bower, *The Will to Lead: Running a business with a network of leaders* (Harvard Business School Press, Boston, Mass., 1997).

G. Bowley, "Silicon Valley's transplanted sapling," *Financial Times,* March 27, 1998, p. 20.

L. Bryan and J. Fraser, *Race for the World* (Harvard Business School Press, Boston, Mass., forthcoming).

P. Butler *et al.,* "A revolution in interaction," *The McKinsey Quarterly,* 1997 Number 1, pp. 4–23.

A. Campbell and M. Alexander, "What's wrong with strategy?" *Harvard Business Review,* November–December 1997, pp. 42–51.

J. Carter, M. van Dijk, and K. Gibson, "Capital investment: How not to build the *Titanic,*" *The McKinsey Quarterly,* 1996 Number 4, pp. 146–59.

J. Champy and N. Nohria, *Fast Forward* (Harvard Business School Press, Boston, Mass., 1996).

A. B. Chan, *Li Ka-Shing: Hong Kong's elusive billionaire* (Macmillan Canada, Toronto, 1996).

H. W. Chesbrough and D. J. Teece, "When is virtual virtuous? Organizing for innovation," *Harvard Business Review,* January–February 1996, pp. 65–73.

C. M. Christensen, *The Innovator's Dilemma: When new technologies cause great firms to fail* (Harvard Business School Press, Boston, Mass., 1997).

J. Cohen and I. Stewart, *The Collapse of Chaos: Discovering simplicity in a complex world* (Viking Penguin, New York, 1994).

J. Collins, "What comes next?" *Inc. Magazine,* October 1997.

J. C. Collins and J. I. Porras, *Built to Last: Successful habits of visionary companies* (Century, London, 1994).

D. Collis, "Corporate advantage: Identifying and exploiting resources," Harvard Business School, Notes 6/10/91, pp. 1–13.

D. J. Collis and C. A. Montgomery, "Competing on resources: Strategy in the 1990s," *Harvard Business Review,* July–August 1995, pp. 118–28.

K. Coyne, S. Hall, and P. Clifford, "Is your core competence a mirage?" *The McKinsey Quarterly,* 1997 Number 1, pp. 40–54.

J. Curran, "GE Capital: Jack Welch's secret weapon," *Fortune,* November 10, 1997, p. 130.

M. A. Cusamano, "How Microsoft makes large teams work like small teams," *Sloan Management Review,* Fall 1997, pp. 9–20.

J. D. Day and J. C. Wendler, "The new economics of organization," *The McKinsey Quarterly,* 1998 Number 1, pp. 4–32.

A. De Geus, *The Living Company: Growth, learning and longevity in business* (Nicholas Brealey, London, 1997).

M. De Pree, *Leadership Is an Art* (Dell, New York, 1989).

L. Edvinsson and M. S. Malone, *Intellectual Capital: Realizing your company's true value by finding its hidden roots* (HarperBusiness, New York, 1997).

W. G. Egelhoff, *Organizing the Multinational Enterprise: An information-processing perspective* (Ballinger, Cambridge, 1988).

K. M. Eisenhardt and S. L. Brown, *Competing on the Edge: Strategy as structured chaos* (Harvard Business School Press, Boston, Mass., 1998).

K. M. Eisenhardt and S. L. Brown, "Time pacing: Competing in markets that won't stand still," *Harvard Business Review,* March 1998, pp. 59–71.

P. B. Evans and T. S. Wurster, "Strategy and the new economics of information," *Harvard Business Review,* September–October 1997, pp. 71–82.

R. Foster, *Innovation: The attacker's advantage* (Summit Books, New York, 1986).

J. W. Gardner, *Self-Renewal: The individual and the innovative society* (W. W. Norton, New York, 1981).

P. Ghemawat, *Commitment: The dynamics of strategy* (Free Press, New York, 1991).

S. Ghoshal and C. A. Bartlett, *The Individualized Corporation: A fundamentally new approach to management* (HarperBusiness, New York, 1997).

S. Ghoshal and H. Mintzberg, "Diversification and diversifact," *California Management Review,* Volume 37, Number 1, Fall 1994, pp. 8–27.

M. Goold, A. Campbell, and M. Alexander, *Corporate-level Strategy: Creating value in the multibusiness company* (John Wiley, New York, 1994).

R. M. Grant, "The resource-based theory of competitive advantage: Implications for strategy formulations," *California Management Review,* Spring 1991, Volume 33, Number 3, pp. 114–34.

R. Grieves, "Greenmailing Mickey Mouse: Disney buys out a threatening investor for $325 million," *Time,* June 25, 1984.

R. Grover, *The Disney Touch: How a daring management team revived an entertainment empire* (Irwin, Homewood, Ill., 1991).

R. G. Hagstrom, Jr., *The Warren Buffet Way* (John Wiley, New York, 1994).

G. Hamel and R. B. Lieber, "Killer strategies that make shareholders rich," *Fortune,* June 23, 1997.

G. Hamel and C. K. Prahalad, *Competing for the Future: Breakthrough strategies for seizing control of your industry and creating the markets of tomorrow* (Harvard Business School Press, Boston, Mass., 1994).

G. Hamel and C. K. Prahalad, "Core competence of the corporation," *Harvard Business Review,* May–June 1990, pp. 79–91.

G. Hamel and C. K. Prahalad, "Strategy as stretch and leverage," *Harvard Business Review,* March–April 1993, pp. 75–84.

M. Hammer and H. Champy, *Reengineering the Corporation: A manifesto for a business revolution* (HarperBusiness, New York, 1993).

J. Heard and J. Keller, "Nokia skates into high tech's big league," *Business Week,* April 4, 1988.

R. Henderson, "Managing innovation in the information age," *Harvard Business Review,* January–February 1994, pp. 100–5.

S. Hensley, "Charles Schwab to start selling life insurance in May," *American Banker,* April 23, 1996.

F. Hesselbein, M. Goldsmith, and R. Beckhard (eds.), *The Organization of the Future* (Jossey-Bass, San Francisco, 1997).

T. R. Horton, *What Works for Me: 16 CEOs talk about their careers and commitments* (Random House, New York, 1986).

Tsun-yan Hsieh, "Prospering Through relationships in Asia," *The McKinsey Quarterly,* 1996 Number 4, pp. 4–13.

M. Iansiti and J. West, "Turning great research into great products," *Harvard Business Review,* May–June 1997, pp. 69–79.

K. Inamori, *A Passion for Success: Practical, inspirational, and spiritual insights from Japan's leading entrepreneur* (McGraw-Hill, New York, 1995).

H. Ishida, "Amoeba management at Kyocera Corporation," *Human Systems Management*, 1994, Volume 13, Number 3, pp. 183–95.

R. M. Kanter, J. Kao, and F. Wiersma, *Business Masters: Innovation – breakthrough thinking at 3M, DuPont, GE, Pfizer, and Rubbermaid* (HarperBusiness, New York, 1997).

R. S. Kaplan and D. P. Norton, *The Balanced Scorecard* (Harvard Business School Press, Boston, Mass., 1996).

J. Katzenbach, *Teams at the Top: Unleashing the potential of both teams and individual leaders* (Harvard Business School Press, Boston, Mass., 1997).

J. Katzenbach *et al.*, *Real Change Leaders: How you can create growth and high performance at your company* (Times Business, New York, 1995).

J. Kay, *Foundations of Corporate Success: How business strategies add value* (Oxford University Press, Oxford, 1993).

D. T. Kearns and D. A. Nadler, *Prophets in the Dark: How Xerox reinvented itself and beat back the Japanese* (HarperCollins, New York, 1992).

J. Kluge *et al.*, *Shrink to Grow: Lessons from innovation and productivity in the electronics industry* (Macmillan, London, 1996).

T. Levitt, *Marketing for Business Growth* (McGraw-Hill, New York, 1974).

T. Levitt, "Marketing myopia," *Harvard Business Review*, reprinted September–October 1975, pp. 26–181.

J. Lowe, *Jack Welch Speaks* (John Wiley, New York, 1998).

J. B. McCoy, L. A. Frieder, and R. B. Hedges, Jr., *Bottom-Line Banking* (Probus, Chicago, 1994).

C. C. Markides, "To diversify or not to diversify," *Harvard Business Review*, November–December 1997, pp. 93–9.

G. G. Marmol and R. M. Murray, Jr., "Leading from the front," *The McKinsey Quarterly*, 1995 Number 3, pp. 18–31.

J. Mickelthwait and A. Wooldridge, *The Witch Doctors* (Heinemann, London, 1996).

P. Milgrom and J. Roberts, "Complementarities and fit: Strategy, structure and organizational change in manufacturing," *Journal of Accounting and Economics,* April 1995, pp. 179–208.

P. Milgrom and J. Roberts, *Economics, Organization and Management* (Prentice Hall, Englewood Cliffs, New Jersey, 1992).

W. H. Miller, "Gillette's secret to sharpness," *Industry Week,* January 3, 1994.

D. Q. Mills and G. B. Friesen, *Broken Promise: An unconventional view of what went wrong at IBM* (Harvard Business School Press, Boston, Mass., 1996).

H. Mintzberg, *The Rise and Fall of Strategic Planning: Reconceiving roles for planning, plans, planners* (Free Press, New York, 1994).

C. A. Montgomery (ed.), *Resource-Based and Evolutionary Theories of the Firm: Towards a synthesis* (Kluwer, Norwell, Mass., 1995).

C. A. Montgomery and S. Hariharan, "Diversified expansion by large established firms," *Journal of Economic Behavior and Organization,* 1991 Number 15, pp. 71–89.

I. Morrison, *The Second Curve: Managing the velocity of change* (Ballantine Books, New York, 1996).

J. Nocera, *A Piece of the Action* (Simon & Schuster, New York, 1994).

T. Pare, "GE monkeys with its money machine," *Fortune,* February 21, 1994, p. 81.

B. A. Pasternack and A. J. Viscio, *The Centerless Corporation: A new model for transforming your organization for growth and prosperity* (Simon & Schuster, New York, 1998).

E. Penrose, *The Theory of the Growth of the Firm* (Oxford University Press, Oxford, third edition, 1995).

M. A. Peteraf, "The cornerstones of competitive advantage: A resource-based view," *Strategic Management Journal,* March 1993, Number 14, pp. 179–91.

T. Peters, *The Circle of Innovation* (Alfred Knopf, New York, 1997).

T. J. Peters and R. H. Waterman, Jr., *In Search of Excellence: Lessons from America's best-run companies* (HarperCollins, Sydney, 1994).

J. Pfeffer, *Competitive Advantage through People: Unleashing the power of the work force* (Harvard Business School Press, Boston, Mass., 1994).

J. Pfeffer, *The Human Equation: Building profits by putting people first* (Harvard Business School Press, Boston, Mass., 1998).

I. Porter, "Village Roadshow shoots for top billing," *Australian Financial Review,* October 12, 1995, p. 23.

M. Porter, *Competitive Strategy: Techniques for analyzing industries and competitors* (Free Press, New York, 1980).

M. Porter, "What is strategy?" *Harvard Business Review,* November–December 1996, pp. 61–78.

F. Reichheld, *The Loyalty Effect* (Harvard Business School Press, Boston, Mass., 1996).

G. Rommel *et al., Simplicity Wins: How Germany's mid-sized industrial companies succeed* (Harvard Business School Press, Boston, Mass., 1995).

D. Rumball, *Peter Munk: The making of a modern tycoon* (Stoddart Publishing, Toronto, 1996).

R. P. Rumelt, D. E. Schendel, and D. J. Teece (eds.), *Fundamental Issues in Strategy: A research agenda* (Harvard Business School Press, Boston, Mass., 1994).

D. Sadtler, A. Campbell, and R. Koch, *Break Up! When large companies are worth more dead than alive* (Capstone, Oxford, 1997).

P. J. H. Schoemaker, "Scenario planning: A tool for strategic thinking," *Sloan Management Review,* Winter 1995, pp. 25–40.

C. Schwab, *How to Be Your Own Stockbroker* (Dell, New York, 1984).

E. C. Shapiro, *Fad Surfing the Boardroom* (Addison-Wesley, Reading, 1995).

R. Slater, *The New GE* (Irwin, Homewood, Ill., 1993).

A. J. Slywotsky, *Value Migration: How to think several moves ahead of the competition* (Harvard Business School Press, Boston, Mass., 1996).

A. J. Slywotsky and D. J. Morrison, *The Profit Zone: How strategic business design will lead you to tomorrow's profits* (Harvard Business School Press, Boston, Mass., 1997).

L. Sproull and S. Kiesler, *Connections* (MIT Press, Cambridge, Mass., 1995).

G. Stalk, Jr., D. K. Pecaut, and B. Burnett, "Breaking compromises, breakaway growth," *Harvard Business Review,* September–October 1996, pp. 131–9.

G. Stalk, Jr., P. Evans, and L. E. Schulman, "Competing on capabilities," *Harvard Business Review,* March–April 1992, pp. 57–69.

T. A. Stewart, *Intellectual Capital: The new wealth of organizations* (Doubleday/Currency, New York, 1997).

J. Stuckey and D. White, "When and when *not* to vertically integrate," *Sloan Management Review,* Spring 1993, Volume 34, Number 3, pp. 71–83.

W. C. Taylor and A. M. Webber, *Going Global: Four entrepreneurs map the new world marketplace* (Viking Penguin, New York, 1996).

D. Teece and G. Pisaro, "The dynamic capabilities of firms: An introduction," *Industrial and Corporate Change,* 1994, Volume 3, Number 3, pp. 537–56.

D. Teece, G. Pisaro, and A. Shuler, "Dynamic capabilities and strategic management," CCC Working Paper No. 94–9, University of California, Berkeley, August 1994.

N. M. Tichy with E. Cohen, *The Leadership Engine: How winning companies build leaders at every level* (HarperBusiness, New York, 1997).

N. M. Tichy and S. Sherman, *Control Your Destiny or Someone Else Will* (Currency/Doubleday, New York, 1993).

R. M. Tomasko, *Downsizing: Reshaping the corporation for the future* (Amacon, New York, 1987).

R. M. Tomasko, *Go for Growth: Five paths to profit and success – choose the right one for you and your company* (John Wiley, New York, 1996).

M. Treacy and F. Wiersma, *The Discipline of Market Leaders: Choose your customers, narrow your focus, and dominate your market* (Addison-Wesley, Reading, 1995).

M. L. Tushman and C. A. O'Reilly III, "Ambidextrous organizations: Managing evolutionary and revolutionary change," *California Management Review,* Summer 1996, Volume 38, Number 4, pp. 8–30.

J. M. Utterback, *Mastering the Dynamics of Innovations: How companies can seize opportunities in the face of technological change* (Harvard Business School Press, Boston, Mass., 1994).

P. Wack, "Scenarios: Uncharted waters ahead," *Harvard Business Review,* September–October 1985, pp. 72–89.

M. M. Waldrop, *Complexity: The emerging science at the edge of order and chaos* (Simon & Schuster, New York, 1992).

M. Weidenbaum and S. Hughes, *The Bamboo Network* (Martin Kessler Books, New York, 1996).

C. B. Wendel, *The New Financiers* (Irwin, Chicago, 1996).

B. Wernerfelt, "A resource-based view of the firm," *Strategic Management Journal,* September–October 1984, Volume 5, pp. 171–80.

R. Whitely and D. Hessan, *Customer Centered Growth: Five proven strategies for building competitive advantage* (Addison-Wesley, Reading, 1996).

P. Williamson and M. Hay, "Strategic staircases," *Long Range Planning,* 1991, Volume 24, Number 4, pp. 36–43.

D. Young, "Illinois Tool still fastened to keep-it-simple formula," *Chicago Tribune,* April 26, 1993.

Index